FRAMED IN MONTE CARLO

HOW I WAS WRONGFULLY CONVICTED
FOR A BILLIONAIRE'S FIERY DEATH

TED MAHER

WITH BILL HAYES AND JENNIFER THOMAS
FOREWORD BY MICHAEL GRIFFITH, ESQ.

Skyhorse Publishing

Dedication

This book is dedicated to my mother and my sister,
who have stood by me through everything.

Thank you for always remembering who I am and what I stand for,
and for never believing an untrue word spoken about me.
—Ted Maher

Skyhorse Publishing books may be purchased in bulk at special discounts for sales promotion, corporate gifts, fund-raising, or educational purposes. Special editions can also be created to specifications. For details, contact the Special Sales Department, Skyhorse Publishing, 307 West 36th Street, 11th Floor, New York, NY 10018 or info@skyhorsepublishing.com.

Skyhorse® and Skyhorse Publishing® are registered trademarks of Skyhorse Publishing, Inc.®, a Delaware corporation.

Visit our website at www.skyhorsepublishing.com.

10 9 8 7 6 5 4 3 2 1

Library of Congress Cataloging-in-Publication Data is available on file.

Cover design by Kai Texel

Print ISBN: 978-1-5107-5586-4
Ebook ISBN: 978-1-5107-5587-1

Printed in the United States of America

CONTENTS

FOREWORD
BY MICHAEL GRIFFITH, ESQ.

This case—the proceedings in which Ted Maher was tried in Monaco for the 1999 death of world banking icon Edmond Safra—is without question the most perplexing and puzzling I've ever been involved in.

I am an international criminal defense lawyer. For the last thirty-five years I have represented Americans imprisoned and beleaguered in foreign countries all over the globe. My very first solo defense case was of Billy Hayes in 1970, which was made into the motion picture *Midnight Express*, earning it infamy across the world. Since then, my work has taken me behind the unforgiving walls and into the cold no-man's-land of *prisiones*, *cezaevleri*, and *maisons de arrest* in over two dozen countries. From defending US soldiers in the Okinawan rape case to exposing corruption in Ecuador, I've been involved in actions and litigations that run the gamut from kidnappings, to robberies, to murders and more—all occurring on some pretty shaky ground.

But in *this* case—Ted's case—the complex circumstances in the chain of events throughout are unprecedented. And they are indisputably compelling—especially to those of us with a hunger-for-truth mindset!

The cast of characters alone is far beyond what even the best fiction mystery writer could come up with: Green Beret–turned–neonatal nurse Ted Maher; insanely wealthy, world-renowned couple Edmond and Lily Safra; the Safras' security team borne from the Israeli Mossad; the Russian mafia; the French and Monegasque legal team of dubious ability and vast inexperience; Ted's intense and mysterious wife, Heidi; the ominous judicial team that ruled Ted's trials in Monaco; the confused and disjointed police and firefighters there; and essentially every other human who placed a fingerprint on this case.

Even more compelling is how that cast of characters was thrown into this doomed drama, which as it climaxed, resulted in the needless deaths of two innocent victims and the collateral destruction of Ted Maher.

I continue to be haunted by this case—by the trial, in particular. Never have I felt such frustration and at times, anger, at the roadblocks that kept me from helping my client to the fullest. Moreover, the public around the world remains in the dark about the most shocking details of this tragic drama.

When Safra died, the media went crazy. Headlines around the world screamed out about the death of one of the world's wealthiest men—and the tangled mystery that scorched every aspect of his murder. When Ted was finally released in 2007, he was interviewed on *Dateline*, *48 Hours*, *Inside Edition*; Dominick Dunne's *Power, Privilege and Justice*, and others. The public interest in this case has been unabated, from its inception up until the present.

It is a saga that appears to have no end, unless and until the truth and nothing but the truth is finally known.

This book is a huge step toward that next installment.

PREFACE

I knew I would forget *nothing* about this entire story. Ever.

But when I was imprisoned, they did everything they could to break me.

When I started a journal, they took it from me.

When I started writing again, they confiscated it again.

Every time I wrote anything down, they took it away. I pissed them off *so* much.

Finally, I was brought before the prison director.

"Why are you doing this, Mr. Maher?" he demanded.

"This is my life," I told him. "I want people to know what's happened to me!"

He looked confused, then arrogant. Matter-of-fact, *indignant.*

"But Mr. Maher, *no one* can know what has been going on in your life . . ."

"Excuse me?!" My senses raged. "*No one can know?* Is that what you're telling me? Well, I'm going to make sure that *everyone* knows!" I screamed. "You can take what I write, you can strip-search me every day, you can tear my cell apart every day—you can take the shit I write every day, every week, every month, for years on end. You can keep me in that cell—*alone*—in my underwear with that hole for a toilet, and you can leave that light on twenty-four hours a day. But you *won't* break me! No matter what you do, I'll never turn into some feeble little nothing, lying curled up in a ball, filthy and shaking in the corner."

I pulled a couple more handwritten scraps of paper out of my shirt and threw them at him.

"Here, take these, too! And come back for the next thing I write! I don't *need* to write it; it's all coming from *here!*" I pointed to my head—my mind, my memory.

"And that's one thing you bastards *can't* take!"

—Ted Maher

INTRODUCTION
BY BILL HAYES

Sixty-seven-year-old Edmond J. Safra was listed by *Forbes* magazine as one of 1999's two hundred wealthiest individuals in the world.[1] With assets in the billions, Safra was high-profile in the international banking community and beyond, for his wealth and business acumen.

Safra owned controlling stakes in both Safra Republic and Republic New York Corporation (RNB)—banks he founded and often referred to as his "children."[2] His legal war with American Express over the sale of his Trade Development Bank in 1983 became legendary and long.

Shortly before his death, he was reportedly collaborating with the FBI to expose a money-laundering operation allegedly perpetrated by the Russian mafia.[3] But decades later, evidence is emerging about the true nature of Safra's "whistleblowing" that indicates it was the actual cause of his demise.

And while it may come as no surprise that Safra's dealings weren't always on the up and up, it is a revelation that the ramifications of his shady transactions extend to today, particularly those involving Russia and the United States's continued face-offs with President Vladmir Putin: from the contentious Magnitsky Act, lobbied by Safra's former partner, Bill Browder, to the controversial Trump Tower meeting during the 2016 presidential election.

His personal life was also one of heavy interest and scrutiny. As Parkinson's disease brought Safra's declining health increasingly into question, the attention to his huge inheritance also increased—by family members and outsiders alike.

Safra's wife, Lily, had long been garnering renown in her own right as "one of the world's richest and most elegant women" (as described later by her unofficial biographer, Isabel Vincent).[4] That title especially applied following the questionable "suicide" of her multimillionaire second husband: Brazilian businessman Alfredo Monteverde.

Possessed of "steely determination," Lily knew from an early age that she wanted "wealth, power, and prestige."[5]

She got all three.

But her marriage to Edmond in 1976 didn't exactly merge Lily and the Safra clan into one big happy family. Several years earlier, Edmond's brother talked Safra out of marrying Lily. That caused more than a little inter—and intra—family friction.

But in the end, Lily—now on her *fourth* husband—got what she wanted, as usual.

The years that followed saw the Safras soar to social status summits that included owning *two* of the world's most opulent dwellings: the dripping-with-history multi-acre Villa La Leopolda on the Côte d'Azur and the 17,500-square-foot palace of a penthouse known as "the world's costliest flat," atop Monaco's La Belle Époque building. [6] This hyper-gilded lifestyle, powered by Safra's relentless banking and business dealings, rose well above legendary—it *defined* extravagance.

In late 1999, in a transaction of mega-proportions, Safra made the final arrangements to sell his banks to the Hong Kong and Shanghai Banking Corporation (HSBC Holdings) for about ten billion dollars.[7] Although the deal was surrounded by controversy, legal battles, and financial finger-pointing, at the time, nobody realized how much dirt was under Safra's own fingernails—despite his curious decision to unload his empire "on the cheap." He also changed his will to leave the bulk of his fortune to Lily. Safra's siblings and the rest of his extended family were left out in the kind of cold seldom felt in Monaco.

And the decision was final.

Not too long after, in the early morning hours of December 3, 1999, Safra was killed—suddenly and mysteriously—in a bizarre blaze that ripped through the Belle Époque's top floor residence. Over the course of three hours, as firemen looked on idly, a tiny fire was allowed to grow into a massive burning blast-furnace with temperatures reaching 1000°F.

Edmond Safra barricaded himself in his bunker-like bathroom with one of his nurses, Vivian Torrente. It became their tomb.

Safra's fiery death in his fortified "flat" generated a heated controversy felt across the globe. Its lack of resolution and ensuing cover-up continue to boil over today.

And in the middle of the whole furtive firestorm was Ted Maher.

Ted is a former Green Beret, a man with obvious incredible toughness. But he is also a street-level, working American, born from pure red, white, and blue Maine stock and raised in upstate New York.

Through a series of circumstances that swelled into the monster perfect storm with countless imperfect twists, Ted rapidly became one of Safra's most appreciated personal nurses, achieving an elite position on the banker's staff in the high-ender heaven that is Monte Carlo, Monaco.

He also became the scapegoat for Safra's death.

He was "condemned"—as the Monegasque refer to prison sentencing—to spending a large part of his life behind bars.

Ted was the easy answer to the hard questions of who, what, when, where, why, and how, regarding Safra's death—questions the Monegasque authorities preferred not to expose to the potentially embarrassing light of bad-PR truth.

By the time Ted was released, he had already suffered seven years and eight months in a foreign prison—a *jail* really, which was never designed with the "amenities" of long-term incarceration in mind. A jail that stood on the shadow side—behind a wall of sunbathed secrets. A jail of degradation and isolation that the sophisticates just outside—and the entire rest of the world, for that matter—could never imagine.

And while Ted finally received some vindication and was released, his reversal of fortune ultimately amounted to little more than a newspaper running a back-page retraction to an unfortunate "mistake" in the previous day's headlines. The damage was done. In Monaco, this was just something else to sweep beneath the Aubusson rug, to once again preserve the sanctity of the world's most celebrated tax haven for the super-rich.

In the United States, Ted appeared on virtually every television news magazine program upon his return—ostensibly to affirm his innocence and celebrate his justified release. The emphasis, however, drifted toward the sensational, and *still* unresolved, death of Edmond Safra.

And that emphasis has proven again and again to have power and sensation of its own.

As Ted strove to pick up the pieces of the profession he once loved, the mountain of articles about Safra's death remained alive on the Internet. *"Fiery death . . . murder . . . imprisonment . . . escape . . . recapture"*—these are words with a hefty shelf-life.

It's hard to get—and keep—a job with that kind of biased baggage.

It's hard to heal all the gaping wounds—both literal and figurative—that were ripped open daily during a near-decade-long incarceration in an isolated cage 4,003 miles from home.

It's hard to put a family together and be a father to kids who have done a lot of growing up without you.

———————————

The chronicle of Ted's journey has more levels of intrigue and seduction than the six-story fortress of Monaco's La Belle Époque Building—described by *Newsweek* as the "impregnable haven for the rich and reclusive" where Edmond Safra lived and died.[8]

It's also where Ted Maher's freedom was choked out by a different kind of thick smokescreen.

This book is the most thorough examination of Safra's death—and Ted's sacrificial skewering—to date. While Ted has spoken out in the past, including the brief publication of another title, critical information has always been excised from his account—usually for fear of retribution. This time, no information has been left on the cutting-room floor or condensed into a media-model sound-bite.

Additionally, new developments have emerged over the past years, including twists that tie Safra's death and Ted's ordeal to none other than Russian president Vladimir Putin.

Here, finally, every detail is complete. Ted's intimate interactions with Safra; the suspicious activities of Safra's controversy-clouded wife, Lily; the violent events and gross incompetence that played into Safra's death; the barrage of damning evidence quashed at trial; the trifecta of savage betrayals by those closest to Ted; the confidential identities of powerful players who know the buried truths and accomplices who helped him regain freedom; and, last but not least, the stunning exposure of behind-the-scenes crimes and machinations that led to Ted's conviction—the same revelations that at long last paved the way for his return to the States.

Two elements of this story burn with an especially intense and haunting heat.

One is the mountain of mysterious details surrounding Safra's death. There are so, *so* many. The other is the psyche-gripping journey into the mind and emotions of Ted Maher as his incredible saga unfolds—from his overnight elevation into a dream job, to becoming prey to an international lynch mob as the murderer of a worldwide banking icon.

Framed in Monte Carlo opens two doors: a platinum portal into the lavish life of a power-paranoid billionaire, and a hard iron cell gate into the 2,814 days of Ted Maher's screaming nightmare.

Welcome to an enlightening walk through both.

CHAPTER 1
DETAINED (PART 1)

I was sitting in JFK.

Alone and isolated.

This feeling wasn't strange at all. It was a feeling that had cut deeply into nearly a quarter of my life as I'd looked at four walls.

Like I was doing now.

But after nearly ten years of stagnant decay in a Monaco jail and French prison, I was finally free!

Or so I thought.

I had landed nearly an hour and a half earlier, but I was being detained.

"You've been gone a very long time, Mr. Maher," the New York cop said before I was taken from the customs line and ushered into the "special room."

I understood that a lot had happened in the United States since 1999: high-alert terrorism, 9/11, Al Qaeda, suspicion of people returning to America after long absences. I had been in an extended coma of prison and politics. Reentering "normalcy" wouldn't be easy.

I cooperated fully as they strip-searched me. I even helped them to go through my two sad duffel bags—the only things I had to show for my years and years in the "luxury" of Monte Carlo.

"Do what you have to," I told them.

I almost smiled.

After what I had been through, they seemed like such amateurs.

CHAPTER 2

THE NEXT LEVEL

I've always taken things to the next level.

It's a drive I was born with—and for most of my life, it's a power that has served me well.

But there were times when it nearly destroyed me.

I've had a lot of time to reflect on this: a decade's worth of thinking in a ten-by-fourteen-foot cell. I've examined my upbringing, my achievements, my history of betrayal by those I've loved and by those jealous of what I've done—all of it.

I've examined everything that aligned with such horrible perfection—those precise factors that collided one deadly night and ripped my life apart.

And every story of vicious truth, every beyond-belief biography, every dissection of crime and murder, and every exposé of icy injustice inevitably paves a simple utilitarian path to the final explosive destination. At that destination—where the blood runs and the permanent effects of the tragedy are vulcanized—hindsight focuses in. When the deadly dust finally settles and the entire picture from the very beginning sharpens up, it's much easier for the ultimate truth to become clear.

The utilitarian path to my own destination of blood and injustice is integral to that entire picture. It was a path that was never without my rare and acute personal drive to that next level—like the gut-push that allowed me to excel in the Green Berets. It was a path that was never without my respect for responsibility and the truth; becoming a single father will reinforce *that* to the fullest. And it was a path that was never without my observation of what makes people tick—from the literal inner workings of barely-breathing infants during on-the-fly triage, to trying to understand some of the worst kind of betrayal.

Even after reaching that explosive end, and even after assessing the effects, I still won't accept not trying to get to that next level.

Trying to do things right and make things right.

Eighty-one miles north of New York City is the hamlet of Pine Bush, with a growing population of about fifteen hundred. I grew up there when the population was about a third of that, after moving as a baby from my birthplace of Auburn, Maine. I'm the oldest of five children. Hard work and a lust for adventure drove my life from the very beginning; it still does. That hard work and adventure got me into many places and situations that I wanted to experience.

But it ultimately led me into places I didn't choose to go.

My father was a telephone repairman and my mother had a full-time job taking care of us and driving a school bus. They did what they could with what they had, but with five mouths to feed on frayed blue-collar wages, we didn't have a lot.

Everything we had was worked for—worked hard for—and I accomplished most things myself.

As a kid, I pulled weeds for a dollar an hour working for a landscaper. I saved that money, bought a lawnmower, and started my own lawn business. I saved *that* money and at sixteen years old I bought my first vehicle.

I always knew I wanted to continue my education past high school. At the close of the Vietnam War, I was seventeen years old, and I knew that the Department of Veterans Affairs would provide benefits if I went into the armed services. With the goal of expanding my knowledge and marching on toward higher learning—that next level—the ends would justify the means for me.

In December 1975, I enlisted in the United States Army under a delayed entry program—to start after I finished high school. By July of '76, I was stationed at Fort Dix, New Jersey, for basic training and was then sent to Fort Sam Houston in San Antonio, Texas.

I realized very quickly that the more things I volunteered for, the more I could advance myself, and the higher rank I would attain.

I eventually went through Airborne School, Advanced Medical training programs, Advanced Rifleman Training, Multi-Vehicle Driving Training—and, of course, the Special Forces training program.

I would go on Temp Duty assignments and there would be orders chasing me around to give me another promotion. In a very short period of time—twenty-three months—I went from being a private to a specialist E5.

When I was just a specialist E1, after Jump School in Fort Benning, Georgia, I was assigned to the 1st Battalion, 505th Parachute Infantry Regiment of the 82nd Airborne. After no more than six months, I knew I wanted more. I wanted to take my training, like everything else, to the next level.

Becoming a Green Beret was the hardest yet most rewarding thing I've ever done in my life.

I heard that Special Forces were looking and had scheduled a meeting at the John F. Kennedy Special Warfare Center and School at Fort Bragg in North Carolina. I attended that meeting with over two thousand other airborne soldiers, all of whom had hopes of completing the Green Beret Special Forces training program.

But "hopes" are very different from "doing," and the two thousand was quickly pared down to seven hundred after a routine background check. And those seven hundred were cut to 320 after a more involved FBI check. The first part of the program was a thirty-day hell training at Camp McCall, North Carolina. It's the kind of "boot camp" where they weed out the mentally weak.

And it worked.

It was repelling. It was survival. It was being assigned a sixty-pound sandbag that was "yours" that you had to take with you everywhere. I weighed between 145 and 165 pounds and I couldn't even pick the damn thing up. So I laid it down on the ground and pushed it.

And *that* worked.

We were up at 0400 running around the racetrack and the airport landing strip, singing the "Ballad of the Green Berets" to our sandbags, asking under our breaths, *What the hell am I doing here?* It was psychological—showing you can do more than you think you can do.

That worked too—for some of us.

By the end of Special Forces training, only sixty remained.

After that came three separate phases of personal training; I chose the medical field. It was really intensive.

My first phase took place at Fort Sam Houston with classes that extended through every level: nursing, surgery, OB/GYN, field sanitation, microbiology, anatomy and physiology, dentistry, improvisation, water sanitation, vet care for animals—you name it. They wanted to make sure you were prepared for anything with a bare minimum of resources.

We attended eight courses a day, five days a week. And if you didn't study through the weekends, you would fail. Period.

Guys were dropping like flies. Sixty-six people started that medical program; thirteen graduated.

Two guys made it all the way to the very last week and then failed the exam.

I was third in my class.

And I stood alone as I traveled to the next phase of my training. Moving onto Phase 2 as a solo was unprecedented.

For this phase, I was stationed in Fort Polk, Louisiana, for an extremely advanced medical training program. Training with doctors and nurses for almost four months straight, I was in the OR, ER, ICU, Labor and Delivery, Lab, everywhere. We covered everything from gunshot wounds to amputations.

Phase Three was Goat Lab. This was an extremely secretive division that used live animals for "study." We also had human simulations of mass emergency scenarios.

For the final thirty days of Green Beret training, all the graduates assembled into adrenaline-pumped groups like in *The A-Team* and competed in serious war games.

In fifty-eight wildcat weeks, my Special Forces training was complete.

I made it through that level with flying colors.

In 1977, right after my first phase of Green Beret training, I met an attractive reservist named Cassandra. She was training at Fort Sam Houston to be a licensed practical nurse.

Cassandra—Sandy—was supposed to be the love of my life.

I saw her as being very down to earth. And she cared for me in a special way that I believe few have felt in life.

At some point, I knew we would be married.

Even though she was very young—in her late teens/early twenties—she suffered from kidney problems. And I realized that coming from a poor family, she wouldn't be able to afford the surgery she needed. So I told her parents I would marry her before I completed my military service so that she could become my dependent and the army would cover it.

So we drove to the South of the Border compound in Dillon, South Carolina. With a path of 175 giant freeway billboards leading the way to its 350 acres of "kitsch, glitz," and weddings performed by a notary public known as "Pedro of the Peace," it was the perfect quick nuptial alternative to, say, Hawaii or the Caribbean. No blood tests, a near drive-thru civil ceremony, and we were done.

It was easy to take our relationship to the next level.

Sandy went back home immediately for the kidney procedure. About six months later, I took my terminal leave from the military, having served my three years, and we had a big official wedding. Our mothers did most of the planning, my grandparents got us a limo, and family traveled in from all over for this ceremony.

Without Pedro.

With us both out of the military, we moved to Las Vegas because I was considering a career in law enforcement.

I was also deciding between medical and forensic science. Las Vegas was a booming city at that point, and they were screening for this work. I knew I would score high in the security and background checks and could rise quickly.

I had been thinking about all of this for a while, so six months earlier, I had gone to Vegas for a police force "pre-test." I flew through all the written, psychological, and background checks and was given a position to start after I left the army. As I waited for my number to come up on the list, I worked security for six weeks at the Circus, Circus hotel. What a trip *that* was—a twenty-four/seven midway of madness! And very, very *pink!*

In September 1979, I became a police officer with Las Vegas Metro.

But that adventure was very short-lived.

As I neared the end of my police academy training, Cassandra—who was working in a neonatal intensive care unit (NICU), continuing her career as a nurse—was exposed to a baby that had spinal meningitis. So naturally, I was exposed as well.

I went from the 195 pounds of muscle I had been as a Special Forces Green Beret down to 145 pounds in just six weeks. I wound up in the hospital, where I could hear the nurses asking, "Is he going to die tonight?"

Things weren't going well. I had meningitis. My wife had meningitis. I had lost so much weight. I suffered six weeks of hell before my symptoms began to subside, and for that entire time, my brain was pretty much cooking.

I tried to return to the police force, but the effects of the meningitis were harsh and lingering. Radio calls would come in and I couldn't remember what was said or reported. I had short-term memory loss. It was scary. I didn't feel as though I could even protect my partner.

Finally, I was given a departmental medical termination.

But those types of medical terminations don't apply to marriage—and the disease had permanent effects on Sandy. She was never the same person that I had married. I would sleep with Dr. Jekyll one night and Mr. Hyde the next.

Throughout my ordeal, I suffered horribly painful meningeal headaches, which I tried everything to relieve—acupuncture, TENS (transcutaneous electrical nerve stimulation) units, bio-feedback, anything I could think of. But nothing worked. And I couldn't go on like that anymore, so I gave in to taking pain meds.

Once I was finally able to think about working again, a friend of mine got me a job in gaming surveillance at the Las Vegas Hilton Hotel. But while my mind was now intact, over the course of eighteen months, I became addicted to the codeine pills I'd been prescribed.

I needed to fix the problem. I decided that I would simply eradicate the entire disease from my body. I did so by working out like a madman. I ran . . . worked out . . . ran . . . worked out. I ran like I was running for my life. Which I was.

After two weeks of "training," I woke up pain-free. Step two was to get off the meds. I stopped them cold turkey and in three days, I was *truly free*. I was healed.

So I was working for the Hilton and the Flamingo—putting in a ton of hours between the two. Plus, as part of my surveillance training, I had to attend casino gaming school in my "off" time. With no compensation.

They gave me two years to finish; I boomed it out in four and a half months. I rose from the low man on the totem pole all the way to the top five in just six months. People were in awe, but that's how I've always done things in my life.

I continued in the very specialized field of Las Vegas surveillance for two and a half years—a specialization that would come back to haunt me two decades later.

What happens in Vegas apparently doesn't always stay there.

The meningitis had been bad—but life's manure pit can always get deeper.

On November 21, 1980, the third worst hotel fire in US history killed eighty-five people in the MGM Grand Hotel on the Strip.[9] One of the collateral casualties was my little Volkswagen Rabbit that was parked right near the base of the fire.

Cars, of course, can be replaced. Some things cannot.

Shortly after the fire, I got clued in by my apartment manager and by some friends at work that I should go home early some night.

I found out that my best friend—who I'd put on the guest list to my apartment building—wasn't just lifting weights in the complex's gym; he was also "exercising" with my wife.

But instead of just busting in on them—*that* would be crude and base—I devised a plan that would settle things more strategically.

Through some help from friends in the Vegas PD, I turned a wall light switch into a microphone. Then I asked the apartment manager if I could install a digital video recorder across from my apartment.

He agreed.

My documentation began.

I would leave for work at 11:00 p.m. At 11:30 p.m., my "best friend" would arrive. At 6:30 or 7:00 in the morning, right before I came home, he would leave.

I was devastated. Betrayed by both my best friend and my wife. Another unpleasant foreshadowing of my future.

I had given this woman everything—I was working all these extra jobs and hours. We had both recovered physically from the meningitis, but she also suffered from scoliosis—a severe curvature of the spine—and maintained that she was too sick to work. Obviously, she was well *enough*!

My best friend soon found out (from yet another friend at work) that I knew what was going on. He left Las Vegas that very night.

I had ideas for my life, too. Casino surveillance wasn't exactly the *ultimate* level for me. My next level would tie in even further to what I had learned and accomplished in the military.

Under Nevada law, you could work with physicians under their general license as a PA—a physician's assistant. An MD named Dr. Hamm was a retired Navy captain, so he knew of me from my success in the Special Forces medical program.

He hired me quickly.

By now, my wife had left. I really *had* cared about her though, so I was still trying to work things out, even after her cheating.

I got her a job. I set her up in her own apartment.

However, on Christmas Eve of 1980, I stopped by her apartment to drop off a gift that my grandmother had sent for her. I knocked and some guy answered the door.

"Sandy doesn't love you anymore," he said arrogantly. "You need to move on."

Now, obviously what he said was true. But here was this stranger, yet another guy in her life, coldly informing me that the love of my life was over. And I'd done nothing to warrant that type of treatment.

I had a .357 in the glove box of my car. I went out and put it in my hand. That's as far as it went though. *Nobody is worth what this would lead to,* I thought. And I was right.

But I did go back for the last word.

"If I ever see you with my wife again," I told him, "I'll kill you."

When we filed for divorce, I still had the surveillance tapes that I had made of Sandy. I transcribed them *all*—fifty-six pages worth—and I went to her attorney's office and asked to see him. *Alone.*

He started jumping all over me, about how they'd tried to serve me, blah, blah, blah . . .

I stopped him.

I laid out *my* conditions for the divorce. Of all the cars, the furniture, the wedding gifts, and everything else we owned, Sandy would get her clothes and personal belongings. That was it.

And I had more to say.

I had spent over eight thousand dollars of *my* money paying for her breast-reduction surgery, which had been necessary to relieve her scoliosis. She was supposedly so sick and in pain because of the condition—but of course not *so* sick that she couldn't screw my friend.

"She's going to start paying me two hundred dollars a month until I'm reimbursed for that money," I told her lawyer. "If you don't agree to that, well, there's the matter of these tapes. And here's the transcript of all of them. Rest assured, pal, if she doesn't sign these divorce papers without changing them in any way, every relative, friend, uncle, and cousin of hers is going to get a copy of the transcript. And being from a rural East Coast town, *everyone* is going to know what a little whore she is."

Cassandra signed the paperwork.

But this particular adventure—like so many other things in my life—would sadly linger on like a cracked violin: no longer soothing, just painful and sour.

———

I worked for Dr. Hamm for a couple of years before I took a vacation. I went back East to go fishing with my grandfather, way up into the northern Maine woods near the Canadian border.

While we were there, we got a call. Well, actually, the park ranger got a call, and he retrieved us from the special fishing spot where he'd set us up.

Our stress-free leisure was about to change.

It was my grandmother. Cassandra had notified her of a "family emergency." So, I called Sandy's mother.

It turned out that the rural postmaster up in her mother's small community was a relative—many in the town were. And apparently, he was the curious type. He couldn't help but "notice" the mail being sent by Sandy to her mother following the divorce—and the contents therein.

I had kept *my* part of the divorce deal, so this had nothing to do with me; it wasn't *my* transcripts that piqued the postman's interest. It was some mother-daughter bonding that he just couldn't resist snooping into—and sharing.

Well—as I had already been certain—news spreads fast in that kind of closed-country closet of a town. People were talking.

Sandy's father couldn't take the fallout. He couldn't take what was being said and what was being thought about his only daughter.

So, he went into the woods and took a shotgun to his head.

And that was the end of that—because of what she did. And she has to live with that for the rest of her life.

Cassandra's father and I had been close—even after the divorce—but Sandy told me not to come to the funeral.

"Just send flowers," she said.

―――――――

I remained back East for a while, but the vacation was definitely over. I flew out of Portland, Maine, with a connecting flight through Chicago to Las Vegas.

The R&R had ended, but this sick adventure had not.

Cassandra had flown back East for her father's funeral, of course, and she, too, was returning to Vegas—the same day.

Also connecting through Chicago.

So there I was at O'Hare airport, and I came around the corner and there she was. She immediately—and loudly—accused me of following her.

"I'm not following you," I told her. "I'm coming back from Maine."

And then I asked her why she was standing by the men's restroom.

My mind quickly went to the promise I had made to that guy at her apartment on that Christmas Eve.

Guess who was in the men's room . . .

Sandy informed me they were engaged and then stood paralyzed as I walked into the restroom to find him.

This guy was standing at the urinal and saw me in the mirror as I came up behind him. He practically pissed on his shoes. He just knew his life was going to end right there on the cold tile floor of that airport bathroom.

He zipped up fast, turned around, and backed against the sink.

I held out my hand and shook his.

I calmly asked how he was doing and then added: "May God have mercy on your soul. Oh, and best wishes—I hear you're getting married!"

I slowly washed my right hand, walked out, brushed past Cassandra, and never looked back.

CHAPTER 3

ADVENTURES ALIGN

I continued to work for Dr. Hamm in Las Vegas for another three and a half years. During that time, Dr. Hamm got called out to Caesars Palace to provide care for Frank Sinatra—a regular performer in the realm of short-toga cocktail waitresses and old-school high-rollers. It turned out that Sinatra had a heel spur.

Now, normally a physician would do surgery and file down the protruding bone, but given his performance schedule, Sinatra just couldn't afford to be laid up like that.

So, Dr. Hamm sent me out to give "Old Blue Eyes" some cortisone shots. When I went down there, the guy had more security than the president of the United States! But once I actually met him, he was the most down-to-earth guy. That was nice to see.

I ended up going out to see Sinatra three or four times.

I was doing well.

Until Dr. Hamm and the other physicians he worked with at the hospital began asking, "Why are we putting our patients in this hospital when we can open up a day surgery center of our own? We could be getting the revenue that the hospital is getting . . ."

One of the hospital directors realized what the doctors' group was planning and became very upset—the hospital would lose thousands of dollars. So, they began cracking down on the doctors—for anything and everything. Including their PAs.

I was doing a closure after an operation, sewing somebody up, when a nurse came in and told me that the hospital director wanted to see me.

No problem.

"Mr. Maher," he said, "we've decided we want to have our PAs certified. You will have to test for your certification if you want to continue working."

So? That didn't bother me.

"I've had more surgical experience than most residents," I told him. "I don't have any problem taking the physician assistant's exam."

But there *was* a problem.

The problem was that when I submitted my records from the Department of Army down in San Antonio and also Baylor University, who had reviewed and accredited our coursework, the transcripts came back mostly blacked out.

This was from the time when they were experimenting with animals. They would take lab animals and shoot them in the hindquarters: *Here is your patient. Here is live tissue; here is dead tissue.* Before the goats, they'd used dogs! They sure didn't want the general populace knowing about these experiments.

So now, all of a sudden, without the specific course listings, I didn't even meet the minimum requirements to take the exam.

My medical adventure was changing.

I knew I had to go back to school and get the full sheepskin. I had to take things to that next level, yet again.

During this time, I had a very low post-divorce opinion of women. I definitely didn't want to be involved in any sort of relationship.

However, I met a girl while working as a PA.

Dr. Hamm and his group *did* open their own place, the Redrock Medical Center, and I went with him. A girl who worked in the office set me up with her cousin, Minnie. We dated and had fun. But it was to be a simple friendship—nothing I intended to take to the next level.

In order to go back to school, I needed one thing: Money.

My grandfather was a bridge contractor up in Maine. He had his own plane and would fly into wherever the next job was. He told me about a huge project—the construction of a dam in Valdez, Alaska. This was in 1986, during the Chernobyl disaster.

The job would solve everything. Twelve-hour shifts, six days a week, making around fifty bucks an hour. If I could do this for even three months, I'd have more than enough money for school.

And it would *certainly* be worth the 3,986-mile trek up the Alcan Highway.

I had a friend in construction who wanted to come with me. So, we all loaded into my tiny Nissan diesel pickup. "We all" being my friend, his wife, his two kids, and me—and bicycles and all kinds of other stuff strapped and packed everywhere. We were a jammed-in, sardine-can version of the Beverly Hillbillies—except that the Clampetts had a lot more room in their 1921 Olds flatbed than we did in my Nissan.

And their money-laden ship had already come in.

After ten days of driving, everybody was ready to kill everybody. To make matters worse, we discovered that oil prices were plummeting, and the industry was suddenly drying up. As we headed north, people kept driving by us heading south—leaving.

We finally rolled into Anchorage, Alaska, with a tired truck and an exhausted crew, only to find that the promised jobs had been put "on hold" by the Environmental Protection Agency. They had to do more "assessments" of the dam project.

Essentially, there were *no* jobs at all there.

Well, almost none.

I ended up delivering pizza for a place called Mafia Mike's Pizza. I had to wear black pants, a white dress shirt, and a black hat.

Mafia Mike's . . . yet another catalyst for hard work and adventure.

Sort of.

My time at the pizza place became what could have been the Parmesan precursor to *Taxicab Confessions*.

One night, I was in my *Sopranos* outfit, delivering a pizza to this upscale house with lots of cars out front; some big-time Mercedes and others. I knocked on the door and a scantily dressed woman answered. I saw people inside doing lines of coke. I gave the woman the pizza and she paid me. Then she said, "Here's your tip!" and threw me the keys to a Porsche! Well, this didn't seem like a good idea, so I gave the keys back to the man who appeared next to her, and he gave me a more-in-line, less-drug-inspired twenty-dollar tip.

Another evening, "dispatch" sent me to deliver a pizza to an Anchorage strip club. Now, prior to this adventure in the Great Northern Frontier, I'd never been to a strip joint in my life. I really don't understand the concept of a strip joint. To me, that's like being obsessed with food and going the best steakhouse in town, and them putting a tender, perfect filet in front of you with potatoes and corn on the cob and a beautiful dessert, and *then* them telling you, "Nope, you can't touch it!"

If I'm going to a restaurant, I'm going to eat!

Anyway, I went to the strip joint—and I'll never forget it. When I walked inside, the song "Black Velvet" was playing. And this eighteen-year-old girl was doing something that (even with all my medical training) I would've thought anatomically impossible—leg up the pole, this and that.

It was more than a performance; it was art.

At least there in the flannel-and-denim outback of Anchorage, Alaska.

Years later, since cell phones have become mandatory, I've always programmed in that song as my ring tone. When shit's really bad and the telephone rings, I smile as I remember that bright little spot in a situation that otherwise pretty much sucked.

But I had to survive.

So I worked up there, hustling pizzas in my *Wise Guy* getup, for almost six weeks.

My patience was wearing. I drove out to the northeast end of Ketchemak Bay on the Kenai Peninsula to check out the jobsite for the Bradley Lake Hydroelectric Project where our end-of-the-rainbow jobs were supposed to have been.

I found out the jobs would be on hold for months.

It was time to go home.

———

I gave the sad news to Mafia Mike, relinquished my Gambino wardrobe, and began my preparations to head south.

Alone.

My friend had found a small job in local construction, so he and his family remained behind (for another two months, anyway).

But even in the midst of chaos, there's always time to fish! And the Alaskan Department of Fish and Game had done a little something to fool Mother Nature. They'd dug this huge trench near the Kenai Peninsula that was three hundred feet wide by five hundred feet long, and three years earlier, they'd dropped about one hundred thousand salmon smelts into it.

Now, if you know anything about salmon, you know they don't spawn in salt water. Well, this was brine water, and as part of some grand experiment, they'd done this to see if the salmon would come back to that particular spot.

And they did! When they swam into this tide pool, they were trapped.

Huge salmon! People would fish using grappling hooks and everything else. Even little kids from Russia would come over since it was so close by, and they'd have a field day.

I knew I just had to land one of those giant salmon, too!

I got a cheap little Zebco reel and I tried and tried, but I couldn't catch anything.

I was exhausted, and it was ten-thirty at night—but it was still light outside due to the Summer Equinox, which up there is twenty-two hours of sunshine! I began talking to one of the locals about my lack of luck with the salmon.

"If you want to catch one of those fish," he said, "get a small piece of Velveeta cheese, put it around some salmon eggs, and put out a bobber . . . but don't tell anybody because it's a local secret!"

So after fishing for about ten hours, I went out armed with Velveeta. And sure enough, here came this huge salmon—like something like out of *Field and Stream*. People were yelling "Look at *that* guy!" so I wound up in a public struggle.

After nearly half an hour with this beast of a fish, he comes 'round, and he's looking tired. He comes up . . . but he breaks the line! I couldn't believe it. Well, I figured I'd lost him, then I saw the bobber go by underneath the water. *There has to be thirty feet of line attached to the bobber,* I thought. *All I need to do is stick a grappling hook out, snatch the line, and I become the Old Man and the Sea!*

Now, the water temperature was only about forty degrees, even in June. But this had become a quest. A redemption! I'd driven four thousand miles to get here, I hadn't gotten a job, and now it was all gonna end with me fishing for ten hours with nothing to show for it? No way! I was getting that damn fish!

I grabbed the line, and everyone started yelling again. My hands were bleeding, but I didn't care. I got the salmon right up to the edge where I was standing, and everything shifted into slow motion. He moved his mouth and the hook slid out— crap! But I reached in and grabbed him.

The thing ended up weighing close to twenty-seven pounds.

But this adventure wasn't over, either. I was about to get my first small claim to fame.

On the way home from Alaska, some hundred miles from Anchorage, I came across a huge sightseeing bus. Japanese tourists were crowded outside of it, in the middle of nowhere, surrounding something and taking a ton of pictures. Cameras were everywhere.

Wondering just what they were photographing, I parked the truck and got out. Why not? I had a little time to satisfy some curiosity.

Well, it was a baby moose. And I mean *baby*. My first thought was that these people were *nuts* to be so close to it—the mother had to be around here somewhere. But it was nearing dusk, so I realized that something wasn't right.

I canvassed the area and saw a big pool of blood. The mother evidently got clipped by a vehicle—you see lots of large train-like caravans of trucks up there—and she bled to death. Now this baby moose was here with the umbilical cord still attached!

Left on its own, I knew it would die. So, I circled around and came up behind it. Then—to the shocked expressions of the tourists and the sound of a million camera clicks—I snatched it up like a little calf in a rodeo and put it in my truck. The little moose didn't struggle at all; it went right to sleep.

Up there, you're more likely to get away with murdering a human than with taking down a game animal like a moose or an eagle—and I didn't want any misunderstandings. So, I called the police and let them know I had a rescue, and that after a long weekend, I would be back in Anchorage standing in front of the zoo first thing Monday morning with a baby moose.

Then I went down to the local emergency room and asked them for some supplies. "I have a baby moose that needs to be fed!" I explained.

I named the moose after my "friend" back home, Minnie—Minnie the Moose.

While working for Mafia Mike's, I had been staying in a mobile home at an old farmhouse in Homer. I took Minnie back there, and for the entire weekend, I had a pet.

One thing I noticed right away was how clean this moose was; no scent at all. I supposed it was a natural defense mechanism, to avoid attracting predators. But then she picked up *my* scent and started following me everywhere. Once, I woke up in the middle of the night with her sucking on my ear!

The local media caught wind of the story and they were all waiting for me when I rolled into the zoo on Monday. They did a big write-up in the newspaper. I still remember the headline: "Transient from Las Vegas saves moose!"

A moose is one of the few animals that will take in another's offspring, and the zoo happened to have a female moose with a two-month-old calf. My little pet had a new mom.

The zoo asked me how old I thought the moose was. I told them that since the umbilical cord had still been attached, I was guessing at most a couple of weeks. It turned out the moose was only about three days old. Left alone, she *definitely* would've died.

A year later, I received a postcard from the Anchorage Zoo. They had just released Minnie back into the wild. By that time, she weighed two thousand pounds!

After that adventure, I had a strange dream: *I was flying into Anchorage in a storm, the plane crashed, and like a behemoth Saint Bernard, Minnie the Moose charged out of the blizzard to save me!* I guess that shows my karmic hope that what goes around eventually comes around.

It's a hope I've struggled hard to hold on to.

———

When I returned to Vegas, my now well-worn truck was repossessed within two days.

"Enough is enough foolishness!" my grandfather called and told me. "You're coming back home. I'm sending you money to rent a moving trailer!"

I loaded up everything I owned into the slow, bulky twenty-four-foot box and rumbled over the 2,600 miles to Middletown, New York, where my parents were. Now I needed another job.

I knew demand was high for nurses, so with my grandfather helping me out, I enrolled in a two-year associate degree nursing program at Orange County Community College, which would allow me to start working and making money quickly.

Plus, if I had to start over, it wasn't going to be at Physician's Assistant 101. I had always liked the nursing side of things and thought that's where I would end up. I admired what they were doing at the "other end" of the surgical table—the anesthesia end. I could become a nurse anesthetist and move forward from there.

I had resumed casually seeing Minnie after returning to Las Vegas. However, a few months later she showed up in New York and moved in with me! I realized she must be in love with me.

I cared about her too and I wanted to give her the attention that she needed. But I was extremely busy.

In addition to school, I was now supporting the both of us by doing carpentry work up in the Catskills for a guy who wanted to transform his newly purchased bungalow colony into a horse ranch. "My son's a jack-of-all-trades," my dad had told him.

Minnie had never completed high school and didn't have many job skills, so I was paying for her to go to cosmetology school, to get a car, and for everything else she wanted.

But she still wasn't happy. What she really wanted was to party!

It takes a lot of commitment to go to school and work full-time. I was busting my ass, pushing myself as hard as I'd pushed that sixty-pound sandbag back in Special Forces training. I had a GPA of 3.85 and was on the dean's list. If I didn't study constantly—what with the complexities of pharmacology and the other heavy medical subjects—I wouldn't get through it.

I didn't need this woman's pressure. I had more important things to deal with; I had a future.

I had more levels.

But it became constant: She accused me of not loving her and not wanting to go out and have any fun with her. It wasn't true; I would have loved to party. But I *needed* to stay on course.

So, she decided that she was going to go "find herself." That little quest of enlightenment involved moving out to live with her friends, totaling the car I gave her, getting arrested for a DWI, and getting involved with married men.

Mother of God, where do I find these people?

I couldn't believe it: I'd finally opened my heart again, and again I was betrayed.

But I *had* to stay focused on work and school.

Soon after, my college hired a new director. She restructured the schedule so that nursing students had to be there every day, at odd hours. I stood up during the information assembly and said, "This won't work. It's unreasonable! How can anyone *hold down a job* with these school hours every day of the week?"

She didn't answer my question, but *I* did—I transferred to Duchess Community College in upstate New York, sixty miles from Middletown.

That is where I met Heidi.

That is what set me up for the *worst* betrayal of my life.

That is when another piece of that savage and perfect alignment slid into place.

CHAPTER 4

BEFORE THE BETRAYAL

Heidi Wustrau was everything you would want in a woman—quiet, beautiful, intelligent. But at first, we were just friends.

I was just finishing my final semester of school when Minnie decided she wanted to return home, to Las Vegas.

Fine.

I even offered to help her move back, since she *did* ostensibly come to New York because of *us*.

We got as far as the Denver foothills before the transmission in her car went. At the same time, she got sick beyond sick, with the flu or something. It was barf, bedlam, and complete disaster.

So I was playing nurse and taking care of her. It took three days and a trunkful of money to get her little throwaway car fixed. All of that led to her saying she was sorry for what she had done to me—and *that* led to something else as well.

After our "final farewell," we drove back to Vegas and within two hours I was on a flight home to New York.

Six weeks later, I got a phone call.

"I'm a little pregnant," said Minnie.

Now, I had only touched her that once since she'd moved out, but I am a man of ethics and if it was my child, I was going to take responsibility for it.

That taking of responsibility led me into doing one of the most genuinely stupid things I've ever done in my life—I married for a child.

After a DNA test to confirm I was the father, we had a quick Vegas wedding (set up by her mother) and took a brief honeymoon to nearby Mt. Charleston. It was a bit better than my "South of the Border" soirée with Sandy under the giant sombrero sign, but not by much.

On June 14, 1989, Minnie gave birth to my son, Matthew.

In the meantime, we'd returned to New York so I could finish my associate degree.

I graduated with honors.

I then sat for the state board exam (the NCLEX) in Albany and passed. After that, I decided I wanted to take my education to the next level: my bachelor's degree.

Minnie was appalled.

Not only because she wanted me to spend more time with her—and now, the baby—but because she was jealous. With my profession being a primarily female field, I was always interacting with a lot of women at work. I was never unfaithful to Minnie, but I have heard it said: "A cheater always worries about being cheated on . . ."

And throughout all this, my relationship with Heidi had remained relatively innocent. We'd seen each other only in the presence of her identical twin sister, who'd served as a de facto chaperone. When Minnie told me she was pregnant, Heidi had sensed something was wrong. She'd then supported me through it and our friendship had remained intact.

Meanwhile, I had gotten a job at Columbia-Presbyterian Medical Center, commonly referred to as Columbia-Presbyterian Hospital. They put me through an orientation program that usually lasted three months; I completed it in six weeks. I actually got the job before I officially graduated—and that, too, was unique and unprecedented.

I excelled at the hospital. I had found my niche. I loved working with preemies in the NICU. This is what I wanted to do.

But my doomed adventure with Minnie lingered.

Our apartment building had increased our rent, so we'd moved to upstate New York, north of Middletown. My parents bought us a trailer and I paid them monthly rent to reimburse them.

But since I was now working in Manhattan, I'd go down, stay for three days on someone's couch that I rented, and then drive back. Sleep, shower, work . . . that was it!

Minnie was left alone upstate with the baby.

She was furious.

So one day, in the dead of winter, Minnie decided to take off—again. I got home from my hour-and-a-half-long commute after an intense three-day workweek to find just my dogs in an empty house. At least she'd left a bunch of food out for them.

That was it.

No note.

Nothing.

But she had taken Matthew—our infant son of just eight weeks.

If she wants to go find herself, I thought, *great! But she's not going to kidnap* my *son!*

I had no idea where she was. She could've been in the Midwest with her grandparents or back in Las Vegas with her mother. I went through three months of hell, just working and wondering and worrying. I had to find my son.

Then one day, I went to the post office up near the trailer my parents had bought for us. I had just planned to send something out, but the guy working there said, "You're Ted Maher. You have some mail here."

"I don't get mail here," I told him.

"You sure do," he replied. "It's certified."

It was a letter postmarked from Nevada. That's where Minnie had landed. And in Nevada, you could become a resident after just three months. You could also execute a divorce by sending a notice to your spouse's last known address. And that's what she did.

I couldn't get to my attorney fast enough.

"Since you're still married," he advised me, "*if* you still had your son, she would have to come back to New York for the proceedings. Now, I'm not telling you that you have to go get your son, but . . . *you have to go get your son.*"

With hardly any money, over spring break, I got on an airplane. I flew to Las Vegas knowing only the PO Box number and zip code from the certified letter. I rented a car, found the post office, and instituted a search like I was trained to in the army. I circled outward from the perimeter, looking for her car.

In two and a half hours, I found it.

I waited until the following morning.

Minnie was living with her mother and stepfather. I waited for her stepfather to leave. Then I waited for her mother to leave. Then I waited for Minnie to come out with my son.

I followed them to a little shopping mall.

And I waited some more.

When they came out, Minnie was holding a balloon. It was the last thing she would buy for our son for quite some time. After she strapped him into his car seat and shut the door, I came up behind her—running. I had keys to her car, so I pushed her out of the way, jumped in, and drove away. It was quick, it was precise, and she never even saw who took the car—and her son.

I got down the road about three blocks from there and my son, whom I hadn't seen in over three months, looked at me and I swore he cooed, "Da Da."

I drove from Las Vegas to Los Angeles, putting 287 miles between us and Minnie. Matthew was now just fifteen weeks old. We boarded a plane at LAX back to New York and at forty thousand feet, I got on the in-flight phone. I called Minnie and asked her if she was missing something.

She was in a panic; I was all business.

First, I told her where I'd left her car.

Next I told her: "If you want a divorce, you can have that, but we're going to share our son. I didn't go out of my way to give you my life so you could steal my son from me. If you want him, you can come back to New York."

She did.

After the legal proceedings, I received full custody—she got visitation rights. I was shown to be a person with income and stability; *she* had DWIs and a history of alcoholism.

She didn't try to press charges for my pushing her.

It was a perfect operation.

I was back in New York, working at Columbia-Presbyterian. I had my son, and I was going to Pace University for my bachelor's degree.

And that was when my relationship with Heidi developed.

She was nine years younger than me and from a strict German family. Very isolated. And she was loyal—I thought.

I fell in love with her.

I also fostered a close friendship with her parents, who saw me as very honorable. I was in the nursing program, and I was a rare single father, who'd received sole custody of his child. Heidi's parents found my relationship with Matthew amazing.

So, her mother approached me with a proposition. She offered to help me take care of Matthew if I would help her daughters with their schooling.

She wanted both of them to get their bachelor's degrees, but she didn't want the twins traveling alone to Pace University in Pleasantville or to Columbia University in the city. So, I got them both jobs at Columbia-Presbyterian with *me*—a big step up from the community hospital where they'd been working—and they enrolled at Pace. Each sister had a small, two-seater car so I traded in *my* car for a minivan. Now I could drive them and all their books and gear over to work and to school.

In exchange, my son and I moved in with their family. Heidi's mom became a grandma to Matthew, who slept every night by their fireplace. I stayed alone in the basement.

Things clicked along very well that way.

After a couple of years, I bought a huge ring for Heidi. It was *twenty-five grand* worth of commitment—for a long time, I would be making bigger ring payments than house payments!

I married Heidi in 1993. We had a wedding up in the Catskills, at the historic Mohonk Mountain House resort, where Anthony Hopkins was filming what turned out to be the much-criticized movie *The Road to Wellville* (described by the *New York Times* as "a lavish, overproduced satire that finds its hilarity in bowel jokes, bowel-touting slogans and bowel-related dinnertime conversation").

The wedding had been planned for thirteen months. All the while, Hopkins kept filming. The resort had huge Victorian suites, no televisions, no phones, magnificent fireplaces—it was a truly awesome place. But the filming went on and on.

Mohonk remained more of a sound stage than the ideal sylvan setting for a wedding.

"They're within days of being done," we were told again and again.

Two days before the wedding, I went up there to check on the progress. That's when I realized that along with the place still looking like the back lot at Universal Studios, my honeymoon suite had been taken over by Anthony Hopkins. I didn't care who the fuck he was—this was *my* honeymoon and I had reserved that suite over a year ago.

"You better get Hopkins' personal manager and get this shit straightened out," I told them, "because I'll be up there pounding at the door!"

They said he would be out by the wedding—no problem.

And he was.

We actually wound up sending him an invitation: "Thank you so much for understanding . . ."

In return, he sent Heidi two dozen long-stem roses with a card that said: "I'm so sorry, but my schedule is full. I can't attend the wedding, but I hope you enjoy the flowers."

On our wedding night, he sent us a huge gourmet platter, with a card reading: "Keep it quiet. Best wishes and regards, Hannibal."

A very different kind of devouring was about to begin.

CHAPTER 5
THE ROAD TO MONACO

Minnie was jealous of Heidi—seriously jealous. It would become another of those imperfect twists in the now well-forming perfect storm.

Matthew was three and a half. Minnie and I were long divorced, and Heidi and I were married.

But Minnie just wouldn't let it all go.

She had remained in New York after the divorce and the custody battle. She saw the nice house in Stormville where her son now lived with Heidi and me. She saw the new SUV that I'd given my wife for Valentine's Day. She saw our lives and her son's life with us.

She finally realized the impact of the sacrifices I had made in working and going to school. But Heidi and I were the ones reaping the rewards. Minnie wanted it. So, she became relentless in her efforts to destroy my marriage to Heidi.

Matthew would come back from visits with Minnie and he'd throw rocks at Heidi's car.

"Mommy told me to do it," he would say.

And then he came back having suffered even more emotional—and now physical—damage with bruises and cigarette burns on him. At that point I went ballistic, and soon there were no visitation rights for Matthew's mother at all.

Minnie remained in upstate New York, kicking around in waitressing jobs, in hopes of being able to see Matthew.

She was also still getting DWIs.

In one of her more impressive performances, she wrapped her car around a telephone pole.

The continued chaos was becoming a huge pain in my ass.

That's when I started the fight—adoption.

God forbid, but if something happened to me, then Matthew would end up having to go back to his biological mother. He knew Heidi as his mother far more than Minnie. And he was getting older. I needed Heidi to adopt Matthew immediately. So, I started down into the black pit of the legal system.

Right away, Minnie secured a court-appointed lawyer. For free, of course. Meantime, I was paying $385 an hour, pro-rated. I fell into that black hole very quickly.

"Oh, Ted, it will just run about five thousand" . . . "Oh, Ted, we need about ten thousand more" . . ."Uh, Ted, things are up to just around twenty-five thousand" . . . Can anyone bid thirty? Do I hear thirty-five?

Added to my tab, I'd been trading even more expensive lawsuits with an obsessive neighbor concerning metes and bounds and other insane property issues. He'd recently had a heart attack—probably from the stress of it—and I wasn't doing much better.

I was paying for all this on a nurse's salary, working twelve-hour shifts back-to-back-to-back with the occasional sixteen-hour shift thrown in. I was killing myself. I wasn't working in standard nursing, either; I was working in the very prestigious ICU at Columbia-Presbyterian Medical Center. And along with prestige came stress— very high stress. Plus, I was driving an hour each way to and from the hospital before and after working these marathon shifts.

The fun quotient was low.

But there was always that next level.

By then, Heidi was pregnant.

It was during this period that a *first* golden opportunity came my way.

I had become familiar with a member of Saudi Arabia's royal family, a Prince Ahmed bin Salman. The third son of the governor of Riyadh Province, Salman was a media executive and a major figure in international thoroughbred horse racing.

Prince Ahmed's wife couldn't conceive, but she became pregnant with triplets through in vitro fertilization at New York Hospital. All three fetuses had been identified as girls, which is not a particularly good thing in their culture.

The wife came to Columbia-Presbyterian as a high-risk pregnancy and delivered the triplets prematurely. The babies all needed special attention and they needed isolation.

But none of the nurses wanted to go into the isolation room to attend to them. The entire area had been cordoned off due to fear of kidnapping. Heavily armed NYPD cops and all kinds of extra security were there on the NICU floor. The nurses were terrified.

Not me.

I was an ex-police officer and a Green Beret.

Take off these little diapers, check the temperature, rotate the tires, no IVs, no antibiotics; they're just little preemies . . .

This was a cushy job.

I was getting these little infant girls bigger and healthier, and after several weeks of doing this, I got word that the governor of Riyadh, along with the babies' father, their publicist, and everybody in the full entourage, was rolling in aboard their own private 737.

So here came the prince who would be seeing his little girls for the first time.

The mother was downstairs, and she hadn't even seen her own daughters yet—she'd been waiting until they were "normal size," trying to cope with the situation in her own way.

So, the father was here, and it was clear we were dealing with royalty. Well, I don't care if you're the prince or the president or a billionaire, I'm going to treat you like anybody else—because you're a human being. Wealth and society-appointed stature doesn't change that.

When the prince entered the room, I jumped into action.

Regardless of the guy's rank and culture, these were his first children. I asked if he wanted to hold them. Before he could say no, I told him, "Here, have a seat in this rocking chair!"

I was working fast. I was drop-kicking all the girls into his arms, and you could see that he was terrified. Some guy was standing right in the middle of everything with a camera; I sidestepped him and plopped the last kid into daddy's arms. "Here you go!"

Even through his shroud of traditional Arab garb, I could see the prince start to smile, just like any first-time dad—because he was indeed a human being.

It all happened so quickly. He wasn't in there for more than two or three minutes, and then he was out of there.

But about an hour later, the prince's publicist came back.

"Ted, do you realize what you did?" he asked. "That man is a Saudi Arabian prince!"

I know.

"You were very aggressive with the babies," he said.

"I know what it's like to be a father," I told him. "I know what it's like to hold your children for the first time. It's wonderful."

"The prince wanted me to tell you something," the publicist said. "Never in his life has anyone ever treated him like you treated him." The publicist continued, "The prince wanted me to tell you that it was the happiest moment in his life."

As the babies were getting discharged, the family offered me a job. Not just any job—a dream job. The position would entail traveling to Switzerland, England, Japan, Saudi Arabia, Brazil, and throughout the rest of South America as the supervisory nurse overseeing their staff of Filipino nurses. It also entailed a salary I couldn't even imagine.

It was big, *big* money.

It was also the first time I realized just how much people with special "research" arms could learn about a person in a very short period of time. I had been exposed to that in my Special Forces training, but now it was directly in my face.

As they offered me the position, it was obvious that they *knew* me.

They knew my background as a police officer.

They knew my background as a Green Beret.

They knew of all my years at Columbia-Presbyterian.

They knew how I'd graduated from Pace University with honors.

They knew me.

In the end, I turned it down. I explained that my wife and I were just starting our own family, so I needed to be with her.

"I'm sorry, but I simply can't."

About a year and a half later is when that type of fortune-charged, once-in-a-lifetime lightning would strike again. That's when this story *really* begins and that's when my path careened sharply into a quick-drop toward that "final explosive destination."

That's when the golden shit began to make its way toward a really big fan.

CHAPTER 6
THE CAMERA

It was 1999. It would be my last year at Columbia-Presbyterian Medical Center. Over the past decade and a half, I had advanced myself to the highest levels in their NICU, in both responsibility and prestige.

I'd been involved in open-heart surgery.

I was an expert with extracorporeal membrane oxygenation (ECMO), used to handle failing respiratory systems of newborns. It's a big-league medical procedure that needs big-league response—it's a no-net tightrope act often referred to as a "last resort." The average nurse may have one or two ECMO cases during their entire career—my records showed that I had fifty.

I was in charge of nineteen other nurses, the entire unit, and everything involved in running it. The nurses in my charge were from all ethnicities and nationalities: Filipino, Black, Caucasian, Irish, Chinese. I worked well within the cross-cultural environment.

At that point—not wanting to use the word "bored"—I simply had no more levels to rise to.

But there *was* one more ultra-demanding, high-test aspect of NICU that I was perfect for. Something that most, if not all, of the nurses feared: *transport*.

Columbia-Presbyterian was a network hospital that had over a hundred other hospitals connected to it. If Yale, for example, had a problem baby, their last resort was to come to us and put him on ECMO. Our job was clear and direct: Go get that kid and save its life.

That is transport.

It was pulse-bursting intensity from start to finish, and it involved super-speed and precision.

The frenzied calls from other hospitals would be cries for life—real blood-and-guts drama that television and movies can't touch: "Hello, Rampart Rescue 51, come and pick up this baby. . . . This baby is this close to dying. . . . The doctors and nurses and everybody else has pushed and done whatever they can, but this baby is going to die very quickly if we don't do something!"

That's why the nurses were horrified to go out on transport: These kids were on death's door. The odds were bad; the over/under was a joke. It was all hanging by a rough-frayed thread from Hospital A to Columbia. It was pure edgework.

I volunteered for it.

And I developed a very good thing, picking up these kids along with an inexperienced doctor or resident who would finally see—and get their hands dirty—in the street-level severity of this stuff. I was able to help so many babies . . .

I come back in with one baby. As soon as I drop that one off, we get another call.

Change these oxygen tanks!

Out again.

Arrive back to Columbia. Third call out. Unprecedented.

I go into a zone—like the quarterback running down the tunnel to the game. With the crowd, the roar. But you see what you have to do and nothing else.

The fathers and mothers are crying.

The babies are dying.

The doctors are screaming.

If I don't get the baby away from this hysteria, there is no way we can function and save this kid's life.

Settle in.

Do what needs to be done.

Focus!

I excel in high stress situations; that has saved my life many times. It helped those babies survive too.

Parents would come back for hospital-sponsored reunions and would thank me for saving their kids' lives. Older children that I'd saved in the NICU would thank me as well.

Some of them told me I was their guardian angel.

I did over one hundred neonatal transports in a single year. Not one of those babies died.

In the summer of '99 I met Harry and Laura Slatkin.

The Slatkins were an older couple by most child-bearing norms.

Laura was a patient at Columbia-Presbyterian, having delivered fraternal twins—one boy and one girl—who were in vitro. At thirty-four weeks, the twins were slightly premature—but not a big deal. They were just a bit sluggish—pokey eaters mainly. Most babies don't have the energy to suckle properly until they're about thirty-six weeks.

The Slatkins owned an elite scented-candle and knickknack business that catered to the celebrity-wealthy. When a Billy Joel or an Elton John wanted a special, fifty-buck-a-pop monogrammed candle or something, Slatkin & Co. was the place to go.

Mr. Slatkin's brother was an interior decorator, working on villas all over the world. Villas and plush residences like those owned by Edmond and Lily Safra . . .

So, I was taking care of this couple's kids along with a nurse, Annie, who was working nights. She was kind of ditzy sometimes, and one day after her shift, I noticed a pile of belongings left behind—some keys, her ID badge, and a camera.

I gathered up the stuff, and the following morning I gave it back to her.

"Annie," I asked her, "I know you come down from upstate New York like I do and you stay with your sister in the city, but how did you get anywhere without your keys?"

Her explanation about the keys is now forgotten small talk, but I will never forget what she told me about the camera: It wasn't hers.

Well, it belonged to someone, so I vowed to find the owner and return it to them.

This camera was quite an expensive model for its time—that long-ago, archaic, pre-digital age. And it was through this camera's lens that the perfect storm could be seen swirling—now taking on the first recognizable forms of its massive shape.

Another looming cloud in that darkening sky was the labor strike that the Medical Center was preparing for.

Columbia-Presbyterian, directly across from the George Washington Bridge, is one of the largest hospitals in the nation and one of the ten most prestigious. They have a large union and a staff of 4500 nurses. Strikes cripple the place.

The NICU, in particular, is a big moneymaker for the hospital. A quarter of a million bucks can be racked up in just a couple of months by *one* kid—and the federal and state governments send the checks.

In addition to my own job at Columbia-Presbyterian, I'd gotten Heidi on as a pediatric nurse. *And* I'd gotten her sister into the chemotherapy department. Add to that, their mother was now caring for Heidi's and my two kids—a three-year-old son and an almost-two-year-old daughter—along with Matthew.

So the upcoming strike threatened the sunny skies of our entire family.

Meanwhile, the camera wasn't Annie's.

But it belonged to *someone*, and I knew I could—and would—find the owner and return it to them.

The schedule at the med center had us working twelve-hour shifts for a few days, and then taking two or three days off. I'd use my next off-time to resolve the camera situation.

I brought the thing home. Realizing there were still some exposures left, I took a few shots of my kids to finish off the roll. Then I unloaded the film and took it to be developed.

I picked up the prints.

Lo and behold, there was Mrs. Slatkin in all her pregnant glory. I see pictures of their beautiful apartment; all very upscale.

I returned to work with the camera, only to discover that Mrs. Slatkin and her twins had been discharged. I tracked down the ward clerk for the unit and told her the story. I asked if it would be possible for her to get me the couple's mailing address.

No problem.

I sent the camera back to the Slatkins, along with the photos and a letter. I explained about finding the camera and about why they'd also see pictures of my kids on the negatives. I added that if they had any questions about the well-being of their children, to please feel free to contact me or any of the nurses at Columbia-Presbyterian.
Sincerely, Ted Maher.

That little task wrapped up, it was back to work in the NICU.

———

A short time later, the same ward clerk approached me out of the blue.

"The Slatkins have been trying to get a hold of you," she said. "I told them you've been busy with transport and all, but that I'd have you call them."

I did.

"We're ecstatic!" Mr. Slatkin began. "Those pictures are impossible to replace—they were the only ones of my wife before the delivery. I don't think we've ever met anybody who would be so honest.

"Ted, I want to do something for you."

I knew he was proposing a reward, but I told him no. If he wanted to make a donation to the Children's Hospital, that would be great, but I wouldn't accept anything for myself.

"Well, Ted, I'd like to take this to *the next level*. Do you mind if I get back to you?"

"Whatever, sir. But I'm not going to take anything just for doing the right thing."

———

A week passed, and Mr. Slatkin called me back.

"Ted," he said, "I know that the staff at Columbia-Presbyterian is going on strike. That means both you and your wife are going to be out of a job."

"Well, you're right," I told him, thinking in the back of my mind that his comment sounded more like research than just something he'd heard casually on the news. And although he'd seen photos of my kids, I didn't recall telling him that I was married, let alone that my wife also worked at the hospital.

"But we'll be okay," I continued. "We'll do what we can do."

"I understand," he said, "but there's something I'd like to present to you. Do you know anything about Parkinson's disease?"

I explained that I knew of it from school and from working as a PA. Although my expertise was in pediatrics, I did understand supportive care—maintaining airways, maintaining medication, all those kinds of things.

"Ted, I know of somebody who hasn't been given the right care. And we can't get quality nurses to take care of this gentleman."

Whoa. Now I was a little curious. The discussion turned a bit more rapid-fire:

"Do you know anything about Edmond Safra?"

"Never heard of him."

"His banking empire?"

"Banking empire? I know nothing about him at all or the banking industry."

"Well." He slowed down. "I know a man who is an international banker and the founder of a huge company, and he has Parkinson's disease and needs good nurses to take care of him."

And then Mr. Slatkin added, "He also needs people with your expertise to take care of him. And seeing how you have a security clearance—"

"Excuse me?" I cut in.

Now I was sure about his "research."

He went on.

They already knew about my background in Special Forces. They knew about my time as a police officer. They had contacts everywhere and they knew it *all*. More than I knew about myself. More than *anybody* should know.

It was the situation with the prince all over again—only deeper in.

I was more than a bit uncomfortable.

But I listened.

"I would like you to come down to Republic National Bank and speak to a man named Luis," continued Mr. Slatkin. "He is one of Mr. Safra's managers, and he will explain what we would like to present to you."

When I arrived the following Thursday to meet with Luis, I went through a full security clearance. I entered the bank offices and was surrounded by grandfather clocks from George Washington, Abraham Lincoln's bureaus, all sorts of priceless antiques. And all the stuff had tags and orange stickers on them—I guessed they were being appraised. Unbeknownst to me at the time, they were starting the process of dismantling the Safra empire.

And I still had no real idea as to who this man Safra was.

I talked with Luis.

He was a bit abrasive, but I listened to what he had to say.

"Mr. Safra is in his Leopolda estate in the French Riviera," he explained, "but I have all the details of our offer to you. The position we are offering is employment as a nurse in Mr. Safra's staff, based in Monaco but with travel back and forth to New York and occasionally other locales. Your basic rotation—subject to adjustments—will be around eight weeks in France, six weeks in Monaco, and twelve weeks in New York City. Then it begins again.

"We will give you an expense account of $120,000 a year, which will pay for your airfare, your meals, your hotel, and your food. We include one bottle of wine that you're allowed every day, an open bar that you're allowed after work, your maid service, et cetera. We will give you a salary of $225,000 a year. You'll work three twelve-hour shifts per week for a total of thirty-six hours."

I was definitely listening.

And thinking.

I've got almost forty grand wrapped up in legal bills with Matthew's custody and adoption battles; and Minnie's still trying to take him after all these years—six months after my neighbor's heart attack, he's back in full swing—hell, I had to have him arrested for tearing up my front lawn and blocking my pregnant wife on our roadway with his car! Heidi and I are both potentially losing our jobs because of the strike . . .

And now this six-figure luxury ship was asking permission to come into port.

Are you kidding me?

The idea of Heidi also joining the nursing team was touched upon; however, I felt that if this position was as interesting as it sounded, I'd go first to assess just what it was like before involving my wife and kids.

These were strange waters indeed, and they needed to be tested.

"Since you already have a current valid passport, as indicated by your trip last year to Aruba, you will just need to get it ready," Luis told me. He looked away and shuffled some paperwork as our discussion drew to a close.

How do you know about my passport and where I've been? I thought.

Then he stopped his busywork and looked right at me.

"Mr. Maher," he added, "Mr. Safra has heard about you and he really does want you over there."

I was still listening, still thinking.

"When?" I asked.

"Monday."

CHAPTER 7

MONDAY

I had forty-eight hours.

Fine.

This offer was too good to pass up, and I could take care of business fast when I needed to.

The passport, the packing, the general "getting things in order" was not a problem. Even taking a leave of absence from Columbia-Presbyterian was simply business. Besides, they were on strike. And thankfully, the finalization—and time consumption—of Matthew's adoption was nearly complete.

But I still had a couple of matters to deal with.

I needed a will and an unlimited power of attorney for Heidi—in case something happened to me over there. That way she could sell the properties, the vehicles, anything.

She would be taken care of.

This proved, of course, to be *the* stupidest thing I've ever done in my life. I was the Kamikaze pilot, mirror-shining his boots before climbing into the cockpit of that one-way ride. Something *did* happen to me over there. But instead of Heidi having my back, all the love and trust I gave and shared with her became the ammunition for the final big-bore blasts of betrayal that took me down when I was trying to limp back home.

But that would hit later.

My own personal *Titanic* had just set sail. The sun was shining, people were waving, and that fatal unknown was still adrift, well beyond the immediate horizon.

The countdown, however, had begun.

———————

It really all felt like a dream—even stranger than the one about the moose.

Dreams last anywhere from a few seconds to forty-five minutes—averaging somewhere in the fifteen-minute range. This dream would last a hell of a lot longer than that—the first forty-eight hours were proof.

———————

It was Monday.

I was in the French Riviera.

The dream was now speeding up—that rapid-eye movement getting even faster. The Air France flight touched down in Nice. The limo was there, and I was driven straight to check-in at a *hôtel de luxe* at the base of the hill that led to the heaven of La Leopolda.

"Here is your key, Mr. Maher."

Now my dream state was like a slow-wave deep sleep. I looked out over my balcony, toward the pool, toward the beautiful women—tan and wet in the warmth.

And this is just my first day here, I thought. *My first hours.*

The dream rolled quickly into a second day—my first actual day of work.

The limo was back.

The driver and I were both well-dressed—suits, ties.

I was far in the back of the long car, alone, wondering if I would finally come face-to-face with my new employer. It seemed like a good possibility as we cruised onto the grounds of the Villa La Leopolda estate, the pinnacle of posh that perfectly characterized *Villefranche-sur-Mer*—a "suburb" of Nice.

I was getting almost seasick in the limo—swerving left, twisting right, turning left again and then right—it was like going up a hill in San Francisco. Again and again. I stared toward the top of the hill where La Leopolda reigned. I saw huge evergreens and hundred-year-old cypress trees.

As I looked around at the pastoral and historical awe that surrounded and *was* La Leopolda, I supposed I could come face-to-face with just about *anyone*—not just this "international banker" but anyone, from the French prime minister to the president of the United States to the specter of Winston Churchill to Great Caesar's Ghost.

Objectively—to the world at large—the "villa" is one of the most expensive homes on the planet, with a price tag far north of $500 million.[10] Set on ten acres with the most "perfect ten" view in all of South France, it was purchased in 1902 by King Leopold of Belgium as a site for a "retreat" for his mistress. The king immediately ordered work on the home's construction, but died before it began.[11] In 1929, the land was purchased by American architect Ogden Codman, Jr., and he constructed *le grand château*. Over the years it has been owned by an Italian car manufacturer and a Canadian financier's widow. The quaint little spot has also been mired in multiple messy attempts by a Russian businessman to buy it.[12]

But to me, this was the lightning bolt that told me I wasn't in upstate New York anymore. It was the ultimate "house up on the hill"—elaborate beyond your wildest dreams.

The grounds were a forest of prime fruit trees. I would learn that Lily Safra wanted fruit trees so that she could make jams and jellies and send them out to friends during the holidays. She could have bought the entire Smucker's jam factory but instead they spent hundreds of thousands of dollars on these fruit trees—which, at that elevation and so close to the sea, required the drilling of special wells to pump water to them.

I eventually became intimately familiar with the mega-lavish "house" itself, too. Its fully air-conditioned, eighty thousand square feet and nineteen bedrooms made it more like a hotel than a home. You needed GPS just to find the kitchen. The marble staircases and immaculate tile throughout enhanced its elegant-excess.

Lily was also adding on to the place, making the cozy Safra cottage even bigger.

Every time I looked at those trees and the ongoing expansion the whole thing blew my mind. You are what you are, I suppose, and that personal essence depends upon one question: Do you have the money to pay?

The Safras did.

———————

All the awe of La Leopolda was not limited to pastoral sensory input, however. We had entered through a sliding gate manned by two armed guards. The gate was an iron portal through huge walls that circled the entire complex, twelve to fourteen feet tall. Other than that gate, you couldn't get into the compound without pole vaulting, parachuting in, or being spring-boarded or catapulted in.

And that posed a pretty edgy risk when—and if—you landed.

The "protection" wasn't limited to brick and mortar, either. Michael Jackson and William Hearst may have had zoos at their estates, but Edmond Safra had a heavily armed security force for his herd. Mossad agents were everywhere—their Israeli Uzis slung with the same ease and comfort as a stateside mall guard's holstered Maglite.

Forty-eight hours had been enough time for "taking care of most business" but it hadn't provided too many leftover minutes for research. I still didn't know much about Edmond Safra. But I was already learning something about the man just by looking at his army.

"Mossad" is short for HaMossad leModi'in uleTafkidim Meyuchadim—the Israeli Institute for Intelligence and Special Operations. And my employer had plenty of both. He had already done his share of intelligence on *me*, and it was obvious that anything involving Edmond Safra was a special operation on some level.

Sitting in the back of that car, I was hit with the smell of realization as to just what all of this insane wealth meant and could mean. It could be as sweet as France's lavender field, or it could carry the stench of extra-moldy *fromage*.

Dealing with—and in—this kind of money is big business. And big business may not always be on the up-and-up. Money has a way of doing that.

It just might produce some enemies along the way.

———————

We arrived at the "business" area of the estate. I was escorted through a set of heavy doors into an office where I prepared myself to meet one of the world's richest men.

That was one fact about Edmond Safra I had quickly learned.

But I was instead introduced to a psychiatrist—Safra's personal psychiatrist.

Questions, examination strategies, raised eyebrows, even some good old back-to-basic Rorschach tests . . .

"So, Ted, what do you think about this? Do you see a flower, or do you see a maniacal serial killer?"

This went on for a while. A long while.

During my many years in the medical field, I had gained a considerable amount of knowledge about psychiatry—and the tactics this man was trying to use on me. So, I was able to turn a lot of it back around on him. It became almost fun for me.

"So, Ted, what would you do about *this* and *that*?"

"I don't know, doctor. What do *you* do about *this* and *that*?"

It worked. *He* knew that *I* knew what these open-ended questions were and that I wasn't quite ready—or willing—to spin in those circles. We actually joked about it, and he could see that my tough breed of ducks were in a pretty straight row.

But we also got serious.

He showed me a painting that I recognized as a Renoir.

Okay . . .

"Seeing a *real* Renoir doesn't affect you?" he asked, somewhat leadingly.

"Well," I explained, "I could have one just like it. It would be a print, of course, but that wouldn't make *me* a different person."

"I never thought about it like that," he admitted.

My reaction seemed to be far from the aesthetic aback I was supposed to have shown.

And I wasn't done.

I explained that "originals" were nice, but when the maid bumped into my Ming vase and shattered it on the floor, I'd be crying. When she did the same to my cheap Chinese copy, I'd probably laugh. Either way, I could still enjoy the artistic essence of the thing, regardless of the authentication of origin.

This was a curious environment indeed to be testifying about my lack of material-istic worship. The South of France isn't exactly known for its restraint when it comes to worldly pleasures. This was like telling the top chef at Le Chateaubriand that you're not really all that impressed with *foie gras*—a burger and fries would be just fine.

But, again, it was me.

And these feelings became even more locked in during the slow-time sludge of my years behind the life-stealing steel of a prison cell door. I had a lot of time to reflect.

There are only three things you can take to the grave with you: your name, your honor, and the way you have loved your family.

Whether you're driving an old VW or a new Mercedes, you're still driving—making it from point A to point B. You're still moving. Whether that's a designer shirt you have on or a Wal-Mart special, it's still a shirt. And none of that should change the person—the *heart* of who you are.

My session with Safra's psychiatrist came to a close, and I seemed to receive his *Good Housekeeping* Seal of Approval. I suppose a by-product of my nonchalance about real master art was that they didn't have to worry about my stealing anything.

The office doors opened, and the driver and the "army" reappeared. I was quickly marshaled back to the hotel in that long car—a car that, for some reason, seemed even longer now.

My first day of work—really just a half-day—was apparently over.

I was returned to my room where I walked back out into the sun of the balcony. The gorgeous women were still out at the pool—they were always at the pool. I was trying to latch onto some reality here, but I could only wonder if I'd awake from this *rêve étrange* before ever meeting the highly insulated Edmond Safra.

———

My second day "on the job" started off like the first—we were almost getting into a routine here. The limo, the drive, the office, the guard legion. But there would be no psychiatrist today.

And no Edmond Safra.

Today I would meet his wife, Lily. We would lunch together—a bit of a formal lunch. Hell, we were ready for it; we were both in suits.

It was a formal meeting because she was a formal woman and *very* upper class. We talked. She asked me questions about what I would do in certain situations.

I met Lily Safra that day, but I certainly didn't even begin to *know* her. Like so many things on this excursion into the unreal, that would take some time.

"Tomorrow," she told me, as our time together was ending, "you will meet my husband."

My second day at work was now over, and as before, I was chauffeured back to the hotel. In my room, my balcony speculations and thoughts again kicked in. Maybe this wasn't a dream after all. I had actually met Lily Safra. And tomorrow, I would finally meet "her husband." I needed to learn more about them both because dream or no dream, they were solidly in my life now.

And I was in theirs.

CHAPTER 8
EDMOND SAFRA

On the third day, I met Edmond Safra.

And the routine of the chauffeured drive to and from that office at La Leopolda was about to expand into a universe that was as foreign to me as the planet Ekos was to Kirk and Spock.

By now I had learned that Edmond Safra was a Jewish-Lebanese banker who owned Trade Development Bank and the Republic National Bank of New York. He was worth about three billion bucks.

Beyond the basic high business stature and renown of Safra, I discovered that in 1983 he sold his Trade Development Bank to American Express—and that it wasn't a smooth *sale*. The long version of this battle royale is spelled out in the 640-page *Vendetta: American Express and the Smearing of Edmond Safra*. But in short, Safra and Amex got into a dispute that became a monster business litigation mess that American Express finally lost, costing them a public apology and the chump change—to them—of eight million dollars in damages to Safra. Edmond gave the money to charities.

While Amex and Edmond may not have seen eye to eye, my meeting with him went quite well. Whenever two people interact in a setting that is business, not social, personality conflicts can arise quickly. There are no friendship circles to fall back on. Edmond Safra and I definitely did not travel in the same friendship circles, but our initial interaction worked.

We hit it off.

He was direct.

He was soft-spoken.

His words were few, but they were well chosen; short and to the point.

I was me.

I was who I am.

It was a good mix.

Most importantly, though, much like the prince of Riyadh, Edmond saw right away that I was able to treat him like a human being, rather than as one of the wealthiest men in the world. He seemed to know that a lot of people are very false and that I wasn't one of them. He probably knew more about me than I knew about myself.

This first meeting touched heavily on intelligence, in both its meanings.

Edmond Safra was a world-strength financer who had been around the corporate-elite block many times. He had seen a lot of good and a lot of bad in people. He could see through bullshit.

He could see that I was straight.

Directly after our meeting on August 13, 1999, I was contacted by Mrs. Safra.

"We would like you to start immediately," she said.

And I did.

I jumped aboard my first rotation at La Leopolda.

I had a quick orientation with Sonia Casiano Herkrath, the head nurse of the staff.

She seemed suspicious of me. I was a white male American, an ex–Green Beret—a very different animal in the nursing world. And things that are different are frightening, or at least unsettling, to most people.

I tried to explain that I was just there to do the job I'd been hired for. But my way of doing a job and pretty much everyone else's has always been a big part of my being different.

And I won't apologize for that.

When I was just two days into the job, Safra was preparing to visit a mogul of the banking community down the peninsula in Beausoleil. It would be a short nine- or ten-mile trip through the side streets in his Mercedes with his chauffeur, and he needed to take along a nurse.

"I want Ted to go with me," he said.

This little field trip was something else that wouldn't endear the "new guy" to the staff.

And more would set me apart.

On the way there, Safra was supposed to take his vitamin D pill for his calcium, along with Sinemet for his Parkinson's disease. He tried to retain some degree of privacy from his business associates, so he was to get the medicines just before meeting his host.

As we arrived, I prepared to give him the pills; then I planned to have lunch with the limo driver.

All in a day's work.

I prepared Mr. Safra's calcium pill.

"I take the Sinemet first," he said.

"Not around me, you won't," I told him.

"Excuse me?!" he snapped.

I told him I wanted him to take the vitamin D pill first.

"No, no," he said. "That's not the way the nurses give it to me. I take it the other way around!"

Not anymore.

The vitamin D was a "horse pill"—a monster.

"If you choke on this, you'll spit it up and out," I explained. "If you take the small Sinemet first, and *then* the vitamin, and *then* you spit it out, what will happen to the Sinemet—the more important drug? They'll *both* be lost.

"Not only that, but we'll have no way of knowing how much Sinemet has been absorbed by your system—and that's critical with the dosage."

Safra nodded.

"How come none of the other nurses ever thought of that?" he asked.

I didn't have *that* answer, but I did have the answer as to why I always seem to be bucking some kind of system: I wasn't trying to kiss this man's ass. I was doing my job. I wanted him to have the same kind of care everyone should have—the *right* kind.

I was making six hundred bucks for a twelve-hour shift and I was going to earn it. I would do the job and do it right.

After that, Edmond began calling me "Teddy"—another nail in my popularity coffin. And that was okay; being adored by the rest of the staff wasn't why I was there.

Sonia and I never did become close. She'd been there for almost three years and was just certain that I was going to become the new charge nurse and take her job away.

The times when we'd work shifts together, I'd try my best to reassure her. *I'm just here to work . . . the money is great and I'm here for my family . . . I'm married; I have three children . . . I don't want your job . . . I don't want your title . . . I don't want anything . . . I just want to work, do my three or four shifts a week, put my money in a bank, and get along with my life . . .*

Variations on that personal mantra would be a plea for peace that I would express so many times throughout the years to come. And just as it was with Sonia, it would generally be in vain.

It didn't matter what I said to her, she continued to feel threatened.

One nurse *not* afflicted with favor-envy was Vivian Torrente. She was also just there to work, and we became friends.

And we were both "just working" the night she and Safra were killed.

CHAPTER 9

LIVING THE DREAM

Edmond Safra was sixty-seven years old when I began working for him. He was truly living the adage that "money can't buy you health, but it *can* buy you *extended* health."

He had four private physicians: one in England, two in Canada, and one in South America. They were some of the best in the world. Some of the nurses were the best, too. Safra had two nurses per shift, not just one. He had help doing *everything*.

And he needed it. Safra's Parkinson's disease was taking a tortuous toll. Parkinson's is a mobility degenerative disease. Your hormones are being replaced by the serotonin related to the illness. When you're on the drug Sinemet, however, the tremor symptoms are controlled. But the thing about Sinemet is that over periods of time, the doses need to be upped. It's like heroin—one day 1g will do the trick, the next day you need 2g, and so on.

That in itself can lead to issues.

At night, the drug dosage would be lessened, but that resulted in Safra having leg cramping and other problems that needed attention.

On most nights, the nurses would genuinely earn their money.

Safra's room would be completely dark. And hot. Hot! Safra was comfortable with ninety-five degrees. Very few of the rest of us shared that particular level of coziness. And our uniform of long sleeves and pants added to the hospice hell.

A nurse had to be with Safra all night—literally, by his side. In the dark. In the heat. And we had to stay awake. Sleeping on the job was something that would send you immediately back to wherever on the globe you may have come from.

I could stay awake.

I would hear him say, "Teddy, Teddy, Teddy!"

I would rub his back and his legs, trying to reduce the Parkinson's cramps that would seize his limbs in the nighttime absence of the Sinemet.

Due to the on-edge stress and the frying discomfort, the nurses would switch out every two hours.

And then you were back.

Teddy, Teddy, Teddy . . .

While working at La Leopolda, the staff stayed in a hotel at the bottom of the hill—"where the poor people are cast," I would joke. The truth is, of course, that there are no actual poor people along the Côte d'Azur, at least in the indigent sense. The hotel worked just fine, and the fast-shuttle closeness sure beat the long commutes I'd endured while working in New York.

And there were other perks.

Every morning I would eat a hotel breakfast, but I would have lunch and dinner at La Leopolda. The food was another of those bellwethers—more lightning that would hit and let you know that the world you came from was a million light years away. Your world's poles have shifted, its axis has reversed, and you're now in Fantasyland.

The kitchen at the estate was half the size of my entire house. Double ovens here, double ovens there, an eight-burner gas-driven range in the middle.

The cooks would whip up a beautiful gourmet spread for the Safras—lasagna or steak or whatever—but they wouldn't cook just one or two meals. They would generally cook for about twenty people, including staff members.

Eventually I had to get back to running because I was gaining weight! In addition to all that eating, I realized that I wasn't doing a whole lot in the physical department on this job—using my brain, yes, but really not much else.

The staff took our meals separately, apart from the main residence dining room. The waiters were usually left out of the staff dinners; they ate later, after they had finished serving. We ate using silverware—real silverware. Our employers, of course, used the gold and platinum ware; so, we were definitely lower-rung. The sting of that low-brow degradation was eased a bit by our use of beautiful china—no Tupperware or paper plates here. The polishing of the silver and the other precious bling occurred in a once-a-month process by the help. This stuff had to shine!

But during our dinners, we still had our duties; helping Safra dress and prepare for his dinner, getting up to administer meds that had to be given on time, regardless of whether you were in the middle of a prime filet or not.

We were working.

And it wasn't just an interruption of the free bone of a world-class meal—there really was pressure to be Johnny-on-the-spot, getting everything right. The drug schedule was inflexible; not watching the clock could cost you your job.

The preservation of as much quality of life that Safra had left was number one.

On my third day at La Leopolda, I met Lily's daughter by her first marriage. She had become Edmond's legal stepdaughter and he'd raised her as his own. She was now around my age—in her forties.

"My name is Adriana," she said. "I've heard so many things about you. The Slatkins speak quite highly of you. I'm the godmother of the babies you took such good care of!"

Until that moment, I'd had no idea about Lily's daughter's connection to the Slatkins. Here was the true bridge between them and the Safras—the reason I had wound up on this dreamlike adventure.

So, in meeting Adriana, I began to fully awaken from my hazy state. I began to understand that this "dream" was totally and completely real.

I saw the web and circle of this connection. I saw why I was where I was. I began to see that maybe, just maybe, a good deed can pay off.

Just maybe.

Dreams *do* come true.

CHAPTER 10
LA BELLE ÉPOQUE

I t's about twenty miles from Nice to Monte Carlo—but there are no spatial gaps in the *beauté absolue*. A chauffeured ride along *rive de la Méditerranée* beats the hell out of stateside freeway commutes.

My time in Monaco would be the first full-length leg of my first rotation, and my inaugural run to this tiniest of countries with the largest of reputations.

At a total land mass of only 1.95 square kilometers, the Principality of Monaco is the most densely populated country on Earth (aside from Vatican City) with the world's highest GDP nominal per capita ($166,726 in 2017).[13] It also has the world's highest life expectancy at almost ninety years[14] and the lowest unemployment rate at 2 percent.[15]

Nobody pushes a shopping cart full of cans and cardboard, or sleeps in doorways in Monaco. And while sumptuousness will vary within Monaco's businesses, every place is comparatively plush (well, *almost* every place—I would eventually spend a lot of time in the only low-rent district in town).

The country also retains a police force of 515 officers to make it one of the safest places on Earth—with one cop for every sixty-eight citizens.[16]

It's sunshine, super-sloops, and sacks of tax-free money for everyone. All the time.

It was in Monte Carlo where Edmond and Lily Safra owned *another* of the most expensive properties in the galaxy—"the world's costliest flat": the penthouse of the La Belle Époque building, a two-story 17,500-square-foot suite overlooking the yacht-lined marina.

As with La Leopolda, the "flat" at La Belle Époque is viewed in real estate terms and with near-voyeurism as a "luxury property for the super-rich."[17] Again like La

Leopolda—it has been the subject of international publicity and super-model-chic style magazine spreads—both before and after the fire.

But for me, it was a second dose of shock therapy. This wasn't a far-removed television special or a vicarious thumb-through of a magazine.

This was where I was employed: *Work station number two.*

In French, *La Belle Époque* means "the beautiful era"—a period in European social history from the late nineteenth century through World War I. Since then, there have been virtually no *non*-beautiful eras in Southern France. But this La Belle Époque was the six-story building that housed one of Safra's banks at street level, and his "local residence" on the top two floors.

My first time to this annex in the Safra universe took me through the same phalanxes of Uzi-bearing guards as the Leopold estate. But this time I wasn't traveling down a pastoral Tara–like path to gain entry, but rather level after level of elevators and security doors.

I was escorted by a guard to a specific elevator designated only for Safra's staff. The place had monitors and cameras everywhere. We exited the elevator into a six-foot-square cubicle—a security system that I had to go through; I couldn't proceed until somebody from the staff and the security cleared me. Once I got through that door, another member of the staff had to open another door to the building to let me in.

I'd heard so much about all the security in Monte Carlo, and now there it was.

La Belle Époque was adjacent to the Hermitage Hotel. On my way through the series of protective hurdles up to the residence I noticed that a pathway on the back of the hotel was in the process of being enclosed to prevent physical access from the hotel to the back of La Belle Époque on the fourth-floor level. *More security.* The flat itself was one of the largest and closest to the sea in Monte Carlo. Easily the most lavish. It had gold- and silver-lined everything and crown molding upon crown molding.

Sure, the suite contained *only* three stadium-sized bedrooms, but they were just for sleeping—when you weren't enjoying the vaulted-ceiling library, the roof terraces and gardens with fifteen-foot trees, the open courtyard, the infinity pool, the walk-in wardrobes, the spa, or the media room.

It was a damned impressive "flat."

Three or four maids were there cleaning each day. They never finished—once "through" they'd start over. It was like the proverbial endless painting of the Forth Bridge.

One of the men who worked in the building explained to me that there was a parking garage below the building, below sea level.

"With no leaks or danger?" I asked him how that was structurally possible and viable.

"Mr. Maher," he answered, "this is Monte Carlo. *Anything's* possible with money."

I would often bring Edmond out into the bright courtyard at La Belle Époque.

"We need to get some air," I'd tell him.

But, as at La Leopolda, the air was always heavy with the breath of security—bodyguards were behind every bush here, too.

I knew one reason was the possibility of kidnapping and extortion and all the rest that goes along with wading through waist-high wealth. But that realization I'd had in the back of the limousine—that cynical smell I'd whiffed on that first day riding into La Leopolda—crept back into my senses: If you've made billions of dollars, there's a *chance* you may have pissed off somebody somewhere.

Whatever the reason, Edmond Safra was a very paranoid man. And here in Monte Carlo I would get my first hard, thick-windowed look into that paranoia.

CHAPTER 11

LILY SAFRA

Edmond Safra's fear of what could happen out there in the world of ridiculous riches was one thing; but I also began to see into his relationship with Lily—and who she was. I was learning a lot and Lily Safra had become a troubling part of this dream—maybe a bit more than one of those fifteen-minute blips.

Lily Watkins was born in Porto Alegre, Brazil, in 1934.[18] She is the daughter of Wolf White Watkins, a British railway engineer, and Annita Noudelman de Castro, a Uruguayan of Russian-Jewish ancestry.

Lily was just seventeen when her marriages began. And none were just marriages; they were renowned nuptial rungs that would help her climb to billionaire status and the eventual rank of the 701st richest person in the world.

Lily's first marriage was to Mario Cohen, an Argentine hosiery magnate, in 1952. Lily and Mario had three children: Claudio, Eduardo, and Adriana. Their spending habits—hers extravagant, his much more conservative—never really jelled. They finally divorced in the early 1960s.

By then Lily had already met her next husband; a man with the very suave and *internacional* name of Alfredo João Monteverde. Alfredo had actually started life in Romania as Alfred Iancu Grunberg before his legal *schimbarea de nume*. "Freddy," as friends called him, owned Ponto Frio, Brazil's most successful appliance store chain. He and Lily married in New York in early 1965—and again, a year and a half later, in Rio, just to cover all the family and friend celebration bases.

It was with Monteverde that things started to get especially interesting.

Three years into their marriage, a divorce was already imminent. On August 25, 1969, more than just a divorce would crash down on the Monteverde family. On that day, Alfredo had a luncheon with Lily and her first husband, Mario. The focus of the luncheon was reportedly Monteverde's desire to continue a relationship with Lily's and Mario's children after the divorce.

That focus would prove moot.

At a little after 3:00 that afternoon, Monteverde's body was discovered in the master bedroom of his and Lily's home by members of their staff. No medical personnel or police were called. Finally, at around 9:45 that night, a company lawyer went to the police station to file a report that Alfredo Monteverde had committed suicide.

Monteverde had supposedly shot himself *twice* in the chest. And from *my* angle, the investigation had a couple of holes in it, too.

No gun powder residue was found on Monteverde's hands, and the coroner's findings were that the right-handed Alfredo *couldn't* have shot himself, given the manner in which the bullets had entered.[19]

But it was ruled a suicide.[20] Instead of a divorce, Lily got somewhere around $300 million in inheritance dumped into her bank account.

And it gets better.

Monteverde was gone so she set her sights on Edmond Safra. Why not? Safra was Alfredo's banker—Monteverde had been Edmond's biggest account for years. That was their connection. But Edmond and Lily's first actual meeting is blurred in the high-beams of high finance and the high-life of big-bucks social interplay.

Some speculate that the pair first met at Safra's brother's wedding in São Paulo in the late 1960s and developed a friendship before Monteverde's death. Regardless, following the "suicide," Edmond told Lily "he would fix everything."[21] He immediately helped Lily assume control of all Monteverde's assets; the rest of the family's bank accounts were canceled within a day.

But Lily and Edmond's pairing was much more than a money merger.

There's a fair amount of corroboration among Safra's friends that—on Edmond's side, at least—it was love at first sight. And he knew she couldn't be just after his money—hell, she had plenty of it herself.

The relationship continued for some time.

But Safra's siblings were vehement in their opinion of Lily. Adamant.

Stay away from this woman!

They hated her.[22]

As much as Edmond may have cared about Lily, he simply couldn't marry her because of the issues with his brothers and sisters. He wanted to just maintain the status quo. But Lily wanted more. So, the pair split.

In short order, Lily married international businessman Samuel Bendahan in Acapulco. It was now early 1972.

When Safra found out, he went absolutely nuts and bombarded Lily with a "fusillade" of calls.

More than one of Lily's acquaintances had a slightly suspicious slant on things—feeling that there was a possibility Lily was just using Sam to make Edmond jealous.[23]

If so, it definitely worked.

After just six weeks, Lily and Sam's marriage began to implode. An ugly end came in the form of a contested divorce, with Lily and Edmond charging Bendahan with extortion for trying to get some sort of settlement from Lily—including thirty-five grand that Lily had commissioned to contractors to redo Bendahan's flat. That attempted extortion resulted in cops nabbing Bendahan as soon as he got off the plane in New York—where he had flown at Lily's lawyers' "request" to negotiate the divorce details in person. Sam spent a nervous night locked up at Rikers Island—not a good place for a mild-mannered man of means to be.

The legal battle between Bendahan and Lily went on for three years until Samuel lost his appeal. Edmond wouldn't marry Lily until the litigation was settled. When it was, in July of 1976, he did—armed with his own legal barricade: a six-hundred-page prenuptial agreement.

So that's the story—that's how Lily nailed Edmond.

But my opinion of Lily was never tainted by the gossip or the extraneous circumstances surrounding her other marriages—and the ensuing death, destruction, and divorces involved. I had never even heard of her before doing my research, and even that was aimed strictly at trying to find out just who these people were in a business sense.

And my personal impression of her started off positively.

It was fall and it was cold. Lily saw me showing up to work in those long sleeves, and she came to me with five or six polo shirts that had been Edmond's. He had gained so much weight that he could no longer wear them; they were brand-new and brand-best.

So she gave them to me, seemingly with genuine concern that I was sweating my ass off in the ninety-five degrees of Safra's room.

It was very human of her.

But things would change over time.

I began to perceive that she was so totally into herself. The rest of the staff warned me not to talk about certain meds that we'd see her take. When I asked why, I was told that their content was "not to be known."

The "certain meds" turned out to be from the Joan Rivers–style treatment camp for the uncomfortably aging. Aging for Lily, and those in that panic-camp, was like a death sentence.

And there were more not-so-quiet whispers about plastic surgery, facial lifts, and other cosmetic "work." But she could afford it and it was her body.

But it was her position that we all had to adjust to.

I don't want to use the word pompous—or maybe I do—but I think she knew she could do whatever she wanted with the power of the money that she had. Period. It was an interesting study. To use another heroin analogy: a little leads to more, and more leads to even more. It seemed to me Lily was hungry for money. The more she had, the more she wanted, and the more she got, the hungrier she became.

I would shake my head. How many houses do you want—*need*? How many *things* do you want and need? Her thirst for wealth seemed never-ending.

But at the end of the plush day, I had a fantastic, well-paying job. There were things I could ignore.

Other things I couldn't.

I was still disturbed by Edmond Safra's pill consumption. I knew that the bigger pills came in a powdered form—you could *drink* the med with orange juice. I was surprised that the other nurses hadn't addressed this.

I explained the situation to Lily and told her to ask their doctor if we could switch the pills to powered form—I knew that the stuff was the same, but we needed to do this right. I wasn't a doctor, after all.

But you don't have to be a doctor to have common sense.

After getting medical approval, I went to the pharmacist—over there you don't need a prescription; you just give them the cash, they give you the stuff—and I used my own money to get the powder for Edmond. I simply did it, and I made him more comfortable.

I wondered how comfortable Lily was making him.

CHAPTER 12

THE COFFIN OF MONTE CARLO

A Sunny Place for Shady People
—W. Somerset Maugham,
describing Monaco and the French Riviera[24]

Two square kilometers.[25]
Less than one square mile.
Smaller than New York's Central Park.[26]
Size just doesn't matter when you're talking about the power of wealth. Signatures and phone calls occupy little space.

Maugham's little commentary bite was taken out of Monaco by the infamous English author in the 1920s. Nearly a century later, his observation still seems to be right on the money.

It was while working at La Belle Époque—in the heart of Monte Carlo—where I began to feel the soul of this land and its people. We were still so close to the fruit-tree-heavy coastal hills of La Leopolda in miles—but far removed in an urban social sense.

Here, employees were placed in a hotel right around the corner from La Belle Époque. And unlike the staff dinners hosted at La Leopolda, we simply signed our names to anything we needed in the area. Our stipends and expense money got "worked out" in the accounting process.

The staff often ate together at the hotel—Vivian, some of the others, and me. But not Sonia. Never Sonia. She simply couldn't seem to get over her fear of my stealing her job. As her apprehension increased, she ordered room service, separating herself from the rest of us more and more.

I also spent a lot of time at Sam's, a little *taverne* near the hotel. It reminded me of Rick's in *Casablanca*. All Safra's staff had to do to eat there was sign the check. They were always pushing wine on us—they were paid extra for that. But I never abused the menu; I was happy with the specials and the salads.

Even with austerity and restraint like mine, it was crazy-expensive keeping a staff maintained in Monaco. And here's where I began another level in my learning—learning about the gilded nuts and bolts of Monaco. I learned that the tiny country is tax-free. If a restaurant makes $100,000, they *keep* $100,000.

Nothing goes to the government—in the way of income.

That provides a big incentive to set up shop there. No service or commodity is cheap in Monaco, and a business owner lives on the gross, not the net. The government gets theirs only when you buy property. The state also retains monopolies in a number of sectors, including tobacco, the telephone network, and the postal service.

The commerce-centered citizenry enjoys other benefits as well. Monaco is always thought of first when visions in the heads of financiers, entrepreneurs, and others of privilege dance toward "tax havens" and the occasional cleansing convenience of money-laundering.

Over the last couple of decades, French parliamentarians Arnaud Montebourg and Vincent Peillon; the Organisation for Economic Co-operation and Development (OECD); the Financial Action Task Force (FATF); the International Monetary Fund (IMF); and the Council of Europe have all expressed concerns and/or have initiated investigations into Monaco's policy of being a city of refuge for those with more money than God.

It's a place of interest indeed.

The three or four days in a row that I had off each week in Monte Carlo quickly changed from a personal exploration of a new city—which just happened to be one of the most celebrated cities in the world—to an expanded study.

I've never understood being able to roll through life with blinders on. Granted, opportunities for the mental and spiritual absorption of life's inner workings might be a bit lower in places like Pine Bush and Stormville as compared to Monte Carlo, but

I seem to have always found them regardless of setting. But now this absorption climbed many levels.

Back home, I went on walks. I did a good amount of exploring and hiking in the all-surrounding steep hills. But when *this* study started, it began in the restaurants, moving into the shops. I can honestly tell you that I've never seen so many people who have so much, yet who always looked so sad.

It's hard to understand that.

I saw people in cafés being treated like royalty, with a lunch bill that was going to be two hundred dollars. They'd have their little French poodle in their lap—patting it. But they all looked so serious. *My god,* I thought, *you've got life by the balls! You should be smiling ear to ear, enjoying absolutely everything!*

I should have heard constant laughter; seen constant joy.

I didn't.

I never heard that. I never saw that. What I saw were people going through the motions of a society—a special society of the extreme wealthy. I saw so little in the way of what I would describe as happiness.

I'll never forget that as long as I live.

———————————

My experience held true to Somerset Maugham's quote and observation. Maybe it's because most everybody there has some sort of bankrolled skeleton in their closet, and maybe they're on edge waiting for the knock at the door or getting tired from looking over their shoulder.

And ultimately, they have to stay within the short boundaries of Monte Carlo—the coffin of Monte Carlo—in order to retain that lifestyle.

They have to toe that state-dictated line. Even though they've been able to wedge themselves into a comfortable spot—at least financially—they still have so much to watch out for and adhere to in the way of *paperwork*, to keep this all working.

I didn't know how personal and literal this connection would be for me at the time, but I saw these people as being in a prison—their own tiny .77-square-mile prison.

A lot of those fears of knocks at the door and over-the-shoulder surveillance had to do with extradition. The currency-cachet Principality of Monaco didn't care how its residents got their money; but some countries did. International laws were the beasts beyond the wall, and other governments *wanted* some of these residents. As a result, these hunted tenants wound up stuck in Monte Carlo's confining couple kilometers, where the principality was happy to protect them—as long as their hundreds of millions of dollars stayed put in Monegasque banks.

CHAPTER 13

THE BUNKER WITH A BILLION-DOLLAR VIEW

The nursing station where I worked in La Belle Époque's penthouse was right next to Edmond's bedroom. Next to that was his personal workout gym. It was about twenty-five-by-thirty feet with a treadmill, free weights, and other special exercising machines that were probably twenty grand a pop at the time. It was a totally professional setup, complete with two physical therapists. These two had also come from New York; they did six-month rotations.

Another sweet gig.

I talked with a therapist who was on duty the same time I was. He was being paid his $225,000 a year to be there for forty-five minutes a day of physical therapy—or a little longer if Mr. Safra required. Either way, he never worked more than an hour and a half a day, tops—and that was just a few days a week.

But it was important work. Safra's doctors said that as long as he kept up his physical aptitudes and his range of motion with his exercising, the longer and better quality of life he'd have.

And all of us on staff wanted that.

When we first met, this physical therapist told me, "Ted, just do your work and save up your money, because you'll never see anything like this again in your life. Ever! And enjoy the food! Every day it's like they cook a feast for a wedding party, but the wedding party never shows up!"

I laughed.

It was just like at La Leopolda.

I thought of the staff as being like the "good and bad" people in the Bible wedding story—the rabble summoned by the servants at the "crossroads" to come to the party that the invited guests snubbed.

At La Belle Époque, two butlers were on duty all the time. There was the cook's crew, security, landscaping, and the ever-present "gofers" to run errands.

Then there were those like Luis—the ones really involved in the business—the investment bankers and other working suits. It was in that realm where I began to really know Anthony Brittain, a young man from South Africa with a strong accent who, like so many others, seldom seemed happy. In his late twenties, he was well-educated in finance, but he also served as an aide to Safra and was letting his other duties get to him.

"I can't believe I'm doing this," he'd moan, as he had to deal with schedules, his employers' emotions, or something else outside of his preferred box. "I'm an investment banker!"

If I could have said it without the risk of being fired, I'd have told him that he was a young kid getting paid up the ass to do something he couldn't even really do, and it was all tax-free!

People would kill to get your job, so shut the hell up and just suck it up!

My job also went beyond my box and job description of nursing—that was simply a part of the deal. At times, I even felt like Sam the Tailor, as I helped Safra out with his clothes.

"Teddy, get the butler; I need a bigger shirt," he said one day.

I told him that I was right there—I'd get it.

I opened his "closet" and it was like Macy's. Racks and racks of clothes. And everything was organized. A section for white shirts, a section for red shirts, blue shirts. And there was suit after suit after suit. And they were all top-notch; three- or four-thousand-dollar threads, many with the tags still on. And none of the tags was marked "Clearance."

Safra's weight and size varied on a fairly constant basis. One day he might have this size waist and collar, the next day he'd need something bigger or smaller. Most of us change our diets when things waver that radically; he just kept a complete wardrobe on hand for each size!

This was one of the most mind-boggling of all the blatant and tangible signs of his monster wealth to me. It was hard to get a grip on—literally having a clothing store for your damn closet! You hear about women having fifty or a hundred pairs of shoes, or you see something like it on TV, but when you come face-to-face with a display like that, there are no words for it.

After all the time I had already spent floating around this *mer de riches*, I didn't think I could be surprised or shocked anymore.

I was wrong.

These power suits, shoes, and shirts represented Safra's life. It was all about the banking and the money and the meetings and looking perfect in that avid arena.

But it was sad to me. Edmond Safra, too, seemed to be in his own prison of his homes and businesses. Sure, they were lavish, but little he did was geared for fun and he spent so much time indoors. With the Mediterranean for a front yard, spending so much time behind walls seemed such a waste—even if those walls were the most beautiful in the world. Artful, man-made architecture and décor is one thing; the immeasurable glory of places like the Côte d'Azur is definitely another.

But some of those walls weren't all that exquisitely appointed. Many were the thick, purposeful stuff of prisons and bunkers. The bullet-and-rocket-proof glass could withstand a .50-caliber shot and much more; with heavy metal valances that closed over them, forming even more layers of hard buffer. There were high-def surveillance systems, the Uzi-slinging guards, and more tiers of security at every turn.

Occasionally, I'd see Safra looking out of those big windows toward the *Mer Méditerranée*—almost as if he were looking toward freedom, like an inmate in a small-windowed cell.

Over and over, I kicked around just what it takes to make multi-billions. I had to keep coming back to the thinking that, along with the idealistic possibility of honest-buck purity, there has to be the *je ne sais quoi;* back door deals and shaky shit.

Just how much depends upon the business and the man.

For example, with his name on the deeds of two million acres of land, Ted Turner has become the largest individual land owner in America. His buffalo herds are the biggest in the world, and free range, too, without barbed wire and fences. I wonder how many rocket-proof windows stand between him and his great outdoors.

Moguls of privilege like these need their security, true; but just what kind of "businessman" needs a full-blown army? I wonder what La Leopolda was like under other people's ownership. Did they also have Uzi posses amongst the trees?

I personally and genuinely liked Edmond Safra. I gave him the best care I could provide and well into levels beyond. But he'd had sixty-plus years and several billion dollars worth of living before we met. Whatever his "utilitarian path to the final explosive destination" may have been, I could never really know.

CHAPTER 14
FIFTH AVENUE PROPHECY

The Safras' Fifth Avenue and East 63rd Street apartment was "nice" but nowhere near as fully-loaded as La Leopolda or La Belle Époque.

Then again, that's probably like comparing a priceless vintage Bugatti Royale to a simple 670K-out-the-door new Ferrari Enzo. And regardless of bottom-line worth, the NYC apartment had the antique charm and power-money heft of all that is Upper East Side New York.

It was about ten thousand square feet of two-story splendor. And, as with all their other love nests, Edmond and Lily had not only their own rooms but their own separate wings.

I used to think about this, too—I knew I'd want my wife next to me in swanky places like these. I guess it was just another part of privilege I couldn't relate to.

When we arrived in New York on my first rotation, however, the temperature in the place was cold—way below Safra's comfort zone.

I stay pretty warm in most situations, but even *I* was chilled there. Workmen had been called and were trying to fix the problem, but whatever they were doing wasn't working.

They must be missing something, I thought. *There has to be a switch or a valve somewhere . . .*

Meanwhile it was getting ridiculous; Mr. Safra had four or five comforters over him to keep warm. I kept looking around, trying to figure out what was keeping the heat out. Finally, in the bathroom, I noticed a valve. The valve. And, no, it wasn't open.

Within an hour of my adjusting it, it was about ninety degrees in the place. "How did it get so hot in here?" Safra asked. "Did we have the heating people come back?"

"No, sir, somebody didn't open the valve," I explained. "Are you sure you're warm enough? If it gets too warm let me know and I'll close it down a little bit . . ."

He just started shaking his head, mumbling something about paying money to people who aren't doing their jobs.

It was another sunny moment for me. It took the nurse to fix the heat in a high-rolling Fifth Avenue apartment!

I did share with Safra that I'd built five houses in my life and about my jack-of-all-trades brand from my father. In many ways stuff like that is like medicine; you need to analyze the signs and symptoms, make a little checklist, and then start troubleshooting and checking things out.

Common sense counts for a lot in most everything. It was something else that Safra truly appreciated.

He shook his head again. "Well, I'm very happy to hear it's all fixed because we've had three people out here . . ."

But I was just doing the right thing because it needed to be done.

Manhattan worked well for me. It was close to home. I'd do my shift on Fifth Avenue, hit the train, head to Stormville, and have Heidi pick me up at the station. When I wasn't working, I actually could live at my house!

It was at least one taste of normalcy in the palate of absentee family life.

It was also in New York where I had a closer opportunity to see Mr. Safra at work. By that point, we would still chat, but more minimally. You could see and hear his speech slurring as his Parkinson's progressed.

But his business meetings were still fierce. He would be talking to bankers or lawyers on the phone and I'd hear him say things like "Just don't bullshit me—tell me the way it is! I don't want to hear the bullshit. Tell me the way it is!"

He'd been around, and all these people with songs and dances weren't making him happy. At this point in his life, he didn't want to hear it.

I appreciated that about him.

I also appreciated that he surrounded himself with the best associates. He had two investment bankers who were constantly changing his assets around; and they were both just in their twenties! Even these guys couldn't believe it themselves that they were there working with Safra, in that kind of league. But they had been top-notch at school, and Safra spotted them at the banks they'd landed in after graduation and scooped them up.

He saw their potential.

And in his field, at least, he took what he wanted.

It was also in New York that a spooky prophecy nearly came to pass. The Ming vase analogy that I had thrown at Safra's shrink early on rose up in eerie ether, threatening to become a shattered reality. And had it happened, it would have been in perfect keeping with the other-worldliness of the entire wild ride.

Among the antiques and the masterworks in the gallery-like home was, yes, a genuine, Xuande porcelain, bona fide Ming. I just happened to be close by as one of the maids was cleaning things up.

The scene unfolded like a Three Stooges skit—except this one had a less messy ending. As the maid nudged the vase and the whole thing began to fall, I caught it.

Now, if it had been the Stooges, Curly would have knocked it over, Moe would have missed grabbing it, and somehow it would have hit Larry in the head, breaking into a million pieces. *Soitenly!* And then the owner—probably some hapless museum curator with a pencil-thin mustache and a bow tie—would have come in crying and screaming, seeing the fortune in ceramic shards all tangled in Larry's clown hair.

Not here.

However, the maid did break out with her fair share of hysterics when I calmly explained to her what had almost happened and the monetary impact of that kind of crash. She really didn't know a Ming from a clay Tijuana bull-bank.

I added the old cliché "accidents will happen" to my pep talk. It apparently didn't provide a lot of solace.

"Panginoon ko! Panginoon ko! Panginoon ko!" she yelled over and over, running around so much that I feared even more demolition in the wake of her panic-dance.

It was just another of those studies, though. A firsthand look at how some people are overwhelmed and paralyzed by this kind of environment—an environment where a bauble on their employer's shelf is worth more than the house they live in at home.

CHAPTER 15

A CELEBRATION OF LARD

More malignant maladies lurked in the health catalog of Edmond Safra—in both the mental strain and the physical deterioration departments.

Safra's banking empire was downsizing—ending actually. His sale of his Republic New York Corporation to HSBC (Hong Kong and Shanghai Banking Corporation), like the American Express deal, hit a couple of complex "snags." One of those snags was that a major client, Martin Armstrong, was being investigated on allegations made by Safra's bank that he'd defrauded investors of nearly $1 billion, using accounts he held at Republic National (though, notably, Republic would eventually take full responsibility for the wrongdoing and pay restitution to Armstrong's clients). Another bothersome wrinkle was that Edmond had previously pledged to honor a long-standing family tradition to turn his banks over to his siblings for them to run;[27] his change of plans was causing quite the familial *désaccord*.

Physically, the Parkinson's was stumbling past its tenth year. And on top of that, Edmond Safra had a 95 percent occlusion in his heart—a degree of blockage that was exposed in his autopsy.

With that kind of statistic, had Safra not died in the accident, there's a good—no, great—chance that he would have suffered a massive heart attack; sooner, definitely not later. Even though some amount of occlusion was known, Safra was not a candidate for open-heart surgery because of the Parkinson's.

I was learning a lot about Edmond Safra, and there was always just that much more.

He loved his cheese sandwiches. But they were more than just cheese—they were a celebration of lard. Safra had lived a lifestyle of decadence, and the heavily seasoned-and-breaded chickens were finally waddling home to roost.

And I was in the middle of it all.

At one point in the New York rotation, the Safras attended another of their many "galas," which was also attended by medical staff to look after Edmond.

And as usual, there were perks.

"Ted, look!" one of the other nurses said. "The cooks have made all this food and there are so many leftovers!"

That particular party had been attended by power-politicians and world diplomats, including Henry Kissinger. Among the "leftovers" was all this caviar—Russian Beluga, the "good" stuff.

I have to tell you, it really was some nasty shit. It was like salted rubber! It was much more about rarity than actual taste. To me it was a stark commentary on the pretense of privilege. Give me an Oreo instead, any day of the week.

Food and privilege were also center stage at yet another celebration of all things monetarily stratospheric. This one was in Washington, DC.

For all the super-focus that Safra had on making money, he was also a very generous and charitable man. Besides the quick eight million from American Express that he gave to charity, Safra was a constant benefactor to educational, religious, medical, cultural, and humanitarian causes and organizations around the world.

He had an especially warm big-bucks spot in his heart for the sick. He donated millions to hospitals around the world—the Hôpital Cantonal de Genève, the Hôpitaux de France, and countless institutions in the United States. He was one of the founders of Albert Einstein Hospital in São Paulo, and in Israel, he initiated the construction of the Edmond and Lily Safra Children's Hospital at Tel Hashomer.

On this trip to DC, Edmond and Lily were being honored by the Trustees of the National Gallery of Art, who were awarding them the Medal for Distinguished Service for their contributions to the Arts in America.

We'd fly down, stay there that night, attend the ceremony, and then head for New York City.

Safra and the whole staff stayed in a hotel directly facing the White House. The card on the back of my room door read "$2,700 a night." We had an entire floor, for just a one-day event. President Bill Clinton was at our hotel that same day for a ceremony of his own, so Secret Service agents were everywhere. Since Safra's staff couldn't come down to the main dining room where the president was, we had to order room service.

That was fine with me.

The evening's restaurant fare mirrored the president's menu: salmon, prime rib, cheesecake, all sorts of stuff. I told them I was working the night shift, so bring up a nice fresh pot of coffee too—along with the beef with potatoes and some green beans and some cheesecake.

As I ate my exquisite dinner, I did some quick calculations—the money being spent just on me for just this night rivaled what I'd made over a good chunk of time when I was struggling to put myself through college. Although I was on American soil in DC, this kind of environment seemed as far into that alternate universe as La Leopolda.

The room phone rang, and it was Anthony Brittain. He went over the upcoming schedule with me and told me I'd be working another night shift—in New York—the following night.

We needed to discuss some logistics. I was working the night in DC, flying back to New York in the morning, and then working the night shift there?

"I'm going to be up for forty-eight hours . . ."

"We didn't think of that," he said.

So, we worked something out.

Instead of leaving with everyone else on the morning flight, I'd sleep in—the room was paid until 1:00 p.m. check-out—and I'd catch a later flight. I'd get some sleep and be ready for the night work in NYC.

Perfect.

But, of course, I couldn't sleep. I had a lot of adrenaline flowing because of the trip. I went out, looked around DC, and just absorbed the whole of this politic-potent environment.

Aboard the plane for New York, I found myself seated next to a familiar face. I wasn't flying first class, but it was DC to New York; anything goes on a line like that. Dan Rather, one of America's most beloved newsmen, settled in to talk with his personal secretary. They had been to Clinton's ceremony and discussed it in piercing journalistic depth.

I adjusted the seatback and just listened, reflecting on how they were working and so was I. None of us was nine-to-five and our workstations were the world.

I guessed there were times when privilege paid off.

The truth was that almost overnight I was in a position to order all the room service, stay in all the expensive hotels, and buy all the caviar—or Oreos—that I wanted, too. From the start, I wired ten thousand bucks every two weeks directly into Heidi's account. And because I was on foreign soil, the tax rates were highly reduced—with the *first* $170,000 completely tax-free!

All of a sudden, the credit card bills were gone. All of a sudden, the attorneys in Matthew's adoption case were paid off. All of a sudden, Minnie's boyfriend was getting upset about the twenty-five-dollar-a-week child support I was still making her pay; they gave up all rights to my son and moved to Florida.

My ship had certainly come in. Of course, there was still the matter of that iceberg floating around out there. But for the moment, the coast was clear and the horizon of my job with Edmond Safra was calm and sunny.

CHAPTER 16
THE FINAL PIECE

I was settled in.

Everything was perfect—and getting better.

My work bet was hedged with Columbia-Presbyterian by the leave of absence and the strike; Matthew's now-completed adoption was no longer a financial and emotional vacuum; Minnie had flitted off with her latest savior; all the bills were being paid off; and I even heard that my crazy upstate New York neighbor with the obsession for metes, bounds, and property lines was finally backing off and not wielding his wicked measuring wheel as wildly as he used to. He was probably worn out from his heart attack—and from my having him arrested.

And I had attained Edmond Safra's respect.

Safra was continually attended to by pairs of those "best in the world" nurses, but he knew the extra steps I took for him—from the "liquidation" of the horse pills, to making sure he spent at least some time in the South-of-France sun and got sufficient physical activity, to everything else that I could possibly do to ease his days of declining health.

And he was never unappreciative. "Oh, thank you, Teddy," he would say over and over.

This man was one of the richest men in the world; he didn't have to even talk to me. He didn't have to acknowledge me or call me by name—just "nurse" would've been good enough. But he took our relationship to a deeper level. He called me "Teddy" because he knew I cared about him.

I, in turn, respected how he treated me and that's what helped push my care for him to my next level.

And my care for those close to him.

The day I met his stepdaughter Adriana wasn't just a cerebral exercise in understanding how I got there; it included a physical exercise, too.

And it set a tone for my level of caring.

Besides Adriana, her brother Eduardo was at La Leopolda that day with one of his children. The setting was some sort of social lunch gathering. Eduardo's little girl was an "energetic" two-and-a-half-year-old—a turbo-charged munchkin. They had a personal maid to watch her and another little girl.

Well, somebody was asking the maid something, and she turned her back on the kids for a second. Now, I was standing outside the little atrium they had by the pool and saw as Eduardo's little girl made a beeline right for the water.

I saw it coming—I knew she was going in and I knew it was a problem. This event was shaping up like the eventual Ming vase situation, but it involved a far more valuable treasure.

I hit my stride and made the pool at the same time she did. It wasn't as pretty as an Olympic gold medal synchronized dive, but the results were worth far more. Her little head never even went underwater. I grabbed her mid-dive and held her up as we went in.

I got more than a "10.0" for that performance.

The maid didn't score as well.

Lily had a fit. She was screaming at the maid in French.

Quel est le problème avec vous?!

Ce que vous pensiez?!

How could you do this?!

I tried to make light of it. "Oh well, she just wanted to cool off. . . . It's so warm out here. . . . Kids will be kids. . . ."

Of course, I was in long pants and a long-sleeve shirt—now soaking wet. I come from freezing New York temperatures, and I was out there on the Côte d'Azur where it'd get so friggin' hot, I'd sweat like a plump duck in a French chef's kitchen. It got damn near unbearable sometimes. So, the dip actually did me some good.

Eventually Lily chilled out. We were all drying off and doing some adrenaline-regrouping when Adriana came up to me.

"We're really happy that you're helping out our dad," she said. "I'm here for whatever you may need."

That was worth so much. I appreciated her support and I sincerely wanted to continue helping the man.

And whenever he needed help, I was there. I became like the near-clairvoyant nurses in high-stress operating rooms—anticipating the surgeon's next move, whether he needs a scalpel or a pair of forceps. When I saw Safra needing something, I could make the presumption of what he needed before he needed it.

I was also in the rotation groove. Now on my second spin at La Leopolda, I was starting to feel comfortable with my new routine that would swirl around the Atlantic, U-turning in Europe, for the foreseeable future.

But I had to consider just how long it would really last. Safra's health was definitely declining. His dosages of daily medications and antidepressants were increasing, and the meds were affecting his abilities. Could he last two, three, or four years? I could put a lot of money in the bank in that time—more than most people see in a lifetime.

My family would be set.

They were the reason for all I was doing, and they were the only piece missing from the puzzle of my new dream-life.

It was such an important part.

I had delivered both of my and Heidi's children. They weren't born in a hospital—they were born in a birthing cottage. No drugs. No monitors. No anesthesia. I'd seen too many C-sections in my time in the NICU, and I wanted their births to be natural. Heidi agreed and I performed the delivery. The first thing those kids saw when they came into the world was me.

I wanted my family together.

CHAPTER 17

DE GAUCHE À DROITE

Four weeks until December 3, 1999

Our stay at La Leopolda had been shorter than anticipated. We'd relocated to La Belle Epoque after just a couple weeks, due to what I'd heard were "security concerns." Given Safra's omnipresent army of guards, that seemed to be the norm, so I didn't think much of it.

I began making plans to bring over my wife and children to be with me.

I interviewed with the director of an international "ABC" preschool and I found a conveniently located apartment in France that was big enough for all of us. Then I prepared a proposal for Anthony Brittain; he'd be the one to look at what I had in mind.

I knew Safra's company was spending over ten grand a month to house and feed me—there was no such thing as cheap rent in Monaco.

I asked Brittain to let *me* be responsible for me. "Give me a ten-grand-a-month stipend, and I'll pay for my own nearby apartment, I'll pay for my ABC school, I'll pay for my children." I offered to do all the paperwork and all the legwork, and the Safra group wouldn't need to worry about paying any of my bills.

Brittain liked the idea. It would save them money and effort in the long run.

And I would have my family.

I had been given the golden goose and we would all share in its eggs.

I was excited. I talked to Heidi about what was going to happen.

But some dark clouds of debate were still brewing back in Stormville—*Should we or shouldn't we?* Heidi's mother was throwing in a lot more than her two cents. She didn't want to be separated from her daughter and grandkids, period—cultural experience or financial benefits be damned.

I tried to explain over and over that this would be a relatively short move. "Look at the opportunity! Can you imagine this break for the kids? Heidi won't have to work; she can just be a mom! The family will be in France. We can go to the beach on the Riviera. Spend weekends in Paris. Go here, go there. Shoot out to Rome. See the Vatican, see the Sistine Chapel, smell the frescoes."

I had all these visions of things I'd only read about back in school. I finally had the ability to do so much for my family. And Safra's team was on board.

Sure, Brittain was still voicing his complaints that "I can't believe I'm an investment banker and I have to deal with this shit!" But what I and others didn't know was that the "shit" surrounding Safra's dealings was a big, steaming mound, and the pile was getting bigger.

Edmond's sale of his Republic New York Corporation bank was still off-track, running into last-minute problems. It had already caused estrangement from his siblings—relationships that had been tight for a lifetime—and, due to the criminal investigation related to Armstrong, the sale price was continuing to drop. But I kept hearing Lily press Edmond to unload it anyway: "We need this, *chéri*—4.6 billion today is better than six billion tomorrow when you're dead. It's a headache; get rid of it!" And so he did, taking a personal loss of $450 million just to push the sale through. [28]

(Her own motivation notwithstanding, Lily's plea may or may not have been a factor: Safra needed to sell before his own dirty deeds were uncovered and the bank lost even more value.)

There would be even more upsets in the Safra family when the details of the eleventh-hour changes in his will became known.

With Safra's health continuing to fail, Lily was gaining even more control—going as far as replacing Safra's cardiologist and physician of thirty years.

Lily and Edmond were into their third decade of marriage. For many of those years, it had looked like Edmond was about to kick the bucket. He had developed the Parkinson's about ten years in and had kept going longer than anticipated.

I wondered if Lily was getting impatient.

———————

Two weeks until December 3, 1999

In November 1999, I was given the best news of my life: The Safras were placing me on permanent staff. That gave me full benefits—insurance, everything. There was virtually no way I could lose my position as long as I continued to do my job and do it right.

That kind of stipulation was never a problem for me.

But with permanent status, I began to notice things.

My W-2 for the first fiscal period listed Spotless and Brite as my employer; for the second it was Platinum Cleaning Company. Edmond Safra could pay for anything; why would he have his nursing staff, including his doctors, paid under two separate subsidiaries? Legally, I was working for a cleaning company based in New York. Evidently, this was another example of how things worked in Monaco. Nurses, I discovered, could only enter Monaco as "tourists," not as professionals—never tainting the pristine labor laws and employment figures.

It was always about that pristine image. It was all about the laundering, the manipulation of things. Still, why would one of the richest men in the world have to go *de gauche à droite,* as the French say ("from the left to the right") in any way, shape or form, when he could just go in a straight line?

Safra could do anything he wanted, in any way he wanted. He made billions in his own way, but what way was that? It was that smell of suspicion again. And it was like when I'd looked at that Renoir and made comments about one's personality not changing—even as one experienced changes in life's different strata.

I'd been pretty sure some kind of constant thread was maintained throughout Safra's dealings, and by that point I was certain that the thread didn't follow such a *ligne droite.*

CHAPTER 18

THE COUNTDOWN CONTINUES

Ten days until December 3, 1999

More straight lines began to curve in strange directions. All of a sudden, security measures started to change at La Belle Époque.

Routinely, at night, all the valances in Edmond's bedroom and along that entire wall were closed—steel valances that shielded Safra from the absolute darkness on that side of the building. They were part of that rocket-and-bomb-proof buffer—hundreds of thousands of dollars worth of protective armor that would stop anything.

If someone down in the marina below La Belle Époque, for example, wanted to kill one of the richest men in the world by firing a rocket into the place, he'd be wasting his time. He'd have better luck trying to take down an F-22 with a slingshot.

But now the valance at the nursing station in the back had to be closed every night as well.

During my first Monte Carlo rotation, if one wanted to step out onto the back porch of the complex to get some fresh air in the dead of night, it was open and available. And there was nothing wrong or dangerous with that—no one could gain entry that way. It wasn't possible physically, and besides, cameras were everywhere. There were armed guards down in the bank. There were separate security elevators. There was a personal elevator that led to another elevator. You had to go through a hallway, through another secure door, through a fire escape to another secure door. There was *no* way anybody could come up to where Safra was. So why were they suddenly mandating that the security valance in that nursing station be closed?

Unless someone knew something we didn't.

Was it pure paranoia or was it a result of how certain deals were made—deals that led to a purse of billions? Billions that wouldn't mean much to Safra if he was dead.

The nurses were starting to talk. "Why are we doing this?" No one was feeling comfortable; it was as if during the course of my nursing work, the chief of security had come up and said, "I want you to start carrying this nine millimeter." It was that blatant. It was yet another part of all the active—and subliminal—signs that indicated something was going on.

And there was more.

My study of Lily Safra and her position went from distracting to disturbing. As she continued to eye more wealth, the effects spilled over onto Edmond's siblings—the final wave rolling in just days before Edmond's death.

I observed and overheard Lily Safra demanding that her husband change his will.

"Oh, *chéri*, you're so sick . . ." she would implore him. "You're going to be giving your brothers and sisters a hundred million each. That's five hundred million. They never see you. Oh, *chéri*, who cares for you? Who loves you? Please, *chéri*, change your will. Change it to give them ten million each instead of a hundred million."

I was witness to her relentless manipulation. I watched it.

And I couldn't believe it.

What do you have to do with telling him how much to give to his siblings? I thought. *Yes, you're married to him, but these are* his *brothers and sisters! This is what he wants.*

But she would milk it and milk it and when he didn't respond, she would storm out of the room like a child.

Eventually, in what would *just happen* to be the final days of Edmond Safra's life, she wore him down and he changed his will, adjusting the hundred million to ten million for each sibling.

One week until December 3, 1999

Things were moving along. I saw so many changes. Security was coming in, adjusting cameras and tweaking everything. *Why are they doing this and why are they doing that?* I wondered. You couldn't put your finger on it, but you knew something was happening.

Something was going down.

Maybe the most bizarre circumstance of all these changes was that Lily was the only person with access to the surveillance equipment. Later, in the trial, the prosecution would hammer at the fact that I had been a surveillance expert in Las Vegas—that I could have easily disabled the system.

Not hardly. In fact, there was no way!

I had *no idea* where the equipment was, and I had no access to it anyway. If I had wanted to disable something, I suppose I could have started in on the cameras in plain sight—cameras that would have recorded me as I took them down. But *that* would have taken me *years* to do—there were big-brother lenses everywhere. In or out of La Belle Époque, you couldn't pick your nose in Monte Carlo without *someone* seeing you.

As long as the equipment was turned on, of course.

CHAPTER 19

THE KIDNAPPING

Thirty-six hours until December 3, 1999

I never took my Safra adventure and all the next levels it produced for granted. That's why I wanted my family with me. In a place amid the high-wire culture-core that escapes most of us who are in the simple-man box. In a place where on my day off I could board a cheap Euro train and shuffle just thirteen miles southwest to Nice—*Nice la Belle;* "Nice the Beautiful"—to yet another jewel in the crown of paradise along the Mediterranean. Of course, on my day off, I could have relaxed in the sun by the pool at the hotel, drinking a high-priced bottle of wine, but on the morning of December 1, I just felt like going to Nice and wandering in the shops and along the Promenade des Anglais.

But after my day of *relâchement,* as I made my way back to the train, those ominous thoughts about "something going on" began to cloud the winter sun (Nice has to sometimes endure up to sixty-five days a year when the sun doesn't shine as brightly as during the other three hundred). That "something going on" had gone beyond the sudden odd actions of Lily and the security personnel: it had been about a week since I first noticed—and *felt*—someone observing me.

It was a calculated and trained sixth sense. The Green Berets, the police department—these are hard callings where eyes in the back of one's head and reaction-connected invisible "feelers" are standard issue. For the survivors.

And I've always been a survivor.

I remembered seeing a white van—a French version of a Dodge Caravan. It was a common type of truck but it—or one just like it—became my four-wheeled shadow, showing up wherever I went. It was at the hotel, the jewelry store, the casino. I *was* being observed.

I knew it.

When I was somewhere between the Promenade and the train station, I walked around a blind corner and in front of me stood a bearded man dressed in black with sunglasses on. And he had a gun.

The white van pulled up quickly.

Now, I can—and have—reacted in nanoseconds to many things; but *this* attack took less than that. Action is always faster than reaction, and this was an action—an operation—that was set into motion with precision. The bunch confronting me wasn't made up of rookies. Nor was I in a movie-thriller where our hero takes away the gun, leaps the moving vehicle, causing it to flip high in the air and crash into a gasoline tanker, and then takes out the thugs one by one as they scramble from the burning van, all in the blink of an exotic Euro-babe's eye.

No.

When the shit went down, it went down fast.

I saw the guy and the gun. The van screeched up with an open door. Masked guys leapt out, threw a hood over my head, heaved me into the van, and we were gone.

Neat and simple.

I listened to them speak. Their language had a strong Eastern European sound— Russian or Czech, perhaps. I tried to assess how many there were. But there were periods of silence.

We drove around for what seemed like forever—maybe thirty or forty minutes, but it felt like an hour and a half. My mind was racing: *Am I going to live?*

Well, if they were going to kill me, I assured myself, *I would already be dead by now. So, there's probably a purpose for my being here.*

I was right.

We got down to business.

With my hood still on, I was told what I was to do.

It was just one thing, really. I was to make sure that the valance in the nursing station in the Safras' flat was left open tomorrow night—*got it?*

I wasn't exactly in a physical position to bargain, so the moral high-ground I was about to take was akin to Oprah trying to explain "inner feelings" to a hungry mastiff.

But I took a shot at it.

I told them that I didn't know where they were going with this, but that it was against my code of ethics to do anything that might end up hurting someone—especially Edmond Safra, the man I was charged with taking care of.

Well, *that* got a reaction. Their reaction was that they dry-cocked and clicked the hammer of a gun into the back of my head several times. That will make your ass pucker a bit.

Evidently my approach hadn't swayed them toward my way of thinking.

At all.

At that point, they enlightened me to the fact that they were definitely in control of the situation and the components of their operation. And they were about to prove their point.

I'd been on my stomach, and I was turned to my side. Then I was pushed into a sitting position with my legs held down. That's when they smashed both my big toes with what felt like a hammer.

My sneakers were not ball-peen resistant.

Then they removed my hood—but not before pushing me face-down onto the floor of the van again with someone's knee in my back. I still had no idea of who they were or how many of them there might be. By that point, wherever we were, it was very dark—and even darker in the van. I got a marginal look at the men as I tried to raise my head, but the two in the back wore masks of their own. The driver kept his back to me and all I could see was that he, like the original gunman, had a beard. *So what?* They gave me nothing to identify them with.

But they did give me something: *Photos.*

They shined a light on a shot of Heidi coming out of Columbia-Presbyterian; another of my two youngest children walking home from preschool up the hill; and one of Matthew walking my little dog, Scottie, out behind my house.

And right there—that little gallery exhibition told me that I was fucked.

I'd always said what I valued most was my family.

I pleaded with the masked SOBs—*again*—that I didn't want to jeopardize anybody's life.

They replied to me, in an atmosphere of pretty damn shaky reassurance considering the masks, the guns, the hood, the kidnapping in a foreign country, and the obvious threats against my family, that I wasn't going to have to do *anything* that would jeopardize *anybody's* life.

"Just make sure the valance is open!"

In very broken English, they supplied more details—more *persuasion* to their request. They added that they were monitoring all of my phone calls—my cellular communications and everything else. If I tried to inform my family of the threat or warn them in any way, I'd be kissing them good-bye without ever actually touching them again.

The photos were new; that was obvious. My kids' lives were just starting, and I wasn't going to end that by doing something stupid.

I couldn't risk it.

I delivered those kids into the world—I wasn't about to deliver them into the hands of this scum.

With a heavy knee still in my back, I tried one more venture into rationality and reason. I mentioned a fact that maybe no one in their little party may have considered: "I'm not scheduled to work tomorrow night."

"Don't worry about that," I was told.

———

Once it was clear that the meeting was indeed over and that I had duly noted all of the bullet-points on their particular agenda, I was unceremoniously freed in the darkness of a side street near the train depot.

"Just make sure the valance is open . . ."

I started to try and put what just happened into some sort of logistical and logical perspective. That valance *used to be* kept open. It was over a set of French doors that allowed the staff and residents to step out for air. We'd always felt that that level of the residence was impenetrable even with the valance open due to its physical position and the legions of armed guards to get through before getting up there.

But then the security was stepped up and the closing of the valance became mandatory. Fears—paranoia—about rockets and airborne hell closed in.

But no one's life would be jeopardized . . .

It was obvious that others knew more than I did.

As I limped to catch the train, I couldn't help but look over my shoulder. I knew I was still being followed. Observed. Tethered and hooked.

For once in my life, I was definitely not me. I was under the control of an unknown; like a disturbing human puppet in an old episode of the *Twilight Zone* that haunts and haunts.

Back at the hotel, I looked at my two black-and-blue big toes. They were a mess but didn't appear broken.

I packed everything. I was leaving. Leaving!

I kept thinking, *What happens if I just go? I haven't said anything. I'm under surveillance but I'm not saying anything.*

I should just go.

But then again, that would be going against their wishes, wouldn't it?

Will something happen to my family if I just go?

Am I saving my own ass but killing my family?

It was a nauseating limbo. I was pacing and packing—unpacking, pacing, and packing again.

Sleep? Are you kidding me?

Early in the morning, the phone rang. This *was* the *Twilight Zone*. This was every cold black-and-white "spine tingler" ever made where the poor bastard who's about to meet his own personal monster just looks at that old ringing phone. He knows he shouldn't answer it, but he has to. The whole thing just had to play out.

My family's lives depended on it.

"Yes?"

It was Anthony Brittain, telling me Lily had changed the schedule for the upcoming night. She was the *only one* with the power to do that.

And I was suddenly on shift.

So was Vivian Torrente, I was told.

But Rod Serling or Alfred Hitchcock didn't appear from the shadows to bring the bent drama back into its fantasy focus. I had to keep living the script.

And I couldn't say a word to anyone. And now I *knew* I couldn't leave. I couldn't even chew off my own arm to get out of the merciless trap I was in. I was wired to the hilt and desperately needed the sleep I couldn't have—and *hadn't* had in going on forty hours.

All I could do was watch the clock.

With each tick, I thought, *Who is doing this? Why?*

Why?

There had to be reasons.

That smell of suspicion was becoming rank.

A lot of those non-straight-line business policies—the *de gauche à droite* way of doing things—of Edmond Safra were first held up, kicked up, and conjured up by that American Express battle that began in 1982 when Amex purchased Safra's Trade Development Bank (TDB). Like most big deals involving big money, the smiles, handshakes, and back-patting turned to frowns and kicks to the groin in a hurry.

Safra had sold one of his "children" for a variety of reasons—including the usual "I need more time to relax"—but a lot had to do with an Andes-sized avalanche of Latin American countries defaulting on bank debts that could hurt TDB. But Safra stayed on as Amex's chief of international banking, so he could continue to give the personal service to his customers. American Express didn't work that way. It was like selling your beloved vintage car to a neighbor and watching him turn it into a dune buggy.

Safra resigned and launched a Swiss extension of his Republic National Bank of New York. That's when a lot of vile slag was thrown: accusations of violating competition clauses, corporate raiding, and all kinds of ugliness led to what has been commonly referred to as American Express' "smear campaign" against Edmond Safra.

Those smears left rancid marks that pointed to Safra being allegedly involved in the 1980s Iran-Contra affair and tainted tax attorney Willard Zucker, and it dredged up bank negotiations from the 1970s linking Safra to New York crime bosses. There were also stains on his rep that were soaked with the money-muck of ex–Panamanian dictator Manuel Noriega and the Colombian drug cartels.

Some very genuine security concerns had crept into the Safras' lives five years ago, in '94, with the kidnapping in Brazil of Edmond's banker nephew, Ezequiel Edmond

Nasser. After seventy-five days of brutal captivity, a ransom was paid and the nephew was released, but the incident led to a step-up of protection throughout the entire Safra empire.[29]

Around that same time, Safra's Parkinson's diagnosis had been confirmed and with it came the disease's side effects—effects like depression, anxiety, and *paranoia*.

In addition, during the past year, Edmond had alerted the FBI to potential money-laundering—everyone assumed by the Russian mafia. So he was cooperating with the feds to get to the root of any international improprieties.[30]

He was also reportedly seen in the company of some big-league Soviets, including dining with two "unnamed Russians" that he "quarreled with"[31] and the so-called "godfather of the Kremlin," oligarch Boris Berezovsky whose status had recently taken a hit when he found himself accused of embezzling money from Aeroflot Airlines."[32] Clearly, Safra had enemies and friends in high Russian places.

I just recently learned that Safra knew exactly where the "laundered" money came from, and that he and Berezovsky (also suspiciously deceased) were involved in a scheme that made both of them enemies of Russian president Vladimir Putin. But even back then, the entanglements Safra had with the Russians and the federal investigation seemed risky, to say the least.

At work, I continued to hear rumblings about a libelous litany of things. Most of it was in French, but I caught enough to get whiffs of the manure: how the red flag raised by Safra on the multi-billion-dollar transfer from Russia had launched one of the largest federal bank investigations in history,[33] more about the Russian mob, and statements like "I'm not going to pay those bastards any money!"

There were surely some motives for "something going on" floating around out there. But I, like many others, couldn't even imagine what was really going down behind the scenes.

Edmond's Parkinson's may have induced his paranoia to an extent—but it seemed pretty damn valid under these particular circumstances.

I thought about the rest of the staff. Why weren't they targets? Why me? I was a former Green Beret and obviously more formidable than any of the other nurses. But was I? Like formidability, there are degrees of vulnerability, and they don't necessarily have anything to do with physical or mental toughness.

I ran down the list of employees. I was the only one on Safra's staff with a family—with young children. I was the only one who could be blackmailed with those kinds of threats. One staff member was retired with no family. Another had a husband she really didn't care about—if someone told her he was going to be killed, she'd say, "Great!" Every one of them had little in the way of actual vulnerability.

I was the winner in that category: I had the most to lose.

Those thugs in that van knew about me and they knew my core values. They knew what I had been throughout my whole life.

They knew who I was.

I reported to work. Vivian was there. The other shift nurses—for some reason—were quickly sent out, as opposed to the usual casual shift transition. Lily was there with Edmond, ready to tuck things in for the night.

I was certainly not my usual self. I was quieter. Withdrawn. Limping, in loosened shoes.

Vivian, however, noticed nothing; she was upbeat.

Perky, even.

"Well, we were supposed to have tonight off but we'll make the best of it!" she said. "I'll get some fruit and we'll keep awake."

She wasn't nervous at all. Why should she have been? She had no clue. I heard some talk about the schedule mix-up being due to one of the other nurses being unexpectedly told she had to return to the Philippines because of a work visa problem. She had to go home, spend one day in the Philippines, and then circle back to Monaco in order to fulfill some sort of obscure bureaucratic residency requirement.

And all of that happened at the last minute.

Now both Vivian and I were on duty as a result of this scheduling emergency. I began to sweat, and it had nothing to do with Edmond's high-temp ambience.

The night nurse we were relieving went out and Lily came in, presumably to shut the valance over the French doors like she did every night.

But she didn't shut it

I looked at Vivian and asked her what we were supposed to do.

"Nothing," she said. "Madame Safra is in charge of that. Don't touch it."

"But it's open!"

"Just leave it," she reaffirmed. "Madame Safra is in control of that."

Just like she was in control of the nurses' schedules.

Lily was in control, and tonight she was in a hurry—weaving more variations into our nightly theme. More anomalies. For example, she was usually calm and pleasant during these casual shift changes, the essence of grace and social schmooze with the help.

"*Bonsoir, chéri.* Good night!"

Not on that night.

Get the earlier nurses out of here!

It was Lily Safra who left that vital portal open on the night of December 3.

My sweating eased and at least a couple of my ripped nerves came together when she performed that duty, after saying goodnight—her last goodnight—to her husband at nine o'clock that evening.

But my sweat and nerves were completely separate from my mind—a badly sleep-deprived mind that I couldn't shut off.

I just kept thinking . . .

I was grateful that Lily left the valance open, of course, instead of me.

It won't be my fault, I thought.

Whatever "it" might eventually become.

And my family is safe.

But I also realized that I'd made no plan B in case the valance couldn't be left open for some reason. I hadn't allowed myself to get to that point. My focus was on my family.

I was thinking and wrestling with the fact that all I'd really done was not tell anyone what was going on and what had happened to me. I was thinking—probably against some true inner reasoning—that nothing could happen now.

I don't have to do anything that will jeopardize anybody's life . . .

Just make sure that the valance is open . . .

Everything was going according to plan. But that was also troubling.

Was Lily involved? Had she been threatened, too?

But how *could* she be threatened? How can you be threatened when you're the sole beneficiary of billions of dollars and the power and control that comes with that? How can you be threatened when you have your own army and you're the general? If I had billions like that, I wouldn't be worried about too much. I could have layer upon layer of guards every hundred feet before the bad guys got to my Alamo.

But in my gut, I felt differently.

Something was going to happen, and I knew it. That fucking valance was as wide open as a fresh-shucked French oyster.

I'd been told one thing, about no life being jeopardized, but this complex plot would expose something altogether different.

Someone *would* get hurt this night amid a shitload of jeopardy; and *they*—whoever *they* were—would draw first blood.

CHAPTER 20

FIRST BLOOD

December 3, 1999
4:30 a.m.

The night had worn on, my nerves and emotions wanting to claw their way out of my body.

Waiting.

Like being chained to railroad tracks—alone, in the dark, and unable to speak.

Or scream.

Waiting to feel the first faint vibrating rumble of the locomotive.

Then hear the shriek of metal wheels.

Louder and louder.

Then the hit.

The cuts may be quick, but the waiting is the hell.

Vivian was now in with Edmond and I was at the nursing station. We changed positions at 4:00 a.m. My last two sweltering hours with Safra had been especially grueling—my head was coming apart in a sweating stream of seared consciousness.

The stress was eating me up.

Is someone going to come in here and start shooting? Am I going to hear the dead-echo pop, pop, pop of a silencer?

I had no gun. That wasn't a part of my job; the massive security force were the ones with tools like that. And they were everywhere around us, right?

And it sure wasn't a part of the "deal" for me to lie in ambush for whomever or whatever might appear that night.

Not with my family at risk.

If you're a real man, you'll sacrifice yourself—what kind of a man would you be if you didn't? If I die, at least they'll be safe.

God, how did I even get into this shit—doing a good deed with a fucking camera? Now I'm over here in Monte Carlo, so far from home, and I'm fucked.

This damned heat is nauseating!

I can't warn Safra—but after all, they said no one would get hurt.

But this kind of money is BIG business. And big business may not always be on the up-and-up.

Is all of this madness caused by some shit Safra caused? Another type of "vendetta" from someone he crossed? The list of potential grudge-holders isn't short and includes plenty of powerful and dangerous people. And all the Russians on that list could be connected with my kidnappers.

Regardless, my family is not going to take the fall because this billionaire has stepped on the wrong toes. I'll do what I can to help Safra or anybody, but I'm not going to give up the lives of my family. I'm being paid an enormous salary, sure, but I didn't sign up to be Safra's bodyguard. Others have that job.

Of course, it wouldn't be long before I discovered none of them were even working tonight.

At least not at La Belle Époque.

The nursing station was about nine feet by twelve feet. Originally a maid's chamber with a small shower and a toilet, when the room was reconfigured, a refrigerator was installed where the shower had been.

That caused a long-running problem.

If you know anything about plumbing (which whoever reworked this room obviously did not), you know that if the sanitary loop in either a toilet or a drain system is left without circulation for a long period, the standing water evaporates and sewer gases come in, and it stinks.

Which it did!

The all-important and busy nursing station in the Safras' zillion-dollar home smelled like a delta swamp outhouse.

I kept trying to explain to the flat's maintenance staff that to make the place not reek, all they had to do was slide the fridge out, put some water into the remaining shower plumbing and then add a non-evaporating liquid, like olive oil, to the standing water so that it wouldn't vaporize. But they just wouldn't get on board with that.

And here's how the issue relates: To counteract the stench, Lily Safra demanded that scented candles (from Slatkin & Co.!) be kept lit almost all the time. So now we're back to the rich and famous with these expensive fifty-dollar-a-pop wax-and-wick wonders that would kill a moose fart at a hundred feet.

One was lit as I sat at the desk in the nursing station.

The desk in the room had the valance-veiled French doors behind it—the valance that was now open.

The valance was simply a roll-up metal shutter. Beyond the valance and the French doors was a balcony. Just below that was the nearby deck of Hôtel Hermitage, which we could easily see when we went onto the landing for fresh air before Lily's nightly closing of the valance.

But we always felt safe out there, even with the deck's elbow-close quarters, because who was going to breach the Hermitage's security *and* the Mossad guard forces of La Belle Époque? And from inside the building, certainly no one could work their way up the labyrinth of elevators and security to get to that landing.

That seemed to cover all the bases.

But what I didn't know were some details concerning the architecture and security-setup of the Hermitage.

It would be a long time before that bit of enlightenment came my way.

Just past 4:30 a.m.
I was sitting at the desk.

Staring.

More thinking.

More of that seared stream of consciousness.

It was a badly unsettled mix. I'm a strong Type A, I'd been awake for thirty-six-plus hours, I was stressed and gnawed-through with that horrible feeling of wired-exhaustion, and I was sitting at that desk . . .

What I routinely did on most nights was walk down the hall to the full workout gym. I'd grab a ten-kilogram barbell (about twenty pounds) and I'd do curls with it to keep myself awake.

That's exactly what I did on this night, too. Although it wasn't to keep me awake as much as to do something, *anything*, to cut this damned stress even a little.

I set the barbell down on the floor, right next to the desk.

And that open valance behind it.

Yes, I was aware that it was open.

That "pop-pop-pop" could be on its way any second.

But we were surrounded by so much security. And I was told no one would get hurt . . .

I never sat for long anyway—tonight or otherwise—with my back to anything. I was always moving around.

Going to the bathroom.

Waiting for the every-two-hour position change.

Making a snack at the refrigerator.

Working the coffee machine.

Doing what I could do to keep myself up.

Finally, it was almost the end of the shift.

This is almost over, I thought.

I really thought I had made it.

Everything was fine.

No.

Just like the split-second kidnapping, the attack came so quick. Call it a sucker-punch, call it an ambush, call it a crying fucking shame that we all don't have 360-degree rotating eyes, call it what you want—but now I was on the floor from a rapid-slam blow to the back of my head.

I was more than dazed—but I'm trained. Survival kicked in. *So this is how it's going to go down?* Here was the lie that they told me, dealt in a hard hand. Here was the first blood—mine.

I was on the floor with this guy standing over me. I grabbed the barbell. Action is faster than reaction. So I took action. I come up with the weight like Thor's hammer to the right side of his fucking head. I did some serious damage.

Now I saw there were two guys—two masked men.

The one I hit went right to his knees. I whacked him solid and put him into another time zone. All bets were off now. I was told that nobody was getting hurt. I'd been hurt. So, that was it. Now we were taking this to a very bad next level.

Later I would hear in the media that the fight "raged" for half an hour. This "fight" happened in a snap of the fingers.

The standing guy pulled out a knife as I fell back from whacking the other guy, the weight still in my hand. I was on the carpet. The guy I hit was in bad shape. He was struggling with a smashed skull and writhing and thrashing like a rundown animal. Instinct and motor-reflex kicked in. He grabbed hold of my leg and was pulling me toward him. And he had a knife. I had on loose-fitting pants and he was ripping at them, so they started to ride up my leg in his death grip.

That became important.

Along with the stupid half-hour death-match portrayal, it would later become a hot topic that I was cut on my thigh but wasn't cut through my pants. Maybe that's because half my pants were up around my ass!

This guy had my leg and I was twisting and turning. I got sliced again. He was trying to get up and I was stabbed again—right in the gut; I'm not sure by which guy.

I was losing blood and my head was pounding.

I lost consciousness. But not for long—not even a couple minutes.

This knife was hanging out of me and I was *really* bleeding now. I looked around and nobody was there.

I didn't know where my attackers had gone.

They might have gone in to get Safra.

My blood was everywhere, but I knew that if I pulled out the knife, I was going to bleed to death because it was stuck in a bad area. I was holding onto the knife, my guts, my blood, and my life.

I reeled over to the switch that controlled the signal light that went from the nurses' station to Safra's room to allow the nurses to communicate with each other silently without disturbing Mr. Safra.

I signaled Vivian that I needed her.

She came.

"My god, Ted, you're bleeding!" she screamed.

I told her that two men came in—*broke* in.

I told her to get Edmond and take him into the bathroom—which is equipped as a safe room—and to close and lock the door!

I stumbled along behind Vivian to the bedroom. She roused Safra while I opened the bathroom door. If you didn't know it was there, the entrance to the bathroom safe room looked like just another part of the wall; an innocuous panel of protection, heavily primed with paranoia.

Safra was fairly alert tonight, and when he saw me covered in blood, his paranoia and panic quickly pulsed. Vivian ushered him into the bathroom and I gave her my cell phone.

"Call for help!" I told her. "I'm going to try to get downstairs and find someone!"

We really had no training for an emergency like this. *Oh, Ted, if there's an emergency, call 911 in Monte Carlo.* No. There was none of that shit here.

I was bleeding and trying to talk. I'd been bashed in the head and sliced on the side. My leg was ripped open, I was holding a knife in the middle of my stomach, and Vivian said the last thing I would ever hear from her: "Ted, everything is going to be okay!"

As I was shutting the panel to the safe room, Safra told me, "Set off the alarm!"

Yeah, okay, okay, the alarm . . .

The alarm?

I was dizzy, and I was coming back past the nursing station. *The alarm?* These guys had already managed to bypass Safra's maze of barriers to get in here. *The alarm?* Then it dawned on me what Safra must have meant: the smoke alarm! That alarm is hooked into a central alarm in the building. If I went down and I passed out, *somebody* would at least have to respond to the damn smoke alarm!

I looked around and saw a small metal trash can—*une poubelle.* It had some banana peels in it, along with some paper and some alcohol from cleaning up stuff.

Nearby on the desk burned that fifty-buck scented candle.

With some tissue paper, I made this little "smoke signal"—*puff, puff,* the alarm went off immediately. I set the can right in the middle of the room, dead center.

I had no intention of starting a fire. I couldn't imagine in any way that the little wastebasket smudge pot *could* start (or as the Monegasque refer to it, *communicate*) a fire.

Hell, if I wanted to *communicate a fire,* I could have done it up right. With the curtains and the abundance of fuel in that place, I could have worked something that would've made the burning of Atlanta look like Cub Scouts cooking s'mores.

What I created was a tiny smoldering "smoke signal," far from anything flammable. I put that *poubelle* in the open center of the room—right underneath the alarm trigger—and it worked.

4:49 a.m.
[La Belle Époque's] *remote surveillance company* [is] *alerted, by means of a telephone transmitter, that the fire alarm in Mr. Safra's apartment* [has] *gone off.*[34]

Eventually, in spite of all the hurdles set up by the Monegasque "justice" system and its authorities, a semi-accurate timeline of the events and even some of the dialogue between the police and firemen would be compiled and included within the official Investigative and Prosecutor's Reports. The media was all over the probe, too.

But right then I was bleeding out. I was thinking I might not make it all the way downstairs. But I knew somebody *had* to come for that alarm.

They did.

Not only were the *sapeurs-pompiers*—the firefighters of Monaco—alerted, but another, completely separate fire department was also notified when that alarm started going off. Within minutes of my triggering the alarm, eighty-six policemen and fifty-six firemen show up.

Of course, eighty-six policemen and fifty-six firemen *showing up* is a very different thing than eighty-six policemen and fifty-six firemen *responding.*

But I had no concept of that right then . . .

Just before 5:00 a.m.
Edmond makes the first call on Maher's phone. He calls Lily and tells her of "aggressors" in the house that have "injured Ted" and that she should "close [herself] in and call police." Lily first calls the Safras' head of security, Samuel Cohen, who is at La Leopolda. Cohen

has already been notified by the Monaco police as to what is going on at La Belle Époque and is already en route.[35]

I was fading.

I still had no idea where the masked men went, or just how severely I hurt that one guy. *Are they going for Lily?* I needed to go downstairs. I was getting the cavalry one way or another—I might not make it, but the cavalry *would* come!

I was getting dizzier. I realized that I could jump the railings in back and head to the Hermitage; but if I passed out and fell and wound up somewhere in the dark shrubbery, nobody was going to see me until the sun came up.

By then I'd be long dead.

I opted for going down a little fire escape to a level where I knew the Israeli bodyguard should be.

And no, he wasn't there.

Great . . .

My mind raced: *Now I need to hit the elevator that will get me down to the other elevator that goes to the bank level. The door will open up and that level's armed guard will be there! And the guard will see me bleeding to death! Yes!—I know I can make it at least that far.*

I was off the first elevator and onto the one that dropped just a single floor to where the bank elevator was. I got to that point and found no one there, either!

Where are all the damn guards?

I realized that—once again— I was screwed.

I *had* to go all the way down to the bank level. It was the logical—and only—choice. I got in the elevator.

Everything I'd done in my military and emergency career had taught me not to panic in any bad situation because it will kill you. Even as I was losing so much blood, my mind was thinking logically like Spock. The endorphins were flowing; a fight for life was going. I was thinking all these different things—*the alarm . . . I'm bleeding . . . they won't find me . . . but wait, I'm in the elevator . . . they'll probably find me, at least . . . maybe even save my life . . . maybe . . .*

This was all happening in seconds, not minutes. You weren't hearing the mellow strains of Muzak elevator music here.

I reached the bank level, the door opened, there *was* a guard! A bank guard—not a Mossad Uzi-warrior. I spoke to him in the best broken French I could choke out. I was literally flopping on the floor. Blood pouring. I saw this guy, eyes wide, start to call someone.

These guys—these guards and cops—are everywhere in Monte Carlo. They just dream of something like this.

5:00 a.m.
Making the second call on Maher's phone, Vivian Torrente calls head nurse Sonia Casiano Herkrath from Safra's dressing room to ask her to call police. She informs Casiano that Maher is injured. Five more calls are made by Torrente during the next 90 minutes.[36]

5:12 a.m.
The first police officers arrive in the lobby of the building. Police begin organizing a floor-by-floor search for intruders.[37]

All of a sudden, the SWAT team showed up, shielded in bulletproof everything. It's like they were protecting the prince or the president. I heard someone yell, "Get down! They're shooting!"

I was going down fast but I was still able to think: *Who's shooting?*

I was on the ground and they had all these guys covering me.

But the truth is that no one was shooting anything!

It was a crazy bandwagon of pumped-up panic and it was just beginning.

Around 5:15 a.m.
Edmond calls Lily a second time[38] *to make sure she has "closed herself in."*[39]

The central alarm was still going off because of the smoke.

Within just a few minutes, medics were starting an IV on me.

I saw the throngs of cops and firemen. I knew the alarm had worked. I knew things would be okay.

Vivian was right.

Semi-conscious, I felt them wheeling me into the ambulance. I was in and out. I heard them talking about surgery. I . . .

5:20 a.m.

Maher is transported to Princess Grace Hospital for treatment of stab wounds.[40]

CHAPTER 21

THE FIRE

Mid-morning, December 3, 1999
Day one in the hospital.

Edmond and Vivian were dead.

But I was not aware.

What wasn't completely destroyed in La Belle Époque had been fouled forever; its elegance reduced to sorry cinders and deluxe debris.

But I was not aware.

Completely lost in my comatose ignorance was that, due to some of the most inexplicable actions and incompetency on the part of a major civil protective force anywhere at any time, my little signal blaze in that tiny *poubelle* was allowed to fatally fan into a fire-and-smoke storm that never should have been.

There was so much I wasn't aware of yet—so much that had occurred.

In the months—and years—to come, I would dig and dig. I would bend my body and brain as I scratched to find every piece to this putrid puzzle. Putting all the foul fragments together, one can see almost exactly what occurred on that December morning in Monaco.

5:24 a.m.
Passersby and neighbours begin flooding emergency phone lines with reports of seeing smoke from the building.[41]

I had been rushed to the hospital and right into emergency surgery. Back at La Belle Époque, the authorities continued to stand idle while Vivian begged for help in call after call from *my* fucking cell phone—the phone I gave her with one hand while holding my guts in with the other.

5:30 a.m.
Torrente makes fourth call to Casiano from the cell phone. She does not mention any smoke. Safra appears calm but requests police intervention.[42]

That intervention didn't happen.

What *did* happen was that when Safra-Security Chief Samuel Cohen showed up at La Belle Époque, he was promptly stopped by the cops on the lower floor of the building and handcuffed, because he was intent on going up into the flat to save his boss. He knew exactly where Safra was, how to get in there, and he even had a key![43]

But Cohen wasn't an official—not one of the insider authorities.

Adding injury to Cohen's insult, after such strong intervention to stop him, none of those "insider authorities" produced any fruitful intervention to aid Safra!

Cohen gave the firefighters specific directions for Safra's location. "Do ten steps to the right . . . find a staircase, go up two flights and . . . find a door." The crew came back after fifteen minutes, saying they couldn't find the door. The no-longer-handcuffed Cohen offered to lead the way and asked for a mask. But again, they refused.

"There was total chaos," Cohen later attested. "People were going up and down the stairs. I saw firemen with a ladder. I shouted which window to go to. They looked at me with . . . arrogance . . . Nobody listened to what I said, and they all refused my help."[44]

Throughout all the "total chaos," the alarm continued to wail out its pleas for help. And it did bring eighty-six policemen and fifty-six firemen out on this "harsh" winter Monaco morning (Monaco in December may actually produce temperatures that drop all the way into the mid-fifties). But for two long, burning hours, the eighty-six policemen and fifty-six firemen did nothing tangible or helpful—like put out the fire.

The firemen were, well, observing, while the police were fully onboard that "bandwagon of pumped-up panic."

I will never forget seeing some initial reports shown to me by my lawyers that laid out the following dialogue between the two agencies:

Fireman: I see a small *poubelle* on fire in the center of the nursing station and the French doors are open . . .

Policeman: Do not advance!

Fireman: I don't have to advance. I have a two-inch water line. I could turn it on and put it out from here.

Policeman: Do not take action!

Then they simply watched as the *poubelle* finally dissolved into fiery ooze and caught the nearby computer on fire. That's when things got bad. The nursing station became the frenzy level of hell.

Still, in reality, that area was the only place that actually had any fire at all—at first. No flames were lapping at Edmond's bedroom door—and definitely not at Lily's.

After alerting Cohen, Lily Safra remained for a few minutes in her bedroom at the other end of the penthouse (about two blocks down from the nursing station!).[45] But soon after—and after her husband's second call to her—Lily looked out her window and saw a policeman on the roof of the Hermitage. "Get out, Madame," the cop told her. "Get out straightaway."[46]

The valance over Lily's windows had raised automatically—possibly because of the smoke alarm—but had jammed halfway up. Following the cop's order, she stepped out through the valance's half opening onto her balcony and went down a flight of adjoining stairs to join the stagnant scene downstairs. All by herself.

Odd?

Maybe we should think about this . . .

No.

No one happened to consider that if this frail older woman could simply waltz out of this "war zone" unescorted and unscathed, maybe some guards with machine guns and bulletproof vests could go back up the same way and get Mr. Safra and Vivian out of that shit they were in.

Nope.

And the shit was getting a lot deeper.

With all the walls and doors and protection, the actual fire couldn't penetrate; but now the smoke was seeping—and then powering—in.

It was the smoke that ultimately branded its stench into the entire scented scape of the immaculate flat.

It was the smoke that found its way everywhere.

It was the smoke that became the first of so, so many dynamics in the "chaos theory" that defined the death of Edmond Safra. The theory that just one small change could have drastically changed everything.

True enough.

5:35 a.m.
Again, using Maher's phone, Edmond Safra speaks with Jean-Marc Farca, Monaco's brigadier chief of police. A "panicky" Safra tells Farca that "a person [has] been assaulted with an axe"[47] and that "they [are] in trouble." Farca tells Safra to go out to the staircase, as there were police there. Fearing his assailants are still inside, Safra refuses. Safra and Vivian tell Farca about the "presence of smoke."[48]

––––––––––

Five years before that morning—before the Safras owned La Belle Époque—the flat had a ceiling entry door over the area that later became the nursing station. It allowed repair access to the heating, air conditioning, and plumbing of the flat. The ceiling way was a wooden web of two-by-fours and other parts of the building's structure.

Five years before that morning, a plumber had been up in that area working on the A/C system, welding. When he went to lunch, he left an unnoticed ember burning up there. That led to the *first* cataclysmic fire at La Belle Époque.[49]

Naturally, the contractors wanted to prevent anything like that from ever happening again. So, during the rebuilding phase, they installed a large fan where the access door was that would drop down in case of fire to suck out the smoke.

No one would *possibly* die from smoke inhalation at La Belle Époque if, *Dieu interdire*, another fire ever erupted.

But then Lily and Edmond bought the estate and rolled in with their own remodeling team.

"What is this?"

"We don't want that thing flopping down!"

They bolted it shut!

So now—here on that chaos-controlled day of December 3, 1999—no fan was available to neutralize the smoke. But the access door remained. Bolted shut or not, it was a weak area directly above the fire. The fire breached that access point and went up into that web of wood, causing the entire ceiling length of the flat to go up.[50]

From the outside, it appeared that the whole building was burning, but really it was just the flat's ceiling and roof that were on fire.

6:15 a.m.

Firefighters make their "first attempt to bring the fire under control."[51]

Finally.

But the question then is the question now: Why didn't the firemen just put out the tiny signal fire when they arrived shortly after 4:49 a.m.?

Was it that they never had this kind of emergency before? I remember being told that five years earlier, they had done a similarly stellar job of not saving the flat. Somehow "inexplicable actions and incompetency" seem to be a kid-gloved part of such a soft society.

Going back just two years earlier, a bicycle shop had caught on fire. The streets in Monte Carlo are like a maze, but the shop was right near the fire station. Unfortunately, it was the wrong way down a one-way street. By the time the fire department took the proper way around—*the long way around*—to get to the fire, the bike shop was razed.

But a destroyed apartment and a store full of charred and melted Peugeots weren't going to make international headlines like the death of Edmond Safra. This incompetency had real ramifications. For once.

On that night and into the morning of December 3, 1999, it was literal *déjà vu* all over again. A Stooges' skit reprise, in which Monsieurs Larry, Moe, and Curly had no idea who was in command, what to do or even how to do it.

The firemen did not want to go by the cornice. One of them said that he "suffered from vertigo."[52]

Vertigo? A firefighter who "doesn't do" heights, in the most densely populated country on Earth with a skyline dominated by residential high-rises?

Meanwhile, back at the fire, keep in mind that the valance on the one side of the flat was open and they had already been aware of and had access to the *poubelle* source fire in the nursing station, but the firemen were having a rough go of it, once they finally made some efforts at actually fighting the fire.

However, with their aerial ladder, they could not enter Edmond Safra's room through a window, because they had trouble raising the rolling blinds and it was impossible for them to break the glass.[53]

Magnificent Monaco and its *force publique* were looking the fool.

6:30 a.m.

Torrente, losing consciousness, makes her sixth and final call from the cell phone, complaining of the smoke and "lack of air."[54] *Safra is heard coughing in the background.*[55]

The smoke from the roof fire was pouring into the "safe room."

"We've been up here forever! This is my sixth call!"

Vivian was in there with Safra, but he was scared to death and wouldn't let her open the door. After all, there were assailants out there!

"But we're dying in here! We're choking! Mr. Safra, I love you very much but you know what, I'm getting the hell out of here because I'm dying!"

Unfortunately, Safra's paranoia was stronger than his reasoning. The posse of potential enemies . . . the sideways side effects of the Sinemet . . .

No way he was letting Vivian open that door. He was now likely consumed with even more of that fear he had poured out to the brigadier chief of police.

Vivian weighed fifty kilos; Edmond, a hundred kilos. Yes, he had Parkinson's, but a hundred-kilo man—sick or not—would be able stop a fifty-kilo nurse from opening a door when he *just knows* there are assassins waiting out there to kill him.

Chaos theory played out so disgustingly well in that scenario. But those uncomfortable details—one more hematoma of horror in Monaco's blackest of black eyes—wouldn't come out until much later.

Also much later, I would even find out that the alarm Edmond was probably telling me to set off was a panic button underneath his bed. A panic button that no one ever told the staff about! Was Safra paranoid enough to want a secret safeguard against his employees? Maybe if that button had been pushed—if Edmond himself had not been too rattled to push it, or to tell Vivian or me to push it, or if he had let us know about it previously—then I wouldn't have needed to trigger the fire alarm. Both alarms were aimed at summoning the "authorities," but I'm guessing with radically different results.

Any one thing could have stopped this entire tragedy.

But nothing did.

After putting a fire hose inside the apartment at 6:39 a.m. and then at 6:55 a.m. tackling the fire in [Edmond's master suite] *that they were able to control at 7:18 a.m., the firemen, equipped with insulated respiratory equipment, proceeded with reconnoitering the premises and more specifically the gym room and Edmond Safra's bedroom. But it took them 5 minutes to open the door, according to Sergeant-Major Sacany, due to the rubble obstructing its access and the volume of the wood of the door.*

Having made a preliminary fruitless inspection of the room, then ventilating the premises, two firemen, informed of the nearby existence . . . of a dressing-room/bathroom, went in at around 7:45 a.m. and discovered the body of a man sitting in an armchair and a woman lying on the floor behind the armchair.[56]

So that was it.

It was over. Done. Lost.

No radiance of riches could outshine this low ember glow of danger and death, and no amount of money was going to buy Safra his life back. The world's toughest body-guards, safe-rooms, and rocket-proof windows had sprung a leak that could squirt and stain far and wide.

And the authorities knew it.

The Monegasque moral of the story now seriously started to become: "Who can we fuck and how can we get out of this shit?"

The idea that two men could break into the heavily secured home of one of the world's wealthiest men, cause his death and leave without trace did not sit well with Monaco's reputation as a crime-free zone for the super-rich . . . Roger Bianchini, a journalist with Nice-Matin, told an author of a book on the

Grimaldis [the Monegasque ruling family that dates back to the 1100s]: "The whole [Monaco money-sheltering] system is well known to the initiated. But when underground deals begin to surface and scandal breaks through, Prince Rainier becomes concerned that the image of the principality could be tarnished."[57]

—Andrew Anthony,

The Observer, October 28, 2000

Well, we sure don't want any part of Monaco "tarnished" now, do we? Those princely authorities began to think:

Look at Ted Maher. He's an opportunist. And he started this fire. Yeah—this could work . . . I mean, how do we know his wounds weren't self-inflicted? He's obviously mentally deranged—schizophrenic, even. Hell, we've already found out that his biological father had a history of mental illness. Of course. This is made to order!

Cela ne pourrait pas être mieux!

No one will look at our refined and profitable paradise with any degree of askance.

And if there were any involvements from the outside, well, "they" will just have to work that out elsewhere.

Lily?

The inheritance?

The Russian mob?

Corporate battlegrounds?

None of that matters.

We have the American.

We have Ted Maher.

CHAPTER 22

LA CONFESSION

December 3, 1999

I awoke in the hospital.

I was in a bed with tubes sticking out of every orifice in my body. But I was coming around, grasping desperately at recall.

What happened?

I remembered some of the ambulance ride. I remembered fading in and out and hearing them talk about surgery and all the blood I lost.

It was ironic; not even three weeks before all of this went down, I'd gotten into an argument with a doctor at a blood bank. I was walking through Monte Carlo late in the afternoon when someone came up to me in the street: "Monsieur, we're collecting blood for Princess Grace Hospital."

This guy was charitably intense and forceful: "It's the end of the day and we've only collected six units of blood."

I guess the rich figure they don't have to give blood, I thought. *Their blood is special.*

But then I thought a little more. *Hell, I'm an American! It's been a while since I gave blood, and I've got some USDA prime blood here . . . the cordon bleu of blood . . . I don't have mad cow or any of the other shit they have over here . . . sure, why not? Let's do it!*

But I had to go through a screening process. Questions were posed:

"Do you have a wife? Children? Ever give blood? Blood type O-positive? Oh, and the name of your mistress?"

"Excuse me?"

"The name of your mistress? Does she have any diseases or issues? Seriously, we need her name."

American culture versus French culture in a blood bank. There I sat, with this doctor grilling my ass about a mistress! In the slick South of France, a guy can have a squeeze or two on the side. It's more than accepted—it's SOP: Standard Operating Procedure. They're worth money and they take care of the guy's needs. And the wife is evidently happy with this because that's the way the moral *boussole* spins.

I thought about La Leopolda having originally been set up as a haven for a king's mistress.

More irony.

And I thought about Minnie's destructive and insane jealousy back home.

I wrestled with this doctor for a long time over the fact that I didn't have a mistress; all this hassle just so I could give blood to him. He finally gave in—fairly condescendingly—and they stuck in the needle to drain me.

Even more irony . . .

Now, lying in that bed, I wondered if I was getting fed back some of my own blood.

I drifted off again.

The next time I woke up, I took a peek at the aftermath of my surgery. It wasn't pretty. Red welts and blood oozed from the wounds.

Damn! The guy who stitched and stapled me back together was probably a drunken veterinarian at best. I had personally sutured up hundreds of guys in the armed services and they'd all looked pretty good. This guy who did mine was like a butcher on barbiturates! (Many years—and thousands of looks at this mess—later, I went to a plastic surgeon in San Antonio to try to get rid of the scars, but he wanted ten grand! So to this day, I still carry the first permanent damage Monaco left me with.)

I looked down toward my feet and saw my leper-looking, still aching toes. But soon all this pain and scarring would be nothing; a far heavier and sharper blade had started to drop.

The good French Doctor Joseph-Ignace Guillotin would've been proud.

December 4, 1999

All of a sudden, I was being interrogated by two French investigators: a Captain Oliver Jude, the only Monegasque cop who could actually speak English, and another gloomy gendarme named Gerard Tiberti. They weren't telling me a thing, but they were sure asking a lot of questions about those short, few minutes that had led up to my being shuttled away in the ambulance.

I still didn't know that Safra was dead.

Or Vivian.

I didn't know about the fire.

I didn't know of any way there *could* be a fire.

I interrupted them and asked what was going on with Mr. Safra. They told me he was also in the hospital and so was Vivian; that they had "a little smoke and dust inhalation."

Smoke inhalation? I wondered. *From what? I mean, even if my little trashcan fire did produce more smoke than necessary to set off that alarm, it would have had to go through the nursing doors, one of Safra's bedroom doors, another bedroom door, another bathroom door, and then yet another bathroom door before it ever got to him. That's five doors.* So there was no way. Something else must have gone down.

But the interrogation went on.

Finally, I stopped them.

I told them I didn't like where this was going and that I hoped they were being honest with me. "You're asking me some really strong questions here, and I really don't feel comfortable talking to you anymore."

"Well, you *are* going to talk to us, Mr. Maher," they told me.

They got forceful.

"We think you fabricated this entire scenario," they accused.

"We think you made up the masked assailants.

"We think you stabbed yourself.

"And we think you lit the fire—all in a plot to save Safra and be a hero in his eyes."

My mind reeled in shock. *Holy shit—you're out of your fucking minds!*

Then they brought out the big guns.

"*You* killed Edmond Safra!"

That stopped my heated rage cold.

"Edmond is dead?" I couldn't believe it.

"Mr. Safra is dead."

"Vivian?"

"Vivian Torrente is dead."

I started crying, *weeping*.

The interrogators gave me a newspaper with photos that showed the entire penthouse enveloped in flames.

I wept even more.

They turned and walked out, leaving me alone in the dark to think and to wonder and to writhe in the torture of all this.

Why?

How?

My God!

December 6, 1999

Day four in the hospital.

I was now shackled to the bed hand and foot, with a urinary catheter. I wasn't going anywhere.

The Monegasque investigators had been back a few times over the past two days, with questions and a "bedside manner" that reeked worse than the sack of urine under my bed.

The morning of day four, they came back armed with an eighty-six-page document all in French for me to sign.

"I'm not signing anything," I told them. "And I want to speak to an attorney *right now!*"

They told me that I *wasn't* going to see an attorney and that I *was* going to sign this document.

"It's not a confession," they assured me. "It's simply a document that explains everything that happened to Mr. Safra."

I told them they could kiss my ass.

But then they produced the passport of my wife.

Something else I didn't know until much later was that the second reports of Edmond's death hit the news, Heidi had placed a panicked call to Lily Safra's personal secretary, Michelle St. Bernard, in New York City.

"Your husband is a hero for trying to save the life of Mr. Safra," St. Bernard told Heidi. "But the suspects are still at large. Would you like to visit Ted in the hospital in Monaco and bring him home?"

"Yes, yes, certainly!" said Heidi. "Thank you!"

St. Bernard also asked Heidi if she would like to bring our children with her. With the danger of suspects still "at large," Heidi declined, asking instead if her brother, Todd, could accompany her.

"But of course, Mrs. Maher," answered the secretary.

With the help of St. Bernard's assistant, full arrangements were made immediately. Heidi and her brother would be provided limousine service from the front door in Stormville to JFK airport, where they'd pick up roundtrip tickets to Nice aboard Delta Airlines. Upon landing in France, another limousine service would take them directly to my bedside at Princess Grace Hospital.

It was a perfect and efficient display of caring benevolence. The same courtesies were extended to the family of Vivian Torrente. They, too, would be on that Delta flight to Nice.

Heidi, Todd, and the Torrente family all arrived in Monaco just as legions of the world's news media were reaching full-swarm. The paparazzi nets were thrown, but none were launched quickly enough to grab Heidi and Todd.

Those two were snared by a much more sinister group.

"We have your wife at our police headquarters here in Monte Carlo, Mr. Maher," Captain Jude told me. "We have been required to strip-search her and she is being subjected to *intense* interrogation of her own."

Lily Safra's "caring benevolence" had made a sudden sharp turn; Michelle St. Bernard's compassionate plan had quickly shifted into a growl and a bite.

The whole story of Heidi's visit to "take me home" would not be known until mid-2001, when Heidi filed an official motion with the Supreme Court in New York against Lily Safra and her employees. Only then would the gory details be added to a sickening summary:

We all understood that my objective was to see my husband, who had been through what must have been a terrifying experience . . . I entrusted my safety and entire itinerary to the Safra organization . . . [but] I suffered shocking and humiliating treatment during the trip which was avoidable and due entirely to the fault of others . . . We were never offered the opportunity to leave any of the interrogations over the next three days, and never offered legal counsel. On the contrary, the coercive context was that if I did not cooperate I would not be granted permission to see my husband . . . They also took our passports.

But all I knew at this time, locked to that goddamned bed, was that these cops *had my wife*!

"And we understand you have some young children back in America," Jude continued. "It's unfortunate, but their mother could stay here for a very, very long time."

The son of a bitch was fingering Heidi's passport.

"None of us wants *that*, do we, Mr. Maher?" he said. "No, of course not. So you are going to sign this document. *Oui?*"

Once again I was completely fucked.

Oui . . .

I signed the document.

A document I couldn't even read.

CHAPTER 23

A PRIVILEGED WITNESS

What even his detractors agree on is that Maher never intended to kill Safra. "If he wanted to," said [chief prosecutor Daniel] Serdet, "he would have had 10,000 chances a day."

—Andrew Anthony, *The Observer*, October 28, 2000

While the quote from Monaco's chief prosecutor came ten months after the deaths of Edmond and Vivian, Daniel Serdet's voice had already started to echo throughout the Côte d'Azur and around *le monde* while the ashes of La Belle Époque were still warm. He had started by keeping his options open.

According to Uri Dan in the *New York Post*, "Serdet . . . suggested the attackers may have had inside help . . . [saying] 'For the moment, the inquiry rests on . . . the nurse.' Asked whether the man was a suspect, Serdet said he was a 'privileged witness.'"[58]

A "privileged witness"? I suppose I had the privilege of witnessing myself get sucker-punched and stabbed. And, with Edmond's and Vivan's lives having gone up in senseless literal flames, I was witnessing my own life get torched.

Serdet soon changed his tune anyway, the voice of his follow-up statements and soothsaying bouncing along nicely with the manic media as every post-fire day brought fresh posturing, postulations, probabilities, possibilities, and preposterous proposals. No one, however, was hearing *my* voice. Other than Jude and Tiberti, I was sequestered from life. No media. No psychiatrists. No newspapers.

While I was still chained to that hospital bed, still peeing in a bag, Serdet held a news conference where he quoted from a police report. According to him and his divine gospel, I had accepted guilt, spilling my guts to the cops.[59] He was right about one thing: my guts had most definitely been spilled—on the floor of La Belle Époque.

And everyone seemed to be blood-thirsty for more. I was being drawn, quartered, and crucified in print and on film. All because of that fucking "document" I was extorted into signing. That document *écrit en français*.

And all because Monaco desperately needed *someone* to pin this on.

Safra aide confesses
Nurse from N.Y. sez he started fatal fire

A New Yorker employed as a nurse by multi-billionaire banker Edmond Safra confessed yesterday to setting the fire in Monaco that killed his boss in a twisted plot to make himself a hero, police said . . . "It was my own dark ideas which led me to do this," a tranquilizer-addled Maher told police, according to Serdet.[60]

—Helen Kennedy, Tracey Tully,
New York Daily News, December 7, 1999

"Dark ideas"?!

The only dark ideas clouding the winter sun in Monte Carlo were those conjured by Serdet and the media.

And "tranquilizer-addled"?!

Ever since I beat down that damned meningitis and its headache-requisite codeine pills years ago, I hadn't *touched* a tranquilizer. If *that's* what they had dug up to brand me as some kind of an addict, then *they* were the ones who are "addled."

News outlets all over the world reported their versions of the story. They certainly hadn't heard the truth from anyone—especially me. No press conferences were being held in my hospital room with the world's most renowned journalists asking me sincere questions about my side of the story. Not the *Daily News* with their hip headlines or anyone else. It wasn't for lack of trying, though. *Newsweek* reported that requests to interview me were denied by Monaco authorities,[61] and I'm sure other media outlets suffered the same fate. They were allowed access only to Serdet and the police.

And like party whispers passed around a room, discussions of my "dark ideas" were soon penned in even bolder ink by the Associated Press. Their article, "Nurse's 'black thoughts' bring rich banker's death," went along with the police's rendition of events: that I had grown resentful of Sonia, and so in an effort to be proclaimed a hero and receive a promotion, I created a "perverse plot" to "fake a break-in, stab [myself], set a fire and hide Safra from the 'intruders.'"[62]

But my plan, according to them, had taken a "tragic turn."

Really, my "plan," *according to them*, had skidded into much more than that; it had sped headfirst over a con-game cliff that only an insecure wimp would even begin to consider.

And that sure as hell wasn't me.

As the speculation and challenges of trying to unravel a messy mystery grew, a few media outlets at least tried to shine some light into the shadows of Monaco. For what it's worth, the Associated Press piece did attempt to counterbalance their "black thoughts" botch-job of me with a slam at the almighty. According to a police source, influential real estate agents flooded officials with calls, worried about optics: The principality ruled by revered Grimaldi blue bloods *had* to maintain its reputation of one of the world's safest places. As such, their urgency to "solve the crime quickly" was clear.[63]

The Observer, too, had a lot more to say about Safra, his fear, and the insane idea being kicked around that I was actually *hired* to kill Edmond:

The strange case of Edmond Safra

When the billionaire banker Edmond Safra died in an apparently bungled robbery at his home in Monte Carlo, the initial suspects ranged from the Russian mafia to the Colombian drug cartels. But then the police arrested one of Safra's 12 nurses and the strange story became stranger still . . . As far back as 1957, Edmond Safra was named as a drug trafficker in a US Bureau of Narcotics report. The accusation was later withdrawn, but until his death Safra was the inspiration for countless unsubstantiated rumours that linked him to drug, gold and currency trafficking, money laundering and organised crime . . . Social acceptance had not lessened Safra's near-phobic paranoia. He always carried blue gemstones to ward off the evil eye, and retained an abiding fear of curses. He was deeply superstitious about the number five and was terrified of being kidnapped. So he must have been deeply scared early that morning . . . Safra must have been paralysed with fear not to feel confident enough to come out. Who did he think was after him? [Lily's lawyer, Marc] Bonnant is quick to scotch any talk of assassins. "Look, if you want to kill a man, you pay $20,000 and you get the job done the right way by a professional. The right way is not to hire a nurse to start a small fire and hope that the police take two hours to get to him."[64]

Bonnant showed some of the only small signs of logic expressed throughout this entire feeding frenzy—"*The right way is not to hire a nurse to start a small fire and hope that the police take two hours to get to him . . .*"

What place in the stage-setting of this tragedy would that fire have had anyway?

And compare that petite pyre with my near disemboweling—a hundred staples had been required to put me back together. If I had stabbed myself as the police were alleging, wouldn't that have been enough? Why add that inconsequential little blaze to the cast? My blood alone would have set the scene for my heroic and martyr-like appearance in front of my employer.

But no one in the media thought this through—they were more focused on my psychological state.

Even the venerable *TIME* magazine:

The Charade of Death

Maher may spend the rest of his days behind bars . . . His life took an irrevocable turn at 5 a.m. on Friday, Dec. 3, when what he later described as "dark ideas" propelled him into a bizarre charade and the death of a female co-worker and his employer, Lebanese-born banker and philanthropist Edmond Safra . . . one of the world's wealthiest men . . . Maher, a heavy user of sedatives whom prosecutors described as "psychologically fragile," did not help matters by frequently changing his story . . . The decision to bring Maher into the Safra household was the biggest blunder of all . . . [Lily's lawyer, Marc] Bonnant says

Maher had been carefully vetted through "in-depth background checks" and a personal interview with Mrs. Safra. "The fact that Maher is unstable became apparent to us only after the accident," Bonnant told *TIME*. "Nothing in Maher's files showed the slightest trace of mental instability."

—Thomas Sancton, *TIME*, Dec. 12, 1999[65]

As all of these attacks of assumption kept advancing, I remained in isolation. These media revelations were still in my grim future; just more sad and maddening things to find out later.

When I did find out, I was fuming. Because, first of all, nothing being printed about the case had been verified by the sole witness and main subject under discussion: me. That made *TIME's* comment that I "did not help matters by frequently changing [my] story" especially frustrating. The *single* change in my story (if one wanted to twist things that far) was when I was forced to go from telling the truth to investigators Jude and Tiberti, to signing their imaginative "document" as they handled my wife's passport—and my wife. What was really "not helping matters" was the story-changing done by the police and the media in this glorified game of Clue, rife with speculations and the salivations as to who killed Colonel Mustard in the library.

As for being "psychologically fragile," something like that *probably* would have crept up on the radar as I was getting top-level security clearance to become a Green Beret, or maybe when I was subjected to a best-money-can-buy background check and shrink eval before joining a billionaire's personal staff. And, since that time, it seems amazing how Marc Bonnant was so sure of my true psychological state. How could *he* affirm my "appearance of instability" when I haven't been "appearing" in front of him or a psychiatrist or *TIME* magazine or anybody?!

I had to try and calm down.

I'd been immediately nailed to *la croix* for the murders of Edmond Safra and Vivian Torrente—by everyone. If the frenzied face-saving Monegasque and I had been cowboys in Dodge City, I'd have already been buzzard lunch, with whatever was left of me swinging in the prairie wind at the end of a quick-noosed rope.

But we were all in the modern safe-haven rapture that is Monaco—no crude lynch mobs here, right? My wife had been abused and I was being filleted like throwaway bait while chained to a sick-bed. I couldn't talk to the media, but somehow, they surmised to know my innermost thoughts. I was pissing down a tube, my family's lifetime of security was swirling toward a similar destination, and I was looking at an eternity of exile in a foreign jail.

But "unstable"?

Not a chance.

Determined? Fucking *furious*? Committed to survival and the truth?

All of the above.

Unfortunately, however, the bandwagon outside was speeding up even more. It was being fed by Serdet and masticated by the media:

Dark ideas.

Tranquilizer-addled.

Black thoughts.

Perverse plot.

Bizarre charade.

Heavy use of sedatives.

Psychologically fragile.

They had it all set up so well.

The message: "Solve the crime quickly; Monaco's reputation is at stake."[66]

I knew I was being made that solution. And I knew that manacled to this bed or penned in a jail cell, catching up with that racing wreck of predetermined condemnation wouldn't be easy. But then again, little of what I'd ever done in life had been easy.

This, though—by any measure—would be the toughest battle yet.

CHAPTER 24
LA MAISON D'ARRÊT

Maisons d'arrêt—literally translated as "houses of arrest"—are by official definition "a category of jails in France which hold prisoners awaiting trial or sentencing, or those being held for less than one year, similar to County Jails in the United States."[67] That makes sense; a county jail, whether in New York, Mississippi, or Monaco is no place for long-term incarceration.

The next phase of things—my post-hospital lockdown—began in one of those *maisons d'arrêt*. It was the only one in Monaco, called the Remand Prison. I was shuttled there soon after I signed "the document."

December 6, 1999

No more hospital.

As I was being taken to Monte Carlo's close-quarters, eighty-one-inmate-capacity slammer, I was told that *le docteur* would come visit me there—to monitor my situation and to eventually remove all those staples that bombed butcher had gouged into my skin.

In my final days in the hospital, I hadn't had the stomach (definitely no pun intended) to face my scabbing-over skinscape and contemplate the cosmetic ramifications. But I was told that the stabbing missed my vital organs by just millimeters.

I was also told something else: That just as quickly as I was being shuffled off to jail, Heidi and Todd had been bum-rushed onto a plane back to New York.

"We got what we wanted from Ted Maher, so let's hurry up and start mopping up the mess."

So there I was, having been attacked, accused, and arrested, and I wouldn't get anywhere near my wife when I needed her most.

Maison d'Arrêt, 4 Avenue Saint-Martin, 98000 Monaco
I arrived at the facility. Heavily guarded and surrounded by an army of cops, I made my way in.

I may not have wanted to peek at my gut, but I had no way to shield my eyes from the bars and walls of what was obviously my new home. La Leopolda, La Belle Époque, and the fine hotels I'd been living in, it was not.

"Check-in" was nowhere near as posh or as cordial, either.

This must have been the nightmare shadow-side of that slipped-reality dream I thought I was having back on that beautiful balcony on my first day in Monaco.

Now it was all about reality—not dreams. I damn sure knew which was which at this point. Reality had hit me with the speed and shock of an RPG flying out of a desert dust cloud.

All in just under six months.

Just under six months—from summer to early December of 1999—since I was at home, working in one of America's finest hospitals. Under six months since I found that camera, walked into job heaven, moved across the Atlantic, and filled my bank accounts. Under six months since I got employed by—and befriended—one of the richest men in the world. Under six months before I tried—and failed—to save that man's life.

I'd gone from Stormville, New York, to Monte Carlo and beyond—with every perk, boost, and bounty that those upward geographic jumps imply. And now the back-end of those jumps had landed me as a stabbed and scarred inmate in a foreign prison.

In under six months.

No rose or chocolate adorned my pillow after this check-in. No fifty-dollar candles graced the room, and no sumptuous background aromas emanated from a five-star kitchen. Instead of a fresh, thick bathrobe waiting in a polished and pristine *salle de bain*, I found myself bent over for a welcome-wagon full-cavity strip search.

It would be the first of many.

In under six months, things had *really* fucking changed.

My new home

Like my sliced-apart belly, this place had plenty of scabs and scars of its own. It had actually been a garrison.

Anybody who was locked up ("condemned," as local law reads) in Monte Carlo for more than ninety days for any crime could opt to be sent from this barred and cozy wonderland to the more expansive French prison system—if you're Monegasque, that is. Because nobody could stay in this closed-in county-jail kind of environment for too long.[68]

There was no real courtyard, a junior-sized gym—certainly no balcony-view swimming pool. Captives had no place to run around, no light. You got to go outside on a dog promenade, which was twelve feet wide by sixty feet long and caged in by fourteen-foot walls, sealed at the top with a net. You got forty-five minutes in the morning to exercise and an hour and a quarter in the afternoon.

When I checked into this penal bed-of-roses, I was still in the grip of *What is going on?* confusion and assessment. "Staying" *anywhere* was not a thought; getting to the truth of this mess and getting home was.

My phone privileges were about as free and easy as my exercise schedule: I was allowed to speak to Heidi once a week for twenty minutes. In our very first conversation, she told me that she knew I couldn't be guilty of any of the things she'd been hearing about and reading. She then began filling me in on the details of what had happened when she and Todd were in Monte Carlo—about the intense interrogation.

She told me about some cops snatching them off the street and a ransacking at the hotel and—

That's when the phone went dead.

I got the guard to redial, but it was as clear as a fifty-dollar glass of Viognier that we were being monitored and that some conversations were simply not going to be had.

Cops?

Ransacking?

It didn't take much of an imagination to see just how locked in I was as Monaco's "solution" to their problem—or the lengths they would go to make this story stick.

Other calls to Heidi allowed me to hear more quick snippets of what had happened to her and Todd, but not many. The phone censors were on the job. What I did glean from her in short bursts were more and more exercises in intimidation.

Two men and a woman in black jumpsuits grabbed Heidi and Todd and forced them into a car . . . They weren't told right away these people were the police . . . they were so frightened . . . Then they were brought to their hotel—the same one I was living at. The shadowy trio went through their room . . . and the room I stayed in . . . and— *Click* . . .

It was the continuing tale of the Monegasque version of CYA: Covering Your Ass. The three cops' ninja spectacle—dressed in all-black and pouncing on my wife—especially made me want to puke.

Besides the basic bullying, their tearing up of my room afforded the authorities the opportunity to leave anything they wanted amongst what I had in there; perhaps something that might help insure that CYA later.

The soft, non-calloused hands of Monaco could be very intimidating when their grip was the sole support preventing—or causing—someone's fall from freedom.

That's a big drop; and their intimidation had worked. I was now in jail with my signature on something, and Heidi was back in New York—hurt, frightened, and bitter—legitimately wondering if she or the kids would ever see me again.

CHAPTER 25

THE LAWYERS

If there was an exact French translation of the American idiom "good ol' boy network," it would define Monaco's *Société des Bains de Mer*—more simply, the SBM Corporation.

The State of Monaco is the main shareholder for SBM, a resort conglomerate that owns five casinos (including the iconic Casino de Monte-Carlo), four hotels (one of which is the now near-and-dear and somewhat infamous neighbor to La Belle Époque, Hôtel Hermitage), and numerous restaurants, spas, and other "trendy and festive addresses"[69] (according to their promo literature)[70]—all in a postage-stamp-sized city-state of corruption; a compressed society with diminutive dimensions but unfathomable power and weight, like the core of the sun. And with devious density. Where owning this amount of prime real estate and controlling this degree of "service" in such a tiny but mega-wealthy country means so much more than just intrinsic upper-echelon status!

SBM owned Monaco's version of Midas' fertile hand.

With their kind of sole-society influence, they also owned attorney Georges Blot.

His name came up when Heidi called the American Consular Office in Marseilles for legal help. They, of course, had their suggestions and helped me to secure court-appointed attorneys.

Enter the French-speaking Blot.

Georges Blot had been in Monte Carlo for many years and knew the culture. He was well-known and established in the hierarchy of Monaco.

I'd soon observe that Blot was at his best when he had a bottle of wine in him; though not top-notch in that shaky state, he was *completely* worthless sober. On top of that, he was a diabetic, so when he hit the wine, his blood sugar would shoot up. He was overweight—260 or 270 pounds, maybe—with a full beard; and in my opinion, his overall image careened *descente* from there. Blot was sixty-something years old and married, but true to the culture he had a forty-something mistress, a doctor at Princess Grace.

That was Georges Blot.

Since Blot had limited English fluency, American ex-pat attorney Donald Manasse was squeezed into the party.

He was bilingual in French, but Manasse's specialty was not criminal procedures; it was business law. Like Blot, he had been in Monaco for years. But he spent his prime-time setting up tax shelters for rock-'n'-roll stars and other biggies who needed to be creative with their fortunes. Manasse, who I'd discover was "Like a Virgin" when it came to criminal cases—he hadn't even *touched* a case like this one —would be the "go-between," balancing this American defendant against the Monegasque system.

These two characters were my representatives. My council. The hand-principality-picked defense team for the sap accused of murdering Edmond Safra—one of Monaco's most prized residents.

Blot and Manasse were my sling-and-stone against the Goliath of Monaco. I was feeling a bit apprehensive about their summoning of divine intervention, but at least they knew the system here, which would be to my benefit.

Sure.

I was lacking so much important knowledge. Added to that growing list of "Things I Didn't Know" was that my only legal weapons had a serious deal with the SBM devil.

"Ted," Blot-Manasse collectively told me, "that document you signed was a confession! It states that you caused this whole thing—that you fabricated the attack and stabbed yourself in order to 'rescue' Edmond Safra and gain favor with him over the other nurses. All of which makes you responsible for everything: the fire, Safra's death, and Vivian's death!"

I felt sick. I wanted to puke. I'd sold my soul by signing that document and now somewhere in his South-of-France den of flames and fortune, the *Diable* was dancing!

"No! That's totally, one hundred percent *untrue!*" I told them. "I signed that thing because I had to! *That's* the truth! Those motherfuckers had my wife!"

But truth didn't enter into the pair's legal strategy.

"In Monaco, Ted," Blot insisted heavily, giving me a whiff of his ever-present booze-breath, "going back on a confession is the worst thing you can do! You can't change your story! Not now. You'll be sentenced to even more time than a guilty plea would get—maybe even life! Just go with the program, Ted, and you'll be out in three years and back with your family. Isn't that what you want, Ted?"

I'm surprised he didn't follow up with a speech about the "meek inheriting the earth." What *I* wanted was the truth. This fucking bogus all-in-French confession had been pulled out of me like a mad dog twisting and snarling with big fangs clamped between my legs.

But since it was a *fait accompli,* the reason *why* I signed it was irrelevant to Blot-Manasse.

Because it was untouchable—apparently.

In America, changes of plea and bargains and judicial jumps are part of the game.

Not in Monaco.

Apparently . . .

I bought what they told me.

I *had* to buy it. Here I was, held captive in a foreign country, where I was entirely unfamiliar with their legal processes and had no else on my side.

So, there we were. Right off the bat, my team's course of battle consisted of just one plan: Don't rock the "guilty" boat.

In hindsight, this was like trying to bail out the starboard side of the Titanic with a crystal champagne glass. Hell, if Blot and Manasse were NFL coaches, they'd call for a fumble on every offensive play. No sense in making those big guys on the other side any madder than they already are—just give 'em the ball! Give 'em what they want!

It was sure doom, right up there with offering that mad dog your nuts just so he won't chomp out your eyes; without even trying to leap to higher ground.

But again, I had no clue.

The pair seemed quite assured of their position and, frankly, they were scaring the crap out of me with all their ominous "life in prison" talk! Because through all this, my family was still number one. They trumped any personal pride or fear of pain or purgatory on my part. If what these "experts" said was true, could I really risk being sent away *forever*—never to see them again? Wasn't it worth three years of my life to ensure we'd be reunited?

Especially after knowing at least some of what they had already suffered?

I was adrift on foreign soil. I was a Green Beret, and good at what I did, but this wasn't a military action. This was firepower-passive and politically-active—no bullets-to-the-brain allowed.

I knew how big-conflict world affairs worked and that the diplomatic strength of the United States was mighty. But what I didn't know was exactly how it might play into a personal skirmish like mine. I was a nurse in private employ charged with a capital crime outside of US borders; and the VIP victim at the center of it all was arguably the world's most well-known and influential banker.

This was a rough-rolling international incident and I was under its wheels. I mean, a lot of shit had gone down already, and I hadn't heard any enraged outcry, so I wasn't feeling super-confident of the cavalry busting in wielding a US flag.

Therefore, once I knew Heidi and the kids were safe, I figured, *Fuck it! Maybe I'd better go along with this confession. This way, that rabid cur will only bite off one nut and I'll still have the other one. I suppose it could be worse.*

These crushing wheels were spinning, I was giving in, and my white flag was dripping with more and more of my own blood.

Blot's breath was still fouling the air when I was first brought before a French magistrate, Patricia Richet.

Only an elite few have the privileged tag of being Monaco citizens, so the state hires French magistrates to serve as judges using Monegasque law.[71] Except for a few tweaks here and there, Monaco's law is virtually identical to that of France. They all *basque* together in the warmth of Napoleonic *Droit Administratif.*

These "borrowed" judges serve a three-year term, and then another three years if they're a good judge.[72] Patricia Richet was just beginning her second term. She had my case. She was the magistrate. She had power.

"Chief Examining Magistrate Patricia Richet . . . is serving essentially as a one-person grand jury who decides which charges Ted Maher will face."[73]

—John Springer, Court TV

My life was basically in her hands.

I was told that interrogation sessions with her were to begin—ostensibly to ready for trial. I heard that an official investigation into the whole terrible tragedy was also well underway.

I knew nothing about Richet. I hadn't (yet) heard the reports floating around the legal community that she was a "violent person [who'd] displayed unstable behavior in the past . . . allegedly with a history of assaulting a fellow judge, putting him in the hospital for a week."[74]

I wanted to believe that our meeting meant we were getting somewhere. I wanted to believe we were still on that fast-track to justice.

I'd have been better off holding onto dreams of the tooth fairy.

My meeting with Richet was not warm. She came in like a pit bull, ready to rip my head off for any answer she didn't like. Her tactic for uncovering "the truth" seemed to be to bark and screech at her prey until they gave in. Well, I wasn't giving in.

It was the beginning of a long three years . . . and I'd just experienced my first week.

Between the Monegasque investigators, the jail, my true-to-the-state lawyers, and the Bastille-inquisition figure of Patricia Richet, it was sinking in deep and sinking in fast that my entire ordeal could and would get worse—much worse.

CHAPTER 26

L'EVIDENCE, QUELLE EVIDENCE?

Early 2000

I was trying to accept that I'd just spent Christmas as an alien in a distant prison. I was trying to double my grip on reality. I was struggling to face the agonizing day-by-day of the first year.

That was when the thinking started. That was when the initial "time-panic" ended. You know, *time-panic:* when something happens and you just can't believe it's happening. Time-panic is when you're bile-tasting nervous, but at the same time almost casual. It's that hazy and pushed period when you say to yourself, *Uh, yes, this is all just a terrible mistake . . . but it will be fine . . . I'm sure it will . . . we just need to get this straightened out.*

Now.

Quick.

Rectify this horrible mistake. And get on with life.

It's the *Phew! That was a close one!* kind of thing.

But then you realize that it wasn't a "close one"; it was a direct hit.

That's when the *thinking* starts. That's when the real work starts. That's when your body and mind must adapt to new environments and new everything. It must, that is, if you're going to survive.

And there was never any question in my mind that I was absolutely going to survive.

As for adapting to the environment: I was in Monaco's county jail of a "prison," dealing with the absence of any stimulation or exercise facilities. The legal face of my "detention" showed me locked up and "awaiting trial." My "awaiting trial" became a lingering limbo with daily strip searches in tandem with the psychological torment of regular face-offs with Patricia Richet.

Okay.

I kept repeating my mantra: *I will survive this . . .*

But it all seemed a useless and plodding treadmill jog—the mental version of the jail's dog run/exercise yard. It was bad enough not making any headway toward truth and freedom, but I wasn't up for leaping even more hurdles on a dead-end road.

My sense of humor and good nature were taking hits, but I was trying to stay positive. More and more would have to be dealt with as I adapted.

Two of the four guards in the regular strip search seemed to enjoy their daily "investigations" with me *too* much. But their taunts and comments couldn't get to me; they only made me stronger. Finally, I turned it around and began taunting *them*. I'd wave my ass suggestively and say, "Are you ready for me, boys?" I went from the highlight of their day to a grindingly vile part of their job description.

They never did touch me beyond what they had to do; they never even tried. Only one guy, a prisoner, *did* try. It was in the shower. He made his move and I turned around; he was unconscious on the floor in a heartbeat.

However, more ominous obstacles loomed in front of me than coping with unwanted garrison gropers.

I had to summon every ounce of the "thinking" and "real work" parts of my personality and combine them with my adapting ability in order to survive the stress-gripped sit-downs with Richet.

Each meeting with that omnipotent magistrate was on the same nerve-effort level as silent-running in a sub during wartime. It was tense and painful, and I couldn't slip up.

These meetings—these depositions—were conducted every five weeks or so at her office, with three special policemen and at least one of my so-called attorneys there. It was a main-stage freak show, especially when Blot was present. When I'd roll my eyes or slap my head at his bumbling, Donald would just tell me, "Well, Ted, you know how George likes his wine."

It was *Sideways* meets *Arrested Development.*

I'd be brought from the jail with a bulletproof vest on, escorted by twenty cops. All the streets to and from Richet's office would be cordoned off, and we never went the same way twice. Every one of these exploratory summits provided quite a logistical show. The authorities were quaking in their jittery, face-saving souls about the possibility of my assassination. If I got blasted to pieces before the trial, the word "conspiracy" would be permanently inked into the headlines.

As that first year dragged on, it became obvious that I had to become a diplomat, a psychologist, and my own representative. Yes, I had to own signing that "document," but I was still bent on trying to point this all-powerful procurer toward the evidence and the truth. And to save my ass while I was at it!

It wasn't going well.

As I brought things up and posed questions, Patricia Richet would call me a liar, excoriate me in French, and yell at me.

"Vous mentez! Vous mentez! Je vais trouver la vérité!"

"You're lying! You're lying!" she'd scream through her interpreter. "I'm going to find the truth!"

Please do!

———

I, however, was the one who knew the *vérité.*

Along with everything else that was so obvious—to me at least—was that I needed to recover all of the Blot-Manasse fumbles. That, and making some big plays of my own, became the "real work" and the only way a legitimate end-run toward the truth could be completed.

By law, all material gathered in the investigation and being readied for the trial had to be shared with me. But also by law, it didn't have to be in English.

I had to sign for everything they delivered to me in the jail. Everything had to be documented. Oh yes, they were doing their jobs. But with my humor and good nature waning, I started to refuse to sign for anything that wasn't in English—and nothing was in English!

Couriers had to leave the material anyway.

Adapt . . . survive . . . think . . .

I was able to get a French-English dictionary. The first word I looked up was "truth."

Vérité.

Truth.

The first documents I translated were the autopsy reports of Edmond and Vivian. It may have been dark in that jail, but I was bringing some high-watt light of my own into things. The details of Vivian's autopsy were especially interesting:

> There are recent traumatic signs in the cervical level [and on] the left rib and especially of the thyroid which is infiltrated by blood. This highly evokes a blow given with the edge of the hand as in some combat sports.[75]
>
> —Autopsy Report on the body of Mrs. Vivian Torrente

I sent for Manasse—the bilingual Donald Manasse. I knew he had copies of all the same documents I did.

As he walked toward my cell, I held up the autopsies on my side of the bars.

"Donald! Did you see this?"

"The autopsy reports? Yes, I saw them."

"But did you read them?"

"Well, yes, I read them."

"Well, why didn't you tell me?!"

"Why didn't I tell you what, Ted?"

I waved the papers at his face.

"This says Vivian was hemorrhaging in her thyroid. The back of her neck was bruised. She had trauma to the top of her head. You don't get that shit from tripping over a toilet or inhaling smoke, buddy!"

Manasse stared at me blankly.

"What part don't you understand?" I asked. "Vivian's throat was crushed, you asshole!"

I couldn't believe this guy.

"Plus," I continued on, "they found DNA under her nails that was Safra's. They found DNA under Safra's nails that was Vivian's. They found blood on her bra, neck, and her clothing that was Safra's. How does his blood get on her bra?! Obviously, there was a struggle."

The report from the biologist of Dr. Dautremepulch stated that the blood test and a little bit of the fingernail, only under the fingernail of the right hand of Vivian Torrente was found her own DNA and under the left hand of her fingernail found a combination of her own DNA and also of Edmond Safra . . . they found that the blood . . . correspond [to] the DNA of Edmond Safra on her bra and on her slip.[76]

—Prosecutor's Report

"It wasn't my fire that killed Vivian, Donald!" I shouted. "It was Edmond's actions that killed Vivian! Doesn't that count for something? Vivian obviously wanted to get the hell out of that death trap but Safra didn't let her; he was too afraid. If not for Safra's insane panic and paranoia, Vivian would have opened that door, and the pair would have been saved!"

Donald said nothing. Even worse, he didn't seem to care about things like that. Things like *facts*! He had that official attitude: *l'évidence, quelle évidence?*

I was wrestling with my lawyers and with the magistrate. I was trying to bare-knuckle people who were armed with crony-backed bazookas when it came to their clout within the system.

But I couldn't and wouldn't give up.

In between each session with Richet, my "real work" was done with the stack of documents and my by then-well-worn dictionary.

Next, I received a copy of the confession I had been coerced into signing. I dug in and I wanted to throw up. *Vérité* may have been the first French word I became familiar with, but now I was also very well-versed with the word *mensonge*: lie. And a lie in any language was still a lie. The confession itself was a jumble of alleged first-person declarations from the two Monegasque investigators and me:

On this day [Dec. 6, 1999] at around 9:15, we [the investigators] go to The Princess Grace Hospital Centre to pick up Ted Maher and take him to our premises, since he has been declared fit to leave the hospital by the doctors. For the transfer, we are assisted by [five officers, each identified by name and title].

We arrive to the 4th floor and proceed to secure his safety by having him wear a bulletproof vest. We then proceeded to extract him from the hospital to our premises.[77]

That wasn't true. I never left that hospital room during their interrogation. The more words of the document I translated, the more their laundry list of allegations came into focus. The scenario posed by the confession had pitted me against Safra's head nurse. It claimed she gave me horrible working hours and made my job difficult to the point where I couldn't sleep at night. The so-called confession also said that I started pilfering tranquilizers from Safra's medicine stash in order to cope:

I wanted to find a way to get attention. I went as far as hurting myself to make it look like I had been attacked . . . I assure you I did not intend to kill them. I only wanted [Safra] to understand that I would never not do good [things].

It's those pills and everything that [the head nurse] put me through that pushed me to do this. In my head I wasn't myself anymore. I realize now, after being in the hospital for three days, what I have done. It's incredible.

I very well confirm what you have discovered. You know quite well what happened. I was alone, there was never an attack. I hit and stabbed myself, I set the fire and it all started by trying to fake an attack by intruders. I did all this to get attention. I would have never done it, though, had I not taken those medications.[78]

The dialogue became more and more over the top:

Investigator: How do you explain the scratches on your face?

Maher: I don't know . . . I know I fell down. I'm trying to remember. I must have hurt myself falling down and that's why I had [a bump or contusion] behind my head. It's coming back to me. I took some sandpaper I had found on the stairs outside while coming to work. I scratched myself with that. I took a small piece that must have been left behind by workers. I took it and put it in my bag.

Investigator: This means that in that precise moment—therefore, prior to starting your shift—you already had the intention of doing what you did? You already had the idea of the fake assault?

Maher: Yes, I thought that I could use it to create marks on my face to make it look like I had been attacked. Yes, I had already planned the scenario of the false assault.[79]

I was in tears. It was an intermingling of sorrow and sheer hilarity at the absurdity of it all. Yet *somehow*, nowhere in this important and damning document was there any mention of my wife or her hijacked passport. However, right near the end of the wordy wreckage was a small parcel of truth, one that created the ultimate in insane irony:

Investigator: How many languages do you speak?

Maher: I only speak English and I understand some words of French.[80]

Perfect, I thought, grimacing at the translation. *Sign here . . .*

While the obligatory and evidently "bothersome" investigation into the deaths of Edmond Safra and Vivian Torrente produced more head-shaking questions than answers, no one really cared. Everyone in that damned deep-tan, shallow-scrupled country was treating the evidence in the case with less concern than a third-division soccer score.

Not me.

At each and every meeting with Patricia Richet, when she swung her third-degree hammer, I blocked and countered with an interrogation of my own. I kept telling her to "go check this, go check that—then you'll find your truth."

But all through every second of this, the word "truth" was an esoteric concept, never a solid state. If Richet asked me point-blank things like "Mr. Maher, you did stab yourself, *non?*" I couldn't deny it outright, because that's what it said in the confession.

Instead, I would take time to digest the question. I would absorb it.

I'd look at Donald or Georges—whoever was there. And at Sandrine Setton, a lawyer added to the team as a gopher for Manasse.

Those looks and all that drama took some time.

Finally, I would answer. With body language full of righteousness, I would look at Richet and say, "You have the confession. I stand by my confession . . . *at this time.*"

But always, I would steer and push and fight and hope for the real truth to come riding in and trample the bogus mea culpa.

My efforts were met with push-back every step of the way.

I made another mental list. And while this discovery-docket expanded, that old list of "Things I Don't Know" got shorter.

"If I can find out things while I'm penned up in this jail hole," I'd ask Patricia Richet, "why can't anyone and everyone outside uncover the same clues? And have those clues *mean* something?"

I started my new list with the basics. First, motive:

1. Before this tragedy unfolded, I had everything I could possibly want in life. I had it made! I was two weeks away from permanent staff status, making secure and abundant money. The plan for my family to come over and my kids to go to school here was in place, as was an apartment for us to live in together. Do people really believe I'd want to endanger or hurt or scare my employer who made this all possible? With the motive of showing myself off as a hero?

2. I didn't need to enact an elaborate scheme to prove myself a hero, because Safra already loved and respected me!

The media had quickly played up the friction between Sonia and me. Exalting her as the almighty head nurse who (they told us over and over) had fired seventeen other nurses in the past sixteen months.

3. She was intimidated and job-threatened by me, not the other way around. I proved myself and my worth to Safra time after time through my actions and abilities. So why would I need to play games?

Then I advanced into the most obvious insanity in the whole mess: the cops and fire department:

4. Just one look at the investigators' event timeline makes you want to slam your head into a wall. Why did the first responders just sit there like idiots, bumbling around in lost logistics, while Lily just strolled down from the penthouse like Free Willy, unscathed and untouched?

"I don't understand why the police allowed me to go down from the sixth floor alone if they were afraid that there were armed intruders," Lily told investigators, "since in the end they let me go down without any protection."[81]
Why indeed?
And the "why's" kept coming:

5. Why didn't a fireman simply hit the *poubelle* with the power-stream of ready water?

6. Why did Safra's security chief, Samuel Cohen, wind up in those handcuffs trying to go up and save his boss? He knew exactly how to find Safra and had keys to everything!

The conspiracy theories came next. I didn't have to look far or open my ears too wide to be aware of them. Jails have pretty damn good eyes and ears of their own, beyond even my own personal stack of documents:

7. First let's get right to the marinated beetroot. Let's talk about Russia . . .

7a. Were the "intruders" Russian contract killers? Safra was openly cooperating with the FBI in the ongoing money-laundering investigation. The idea of a pissed off Russian gangster should at least be entertained as a viable possibility, no?

7b. What about Safra's implication in the Money Plane scandal, where planeloads of cash from the US Federal Reserve were flown daily from JFK to Russia, supposedly to fund the Russian mob?[82] Surely that ruffled somebody's feathers!

7c. With Hermitage Management, a financial management company cofounded by Safra and Bill Browder, the pair became the largest investors in Russia. Could that have upset other power-hungry individuals in a land of voracious bears and ravenous wolves?

7d. What kind of business were Safra and Russian oligarch Berezovsky involved with? The latter was making more and more enemies at the Kremlin, and there even rumors that newly appointed President Putin might try to "prove his independence by making a great show of cutting ties with the powerful tycoons who wielded so much influence over Yeltsin."[83] Certainly the "godfather of the Kremlin" was in that group, along with Safra and Browder, Russia's "largest investors"!

8. How about other countries? For example, why does a tiny country like Monte Carlo have an embassy in Bogotá, Colombia? Could there be the *slight* possibility that some of Colombia's drug lords did a little business with Monaco—the world's tax-sheltering, money-laundering mecca?

9. Did Prince Rainier have something to do with all of this—before and/or after the fire?

9a. Before: One kicked-around consideration was the mammoth portion of Safra's cash that was stationed in Monte Carlo—could that have entangled the Monegasque government?

9b. After: bad press and bad publicity just might attract some bad attention on this sunny slice of Southern France—and that just might interfere with smooth-running business-as-usual.

Last but definitely not least, I needed to take a close look at the grieving widow:

10. Why—especially in the midst of Safra's recent paranoid precautions—did Lily give all dozen or so members of his Mossad-trained security team the night off?

11. Why did Lily change the nurses' shifts, putting me on the schedule for that night—a night I was supposed to be off? And how did my kidnappers know "[I wouldn't need to] worry about that"?

12. Why did Lily leave that valance open—after religiously closing it every night—in strange-sync with my kidnappers' wishes?

Since the tragedy, I'd come across two more niggling nuggets about Lily that had me wanting to unearth more:

Lily had been rumored to be having an "inappropriate relationship" with one of Edmond's bank managers; after the fire, I heard that a mysterious post-it note had been found in her bedroom saying "I Love You" to an "unidentified person." Of course, both those claims never saw the light of day.

Another, more solid, cause for pause was that Lily had hastily paid off the Torrente family for Vivian's death. Why? Was she afraid of them seeing the true autopsy results, knowing Edmond's culpability would be worth a much prettier penny than what they'd agreed to? On that front, my musings were apparently right on the money. In two years, Vivian's children would file suit against Lily for $96 million,[84] claiming they'd been "fraudulently deceived and misled into signing a so-called settlement agreement with the named defendants wherein critical information, including the autopsy report was intentionally withheld from them."[85]

But getting back to the more blatant questions . . .

13. How much did Edmond's changing of his will in Lily's favor over his siblings (or the coercion I witnessed firsthand!) have to do with his sudden death?

14. What about those *Twilight Zone*-like "coincidences" involving the Safras' statehood status becoming super-solid, just as Edmond financially became very liquid, having hurriedly sold his Republic National Bank—as Lily desired?

"It is an interesting fact that Edmond and Lily Safra's Monegasque citizenship papers came through the day before he was killed. The sale of his Republic New York Corporation and Safra Republic Holdings had been approved by shareholders just days before that."[86]

—Dominick Dunne, "Death in Monaco,"
Vanity Fair, December 2000

Interesting indeed. As new citizens of Monaco, Edmond and Lily had achieved an elite of the elite status—given only to roughly 19 percent[87] of the principality's privileged population and about 0.000075% of everyone on Earth. It was the kind of very rare air Lily loved to inhale. It was also a designation that came with *une richesse* of financial perks, such as no income tax, no wealth tax, no local tax, no capital gains tax, a corporate income tax[88] that's a fraction of the rest of the globe—and an *inheritance* tax that's zero for spouses.[89]

It was so *bien* being Monegasque.

Added to all that, Edmond's bank sale allowed him to will a neat sum of cash to his wife, without her becoming embroiled in the business venture or having to sell off assets after his death—*très convenient!*

Many posited that Mr. Safra was getting to the point where he couldn't control his banking empire anymore; providing at least one reason it was being sold. And then-CNBC commentator Maria Bartiromo was just one of the money pundits amazed that it was being sold so cheap.[90] While I'd later learn the story behind the "cheap" part, I already knew the answer to *why* he'd initiated the sale to begin with. I had heard Lily cajole Edmond to sell it off, despite his siblings' protests. And the deal was finally approved *the week before his death* for "only" $9.85 billion "generating $2.8 billion for Safra's heirs."[91]

And all *that* money would be sitting in escrow in Monte Carlo, tax-free. All of it. Tax-free.

As the investigative saying goes: follow the money! One didn't need look far to find a motive in this case . . .

Finally, let's talk about the kidnappers snatching me off that street in Nice and my attackers the next night—obviously from the same party-loving fraternity of Tau Theta Thug:

15. It made sense to leverage me: I was the nurse with the most to lose and the one ballsy enough to make their plan work by opening the security valance against the Safras' protocol.

16. Of course, the prevailing self-attack "theory" would mean I was never kidnapped; but my hospital records showed bruising on my big toes. Yeah—the ones the kidnappers smashed! More evidence in my favor cut to the quick.

17. Obviously I messed up the plans of whoever came in the residence. Judging by how I was attacked, they were banking on my being knocked unconscious—or dead. There was no way they wanted to get tangled up in a battle royale when time was of the essence and they had a bigger "fromage" to deal with than a nurse.

18. If the kidnappers/attackers were in cahoots with Lily, and she was going to take care of their damn valance, why bother to kidnap and blackmail me?

18a. My best guess is that they needed assurance nobody would close the valance once Lily walked away. And I was the one to worry about because I'd be the type to notice—and fix—the security breach.

18b. But also, you can't cheat at blackjack unless every card is marked to ensure that all the cards are known. And it never hurts to double your insurance.

They did their best to stack the deck but, in the end, I was the one draw that didn't flip quite right—the ultimate wildcard.

And then I was in jail, an openly marked man. And I wasn't about to fold.

———

"Don't you find ANY of this the least bit suspicious, Patricia Richet?!

"Hey—you know what might really help clear things up? How about the recordings of the police and fire department communications for that morning? Have you bothered to examine those? Or what about the feed from all the cameras on the street and the apartment? Surely my attackers could be seen somewhere on there!

"Have you tried pursuing ANY of the avenues I've listed? Why all the focus on ME? How the hell is Ted the nurse—sitting and rotting in this jail—supposed to provide the answers to any of these questions?!

"How?!

"Why?!"

"I'll be the one asking the questions here, Mr. Maher, not you!"

"Fine!" I screamed. "But ask them somewhere else, too. Get me some answers, Patricia Richet. Get *all* of us some answers, Patricia Richet!"

CHAPTER 27

UN SPECTACLE DE CHIEN ET DE PONEY: THE REENACTMENT

May 2000

I was *still* sitting behind bars and *still* nothing solid was being done to get me the fuck out of jail!

Especially by the crack-duo of Blot-Manasse.

I was foolishly trusting those weak, idiotic men, instead of doing what I had done all my life—relying on my own (although now ripped-apart) gut. I was getting more help and support from the crook sharing my cell.

Although the jail held an official maximum of eighty-one inmates, usually only about twenty or thirty were in there at any given time. Most of them for check fraud, shoplifting, bank scams, alcohol, drunk driving—Monte Carlo fluff stuff. For the better part of every year, the *de luxe* suites at 4 Avenue Saint-Martin remained lonely and empty.

But suddenly, a rush of perpetrators were brought in who fell into those fluff categories dealing with currency and cheating issues. Monegasque authorities and the citizenry are especially un-warm toward that kind of evil. It's a sacrilege before their exalted God of Money.

It would not be tolerated!

So we had the nuisance of a few double-bookings at the inn, and for two or three weeks I was paired with a French inmate named (yes, *but of course*) Jacques. Obviously, we talked—as best as our language skills allowed. And just as obviously we found out things about one another. Jacques was in there, like many in the current wave, because he'd bounced some checks on the locals.

And, *en ce moment*, I discovered that Jacques knew Edmond Safra—peripherally at least.

Fifteen years prior to his inconvenient interlude with me in Monte Carlo, Jacques was involved in a real estate deal in Miami. It was a bit more complicated than his bounced checks. You see, he and a South American were buying a hotel. They needed about $650,000. Guess which bank they went to for seed money?

"No problem!" Jacques and his partner were told by Safra associates. "We'll get this loan done for you . . . it'll take about six weeks."

Great.

But just before the transaction was to close, Jacques showed up at the bank to finalize everything.

Nope.

Sorry.

It seems that a subsidiary of the bank—using the insider info from Jacques—came up with a third-party business that contacted the seller directly and "worked something out," screwing Jacques and his partner out of a deal.

Jacques lost everything.

"Edmond Safra's way of doing business cost me $650,000! When I heard that he had died, I did not shed a tear. *Reposer en paix, Monsieur Safra!*"

It's a small world, and it was even smaller in that cell. But the tale of the lost bucks wasn't the only thing Jacques had to say to me within those walls.

"Vous avez besoin d'un avocat réel!"

He was right: I needed a *real* lawyer.

He told me I needed another Jacques: Jacques Vergès.

I wasn't aware of Vergès, but everyone in the international community of top-level judicial juice was. This French-Vietnamese Communism-espousing defense shark drew a lot of prosecutorial blood as he protected a controversial cast of characters. His client list included Khmer Rouge head of state Khieu Samphan, Nazi war criminal Klaus Barbie, and terrorist Ilich Ramírez Sánchez (a.k.a. Carlos the Jackal).

So why not me?

I figured if nothing else, a Communist probably wouldn't be able to be bought off by the super-capitalist State of Monaco.

It just wouldn't be ethical.

And it so happened that my cellmate's girlfriend was Vergès' secretary in Paris. I did wonder briefly why my buddy here hadn't contacted Vergès for *his own* defense since he claimed to have this "in." But the more I found out about Vergès, the more obvious it became that he was only interested in clients who went well beyond the bush leagues of bad checks. With a billionaire's skeleton in my closet, I knew I'd qualify.

"Ted," said Jacques, "do you want me to contact Vergès?"

Not just yes, but "Fuck, yes!"

Jacques wrote a letter to Vergès in English, via his girlfriend.

Nothing.

He wrote a letter to Vergès in French, via his girlfriend.

Nothing.

Then Jacques wrote a letter to Vergès in French via the minister of justice and the consular agent.

Still nothing from Vergès.

Eventually, we figured out that everything we'd mailed out had never seen the light of day. The prison bastards were intercepting it, deciding that no one around there needed a weapon like Jacques Vergès.

I wrote one more letter. This time we gave it to my roomie's lawyer to smuggle out.

That one got through and Vergès sent an immediate response. Except we didn't know it. Others did, though; the ones who intercepted my incoming mail.

Surprise, surprise—Donald and George soon showed up at the jail.

"Hey, Ted, how's things?"

They never came together like that, so I knew something was up. And they surely weren't there to give me any good news about the incredible progress they had been making toward turning the key to my steel door. Their message was somewhat colder than that:

"Oh, by the way, Ted, we heard from the minister of justice. He was telling us over a bottle of wine at lunch that you're going to have Jacques Vergès as your attorney."

I commended them on their amazing investigative ability to find out *that* when they didn't seem to be able to find out a damn thing about this case!

"I'm trying to get Vergès because you two are just puppets of this whole system that has me behind these bars!"

They weren't happy.

"Jacques Vergès is the worst media hound in this business! If you want to do twenty-five to life, have at it! Get him! Even if he puts on a good show—which he will—you'll be in jail forever!

"We've already told you what you have to do. You've signed that document. Now you just need to plead guilty, take the few years, and then get on with your life. Is it worth it to spend the rest of your life in prison for the sake of a good show?"

No.

No, it wasn't.

I hated them and I hated all of it, but I supposed I had to grab the facts by the throat and deal with them. That was how it was. Just let me do a few years and then get the fuck out of that damned country.

My head was in my hands when I finally heard from Vergès. As Blot-Manasse already knew, Vergès' answer was yes. He would slide me right in there with Samphan, Barbie, and Carlos the Jackal. It was a perfect fit.

But I had to decline. No, my life wasn't worth a "show." But it *was* worth the truth. At what price would that truth come?

October 20, 2000

Eleven months in that miserable "county jail."

Still no trial.

But many interrogations with Patricia Richet had come and gruelingly gone. And I had not one, but two, sterling lawyers: one who drank like a fish, and both of whom bowed down like limp lackeys for the company store. Ain't life grand?

And it was time for something more.

The Monegasque judicial powers felt that the condemning cherry on top of the *mousse au chocolat* would be to conduct a reenactment—a reconstruction of exactly what happened in the early morning hours of December 3, 1999.

The reenactment was later covered by some in the media, including Dominick Dunne.[92] But a little was lost in translation.

To be blunt, it was the most ridiculous thing I have ever been a part of. "We're going to absolutely *prove* what occurred," the police and the prosecutors told me.

I bet.

The day before the reenactment, I asked, "What's going to happen with the firemen and the policemen—where's everybody going to be?"

"Mr. Maher," they answered, "there will be no firemen or policemen there."

"Excuse me?" I said. "I thought we were reconstructing this! 'My person' was only at the scene for five or ten minutes, tops! Then I was on my way to the hospital! What the police and the firefighters did, and especially *didn't* do after that, is kind of key here! You mean you're not going to have eighty-six policemen and fifty-six firemen just standing around? And aren't you going to have Lily relive her last two conversations with her husband? *On MY phone! And what about Safra's head of security being handcuffed so he couldn't get up to save his boss?* Who's going to play the frustrated and angry Samuel Cohen? Just what exactly are you going to reconstruct here? What?"

It was all fantasy-choreography with cameras and microphones centered on me—nobody else. If these guys were producers on Broadway, they'd turn *The Music Man* into a solo performance; "Seventy-Six Trombones" would be marched by one poor sap with a piccolo.

Darkness had long set in on this Friday of fabrication and fools.

It was 10:30 at night.

I was brought to 15 Bis 17 Avenue D'ostende: La Belle Époque. All the streets were cordoned off. Legions of police were there—not to play the roles of themselves in this badly re-edited rerun, but in case I tried to escape.

A new roof was under construction over the penthouse, but otherwise its appearance and smell still reeked of the December 3 aftermath, eleven months later.

And there was Lily—accompanied by three lawyers. She wasn't there to play herself, either; she was simply a part of the audience. To watch as I relived the kindling of the alarm fire in *une poubelle*.

Then we all had to nervously deal with a little exposure; that's evidently why I'd again been forced to wear a bulletproof vest. I had to show everyone the French doors and the valance, and I guess they didn't want me to be opened up to the public without protection.

So they claimed. I suppose some random nut out there in the citizenry could've actually posed a threat of danger. But what was *really* hard to ignore were the five red laser sights trained on my heart from the *cops'* high-powered rifles—high-powered enough to penetrate the vest they'd given me.

This was an FYI, just to let me know where things were at.

"Mr. Maher, if you decide to try to escape by swan-diving over the balcony, landing perfectly in a speeding delivery truck stacked with mattresses like they do in the movies, well, you'll be dead before your ass hits the first feather!"

Okay.

They had me there.

So I expressed what could have been my last act of defiance: I flipped off each Monegasque sniper, one by one.

Sun-up, October 21, 2000

The limping dog and pony spectacle dragged on and on. Finally, the police and the court officials brought me into the stench-ridden bathroom where I saw the marked silhouettes of Safra and Vivian, draped in their final positions.

It hit me.

It hit me hard.

As if one of those snipers had just open-fired.

I wept like a baby.

"Why did you have to bring me in here?" I choked. "Safra was really my friend, and Vivian . . . Vivian was like a mother figure to me."

"Because Mr. Maher," a cop answered calmly, "this is where they died."

CHAPTER 28
LE DÉSACCORD

Late 2000

Respected attorney Michael Jeffrey Griffith—another New Yorker—was driving near his home listening to news on the radio. Griffith was a partner in a firm called the International Legal Defense Counsel (ILDC). The group has a highly refined specialization, representing Americans who get arrested in foreign countries.

Griffith turned up the radio as he heard a story—*my* story. He listened. He was interested, naturally. It was right up his multinational alley, and he knew the name of Edmond Safra. Griffith, in fact, was introduced to Safra years before. They met only the one time, but to Griffith, Edmond was kind of a hero. Griffith liked Safra's legal chutzpah, standing up for himself in the American Express situation, prevailing, and then donating his judgment to charity.[93]

But the news moved on and Griffith filed the complex mess in Monaco into the back of his mind—*there's probably no way we could get that case . . .*

Besides, other than what he'd heard on the news, Michael Griffith didn't know me, and I didn't know him. What I *did* know was that I'd had it with the defense disasters that were George Blot and Donald Manasse.

I should have brought Jacques Vergès into this. Nothing was happening! Nothing! No trial!

Nothing!

Through letters and the few calls I was allowed, I told Heidi that I was simply rotting away there. One of the few positive moments came with a photo Heidi sent.

It was of her with Matthew and the judge at the final stage of his adoption, when all of Minnie's rights to him were officially gone.

I just want to go home! I have my life there! I have love!

But the tragic-comedy Blot-Manasse team allowed everything to explode directly into my face. And it wasn't *them* headed for a long-term pratfall in the miserable bomb of a jurisprudence joke; it was me! I was recalculating the price and value of the truth.

I went over and over the facts of the case.

I even pleaded to Donald as a fellow American. I tried to appeal to emotion and logic. I told him that Americans don't screw Americans!

"I'm in trouble here, Donald!" I screamed.

"Yes, Ted," he softly countered. "I understand. And don't worry. I'm going to treat you just like you're my son."

Well, that was real sweet.

But as we all know, talk is cheap. Damn cheap.

The Blot-Manasse duck-and-cover cowardice and impotence mystified Heidi and her mother. Their lack of understanding of the guilty plea I'd been forced into was killing them like it was killing me.

Help me!

Heidi and her mom did some research and contacted Amnesty International.

"Fighting injustice . . . promoting human rights . . ."[94]

What I was suffering slid right in there with Amnesty's mottoes and goals; I was buried headfirst in injustice and I sure as hell didn't see my human rights being promoted.

Heidi told them the entire story. They listened. In turn, Amnesty International called a law firm they worked closely with: ILDC.

Michael Griffith didn't know it, but with or without that car or the news on its radio, he was on a collision course that would bounce that "complex mess" of Safra's death and my arrest from the back of his mind to all-consuming status in the driver's seat.

Amnesty talked to Griffith's partner in Philadelphia.

"Would you be interested in this case?"

The partner called Griffith.

"Would you be interested in this case?"

Our paths began to cross and merge.

And Griffith and I were a fit.

Griffith started in the field of international criminal law with a frantic and frenetic first case, the 1970 Turkish drug prison-atrocity of American student Billy Hayes that became the book and Academy-Award-winning movie *Midnight Express*.[95]

It was quite the career "all aboard!"

Besides his three thousand cases of earth-circling experience, Griffith testified before the US Senate concerning the transfer of prisoners between the United States and Mexico, enabling them to be closer to families and friends, and to get decent food and college credits while incarcerated. His testimony led to the Council of Europe Transfer Treaty, still in place today, which allows the United States and forty other countries across the globe to transfer their inmates back and forth.[96]

Michael must also hold some kind of *ex aequo et bono* ("according to the right and good") world record for his work representing clients in prisons in over two dozen countries. He represented Kendrick Ledet and Rodrico Harp, two of the United States servicemen charged in 1995's infamous "Okinawan Rape Trial."

Beyond that, after my trial, Griffith would go on to be one of the attorneys for US Marine Corps Major Michael Brown, charged for a crime similar to that of Ledet and Harp; also in Okinawa. He would represent James Williams in Ecuador, an American citizen being held without trial, one of many victims of corrupt bribe-demanding judges and officials. He would also coordinate the defense of Americans wrongfully accused of murder in Tortola, British West Indies.[97]

You won't see attorneys like this on a bus-side banner ad with a smarmy grin screaming, *"Accident? DUI? I can help!"*

Griffith called Heidi. "Let's start to get the facts—all of them."

He was told about the law team of the lame that was sinking me. He was told about that jugular-gnawing, arm-twist plea. He was told that a "fresh face" was desperately needed over there on that defense team.

He agreed.

He even took the case pro bono. But the money needed for his expenses wasn't easy for my family. My aunt, a retired army lieutenant colonel, put up twenty-five grand; my mother, an additional fifteen. Everyone was involved and everyone wanted me home and vindicated. So, Michael Griffith was on his way to Monaco; and he eventually tallied two more trips to Monaco on his own dime.

Michael Griffith was intent on digging into Safra's death with a heavy shovel. Meanwhile, the Blot-Manasse stall-and-stonewall twins were still doing *their* groundbreaking probing with *fromage* appetizer spoons.

Early 2001

Griffith landed in Monaco with focus. He knew who he was, what he'd done, and what he was capable of.

He's a good hired gun to have on your side.

But unfortunately, I had no way of knowing this. I was still sequestered and separated from so much, caught up only in the immediacy of living out the repercussions of the *papier* I signed, coupled with the paradox of trying to get the real truth known and exposed. I was in a complexly woven distorted world, and I trusted no one but myself to pull me out of it.

Enter Michael Griffith.

He and I met.

So what? I thought. I had little interest in him at first, and little faith that he could do anything for me.

I was settled in.

I was nervous.

I'd been jack-hammered and brainwashed with the reality of *ma confession*.

. . . maybe that rabid cur will only bite off one nut . . . I suppose it could be worse . . .

While Griffith was ready for all-out legal war, he was trying hard to get a grip on how legal motion flowed within this monarchy. Coming into the sorry spectacle a year after it began made for some slippery attempts at catching up.

My first priority was to paint for Griffith the surreal abstraction that was my current legal representation. Here, so close to the Louvre, the defense that Blot and

Manasse had crafted had none of the order and dignity of da Vinci's *Mona Lisa*; it evoked more the monkey-screech moronics of Alexandre Gabriel Decamps' *Le Désaccord*.

After I laid out all the sad details, Griffith took a professional look into my dream team. He discovered that Donald Manasse had tried exactly *one* criminal case, some sort of misdemeanor. And Griffith's axiom "one criminal case does *not* make you a criminal lawyer" haunted with truth.

The worst was the pitiful puzzle Griffith was hit with: Regardless of the stains on their souls and brains, my current "representatives" had not a concern at my signing of a confession in a foreign language. Not wanting to upset *le panier de pommes* by backtracking on that guilty admission was, for them, always mission number one.

"Ted," Griffith told me, "when anyone is forced to sign a confession—especially a confession written in a language they don't understand—I'm the kind of attorney that stays up at night just dreaming about what I can do in that kind of situation! I can't wait to get going!"

"No, no, no," I told him. "We can't recant the confession now. We can't touch that!"

Blot-Manasse had spent the past year doing their Monagasque-loyal best to convince me to go along with this—and had succeeded.

"You cannot risk a possible life sentence!"

I guess the "sunny but shady" land of Monaco liked to exalt itself as having silver scruples and platinum principles. The government would do the lying, here! Anyone else would be punished to the fullest extent!

And by that point I had met with Patricia Richet a half-dozen or so times already. She had pushed in her own quiver of mental bamboo splinters. How could I possibly go back to her at this point and say, "No, I actually *am* changing my story"? How long would things drag out then?

It was a bad movie for Michael to come into the middle of.

The darkness of the Monegasque culture and its legal leanings was also examined by Griffith. He wanted to understand just *why* Blot-Manasse were hunkered down in the fear and hullabaloo of what any type of plea change might lead to.

"What do you mean I can't reverse a confession?" Griffith chafed. "There is no confession!"

It made Griffith sick to see Blot-Manasse nearly crying: "Oh my god, how are we going to overturn this? This is difficult. If we try to do it, Ted will get more time in jail."

Was this a mandated-by-the-state act? Were they truly this inept? Or both?

Another awkward intermission for Griffith consisted of my telling him about the absurd "reenactment." He was in shock.

After that, it was time to get educated as to how French and Monegasque law commissions the judge to do the criminal investigation, not the prosecutor as in the States. Pile it on!

It was quickly clear that Griffith (a *foreign* lawyer, at that) would be in a very difficult position to undo everything, all the statements and all that had been done—including that stupid reconstruction of the crime.

Could it be that I was a tougher *noix* to crack than the "Okinawan Rapists" or even international drug smugglers?

Michael's "difficult position" became a nearly crippling contortion when considering just *what* Monaco's Société des Bains de Mer is, and how SBM owned the country and my lawyers.

Then Michael Griffith met Georges Blot and Donald Manasse.

It was apparent from the first inter-attorney interactions that the Abbott and Costello of the Monegasque court system weren't about to "empty their cups" to learn anything from the extensive experience of a *real* international lawyer.

Blot-Manasse had wanted no part of Jacques Vergès, and Griffith was even worse for them. Because Griffith was in their face. His involvement was happening; it wasn't just a theoretical.

Think about when Moe and Larry had to replace Curly: what if they hadn't come back with Shemp? What if Sir Laurence Olivier had arrived instead?

Dynamics would change.

CHAPTER 29

THE PRICE OF TRUTH

I was counting every one of the 525,600 minutes in the year 2001.
Slowly.
Day by day.

Meanwhile, Griffith was spending *his* time doing research.

After some initial digging, he boiled down the suspect *ingrédients* into one thick *soupe à l'oignonit*, identifying three major groups with reason to harm Mr. Safra: some Russians involved in alleged money-laundering; Palestine organizations who objected to his charities for Israel; and those (on various sides) who weren't thrilled about Safra's bank's involvement in the Iran-Contra affair.

Griffith learned more . . .

And in everything he absorbed, he discerned that it was all about the money. It's always about the money, with maybe some politics thrown in.

Griffith waded further into Safra's messy battle with the Russians that involved Safra getting in bed with the US Justice Department to take down a Soviet crime syndicate.

It all began with Safra blowing the whistle on a massive money transfer he saw going through the Bank of New York. He flagged the Russia-initiated transaction as potential money-laundering. The Feds launched an investigation, openly assuming the involvement of the Russian mafia. Such a vast blast of money from Kremlin-country—who else could it be?

Some fifteen years later, I'd get a behind-the-curtain peek into the perilous game Safra was really playing with other powerful Russians, but for now—and no matter which side of the curtain you viewed it from—Safra was screwing with some extremely dangerous *lyudi*. This of course, got Griffith's attention because now we had some really compelling candidates for who wanted—and had the potency to arrange— Safra's death.

But, of course, always nagging was another line-item: Lily's complicit actions and her intense suggestions to Edmond concerning the bountiful bottom line of his will.

Maybe the real bottom line to the entire disaster was what I instinctively felt from the very beginning: that Edmond Safra had his fair share of enemies. And he arguably had *more* than his share of that ever-troublesome money that breeds them.

———————————

Griffith decided to expand his honesty-hunt horizons in regard to Lily. He looked into that *other* awkward and still-unexplained death of another of Lily's cash-stuffed husbands, Alfredo Monteverde.

Despite all the bizarre bumps and grinds in that one, apparently no investigation of Lily—the wife—was conducted. And apparently this same oversight—seasoned with a pinch of privilege of position—was occurring this time, too.

It made zero sense to Michael. SOP in cases like this is to immediately look at a spouse as a "person of interest." Especially when their loved one has died suspiciously or when a lot of money has been inherited. Or both!

If the Manolo Blahnik shoe fits . . .

Now, cops aren't *necessarily* suggesting a widow or widower actually did anything, but that's the way a police investigation is conducted. You corroborate things. And usually police try to interrogate these people to *eliminate* them from suspicion. But if there's a blip on that suspicious-activity radar, you keep going down that road. If there's no smudge of dirty deeds—great, they're in the clear.

Griffith didn't know exactly what Lily's cut of Safra's billions would add up to, but obviously it was hefty. In a situation like that—again, *normally*—an investigation would check the widow's phone calls, where she was, who she talked to in recent days . . . You'd give her a concise, bare-bulb interview.

Not Lily Safra.

What we did have were some of our first-act inter-attorney interactions with Moe, Larry, and Hamlet.

> I would not hear your enemy say so,
> Nor shall you do mine ear that violence . . . [98]

Michael opened by speaking to Donald Manasse about the surveillance videos from the Safras' flat being empty. Griffith posited that footage from cameras had been erased, purposefully or by "accident" by someone with access to it. Someone at the flat, or the police.

The reply from Manasse was: "We don't know when and where or how it was erased."

Okay.

Griffith had a couple more inquiries about the surveillance system—or lack of it. What about the camera that wasn't working at all? What about yet another camera that was facing in an opposite direction from any area of activity?

"We don't know . . ."

Griffith was facing daily frustration that would only intensify. He was digging, blasting, and exhuming. He was part of the "team"—sort of—but he did not yet have the key to the lock on the done-and-done guilty plea.

Griffith's initial impulse had been to fight this thing with every legal claw and fang in his arsenal. He railed at me. He gave me advice and pep talks—"I can't wait to get going, Ted!"

He was even serious about bringing in the FBI. He wanted to get with the Monegasque government and have the Bureau come in and administer a polygraph test, which I had always agreed to do: anytime, anywhere.

He also tried to figure out a way in which I could be used by the FBI as a witness in the Russian mob money-laundering mess. Maybe I could be called for questioning to determine if I'd heard or seen anything in and around Safra's various meetings or calls. That would have pulled me out of this mess immediately.

But Griffith couldn't get anything going because of the "so-called" confession and how deeply that had buried me.

I was frustrated right along with him. I was in the middle of it all. I was in the middle of so much. I was reevaluating. I was recalculating that price and value of the truth.

I wanted Griffith to break through to that truth. I wanted Patricia Richet to break through to that truth. But what would that do? As much as I hated Blot-Manasse, I had to rely at least *somewhat* on their Monegasque-native know-how that going against my confession could doom me for life; they banged that stick at me hard! And meanwhile, they dangled the enticing carrot that with this plea I could be out in just a few years—and I had already served most of that!

I was back to that *thinking*, the realization that this wasn't a "close one," it was a direct hit. Survive.

Survive!

I never doubted that I would survive, but it's good to have some help that flies higher than even the toughest hired legal guns; it's good to have a well-equipped guardian angel in the wings.

Kate was a beautiful young Monegasque woman. Half my age, Kate was interning at the prison; learning the security industry and earning credits for the French college she attended. She helped deal with the two or three female prisoners who might be there at any given time.

She didn't interact regularly with the male prisoners, but at times she would accompany a male guard taking an inmate to see a social worker or something like that; but she was never alone with an inmate unless that inmate was a woman.

Holiday gatherings, church services, and other mixed "events" gave Kate and I chances to talk and get to know each other. Sometimes the various Catholic groups would pass out bunches of flowers and I'd make sure mine went to Kate: "They're just going to die here; please take them home."

Our relationship wasn't about physical attraction or anything like that. It was an innocent intimacy that grew because she was human. She'd talk to me. She was nice to me.

Her mother was also the secretary to Monaco's minister of justice.

As things unfolded, Kate's family connection would be *très bénéfique.*

Michael flew back to New York.

On the plane, he mentally ran through everything. He thought about the autopsy reports. He thought about the evident struggle between Safra and Vivian; of Safra's Parkinson's-and-drug-fueled paranoia.

Midflight into the mental rewind, Griffith got into a conversation with the man seated next to him. The man was a pharmaceuticals salesman. They discussed the drugs used to treat Parkinson's. The "expert" sitting next to Michael reaffirmed what I already knew: "Sinemet, carbidopa-levodopa, will definitely induce paranoia. And much more."

In New York, Michael reported back to Heidi and her mother. He told them about the deadbolt on the guilty plea.

"Ted is standing firm," he said. "He signed the confession and he's going to deal with it."

They weren't happy.

"According to local counsel," he tried to explain, "it's tough if not impossible to overturn a confession. So you've got two choices: go with the confession or try to overturn the confession and have them think that you're lying. There's also very little chance of a confession being overturned, anyway. So with that in mind, we're going to go with the confession. Again, *according to local counsel,* Ted will be out in two or three years, maybe less, and then we all go home."

Heidi's unhappiness turned to accusations that Griffith was in league with Blot-Manasse and Monaco; brainwashed, bribed, or both.

Griffith's frustration built. He was perplexed and disgusted.

"The defendant is the master," he explained to them. "The attorney is the servant. And right now, the orders in the castle are to ride out the remainder of this sentence."

Heidi and her mother softened in their venom toward Michael. But still, we were all languishing in this vicious vacuum. It's so hard to just wait for something, especially when you don't know what it is you're waiting for.

April 17, 2001

Even with the confession stalemate biting down hard, Michael Griffith was trying to break free with something. He knew that Heidi's complete and unabridged version of what happened to her and her brother on that first rushed trip into Monaco was such a distasteful and outrageous part of all this.

Everyone needed to hear it.

Especially Lily.

And Lily should pay. If nothing else, we needed to work this!

Griffith went to work with a local attorney and prepared a commencement of action that named Lily, Brittan, St. Bernard, and essentially all of Lily's staff. Three weeks later, on May 8, 2001, he added the formal complaint to the State Department to his attack. Both contained Heidi's full affidavit—the rest of the story about her first touchdown in Monaco:

THE ILL-FATED AND TERRYIFYING TRIP TO MONACO AND ITS AFTERMATH

I [Heidi Maher] *was met at the Nice airport by Safra staff. The welcoming party consisted of Anthony Brittain . . . Sonia Casiano* [Herkrath], *Cecilia Min (two of Mr. Safra's nurses) . . . and a driver named Mark. Two limousines were waiting.*

Anthony Brittain took our luggage to one car and accompanied the Torrente family to the Hotel Balmoral. In the interest of saving time and in view of the urgency of the situation, my brother and I were invited to travel with Sonia Casiano and Mark in the second car. Without our luggage, we could travel directly to Ted's hospital bedside in Monaco. We never got there and I never saw Ted before leaving.

After three days of dreadful interrogation and broken promises, having misplaced my trust in those with whom I dealt, I had no choice but to return home to Stormville, New York.

THE CHANGE IN DIRECTION AND THE TELEPHONE CALL

Mark drove very quickly (approximately 95 kilometers [60 miles] per hour) toward the hospital. Suddenly, after we cleared the tunnel which connects France and Monaco, he received a call from Anthony Brittain on his cellular telephone. Brittain ordered Mark to

THE PRICE OF TRUTH

change direction abruptly and take us to the Hotel Balmoral. Ted and other Safra staff had been housed there and arrangements were made there for us as well. We were not given any option to refuse this change, nor could we have left the speeding limousine. Brittain's directions proved to be a very fateful change of course.

THE FIRST MONACO POLICE INTERROGATION

After some time at the hotel, Anthony Brittain took my brother and me to the Monaco Police Station. Since Brittain said that the police would help us to see Ted, we complied. This representation was false. I was interrogated about my husband by an Inspector Rousset. She showed me a knife with a six-inch blade. She stated that it was found in Ted's pocket thereby suggesting that he was culpable in some way in the two deaths . . .

I denied any knowledge of the knife. I had never seen it before. I began to cry and asked again to see my husband. The police ignored my request . . . My brother and I were then instructed by the police to wait outside while Safra nurse Sonia Casiano, who spoke French (we did not), sought permission for me to visit my husband. While waiting, I called home on Mark's cellular phone to speak with my children only to learn that one of them was very ill and very upset.

THE ABDUCTION NEAR THE POLICE STATION

While we were waiting for Sonia to emerge from the interrogation room and out of nowhere, two men and a woman in black jumpsuits bearing no identifying markings grabbed me and my brother and forced us into a car. I did not know whether these were the people suspected of killing Mr. Safra and Vivian Torrente. Our driver, Mark, ran after us screaming, but could not help. I cannot convey in words for the Court, even in the context of this already terrifying day, how this episode was so deathly terrible. We were both being kidnapped and I thought we were going to die.

The three took us back to the Hotel Balmoral and gained access to my and my husband's rooms and possessions. They rifled through our things which were in the luggage we had left at the hotel. They had Ted's small tape recorder on which he stored one of our children's "I love you, Dad" telephone conversations. They played it for me; the emotion was over-whelming. They also took our passports. The female stated that this was her job. We were then released and told to report back to the police station later in the day . . .

On the evening of December 5, 1999, Michelle St. Bernard told me that in view of my desire to leave and go home, she and/or Sandra, a Safra secretary, would make the *arrangements for replacement tickets for the return trip to be waiting for us at the Nice airport. When we actually arrived at the ticket counter, the Delta representative demanded $2,400 in payment. I immediately called Sandra who refused me. I covered this expense on my credit card and returned home. The expense has never been reimbursed.*

I learned later that Ted had been shown my passport, which was taken from me during the abduction from the police station, and told that I had been strip searched and tortured. At the time this all happened, his legs and arms were tied to his hospital bed and he was connected to a urinary catheter.

Ted neither reads nor writes French. Nevertheless, he was handed a French confession by the Monaco police. He signed it to spare me from what he thought would be further abuse by the Monaco authorities.

CONCLUSION

We still do not know who orchestrated these events and why. For example: who actually paid for and later cancelled the Delta return flight tickets; who is responsible for the sudden change in our limousine's itinerary; who arranged to deceive me into the coercive police interrogation room; and who converted my trip into a Monaco police investigation without my prior informed consent or knowledge . . . [99]

The requested disposition and documents will lead us to the truth and to those truly responsible for, among other things, the utter lack of due care and breach of duty to me.[100]

It's a damning story and a damning truth; the damages here are monumental. Griffith knows it, and it's a solid bet that Lily's legal lemmings know it too. Now Griffith has at least something to get him going.

The suit has steam and is headed for court. But within just days of the proceedings, Heidi pulls out.

Griffith goes nuts!

"What is wrong with you?!" he asks. "Do this for your kids, at least! Lily is not going to go to that courtroom! She will settle! We need to see this through!"

With murky explanations like "I need to get on with my life!" and "I just want all this to end!" Heidi pulls the plug on the action.

That's it.

Shred the paperwork and go home.

Michael and the local lawyer miss out on a nice payday and Heidi's gutsy narrative never has the opportunity to string up Lily and make her squirm and dance.

Griffith can't help but surmise: "There has to be a *real* reason for Heidi to do this; there just has to . . ."

CHAPTER 30

THE BREAKING POINT

2001 limps like a wounded animal into mid-2002

218,013 minutes . . .

218,014 . . .

I was going on three years entombed behind these prison walls.

The vacuum of downed-hope I was living in was never a complete void. The eventual end was still a mystery, but the daily attempts to break me were certain and mounting.

Strip searches never stopped: Bend over, spread my cheeks, lift up my penis, move my balls. Stick out my tongue.

It was all psychological.

They were trying to break me.

Well, fuck them.

They weren't looking for anything. They knew I couldn't *have* anything. There was no way anything obvious and quick could get into that place. It wasn't that kind of place. This wasn't Men's Central in downtown Los Angeles, or Angola in Louisiana, where so much can get lost in the contraband shuffle.

Nothing can go unseen in a forest that has at most eighty-one trees.

Even when the lawyers or anyone came in from the outside, they had to go through two locked doors, and then another locked door, and then two more, and then be escorted by guards. By the time they got to me, they had passed through eight locked doors, eight levels of security, and metal detection.

One of that "anyone" from the outside was the vice consulate in Marseille, France, representing the United States of America: Ellen Thorburn. She—the State Department in human form—would visit me about once a month, to see how Monaco was treating me; if there were any abuses.

Great.

Thanks.

Wonderful.

I'm still here, Ellen.

And Blot-Manasse would swing by, dragging along their own decaying carcasses. Their message was always cheery: "Well, this or that has come up and now we may be looking at five years . . . oh, and hey, something else has surfaced and it may be seven years, but that's better than life in here, no?"

Their little visits were nothing more than *mental* strip searches.

I wrote a letter to Michael because I had begun to see: he had been so right in his frustration and disgust with this "program."

TED MAHER
BP 532 Maison D'Arret
Monaco, Cedex 98015

Dear Michael,
I wish that I had followed your advice. Everything you said to me appears to be coming true. Not ONE thing that Georges has told me has come true. I was very foolish and scared to change anything for what I was told "would happen" . . .
Again, you were right. It seems that for whatever reason, [Blot-Manasse] are going with the flow. It stinks from every direction. To hold me 100% responsible for this accident will polish Monaco's golden image.
Over two years ago, Georges told me a story of a shepherd who burnt his fields. He stated that the shepherd had no intention to kill anyone or to have his fire spread to a home; all of which happened. He told me that this man received two years. Then later, I was told my case would be looked at around four years. Over the last six months, I've been told to look at a maximum of six years. As of last week, Georges

tells me, over lunch, with alcohol on his breath, he wants to convince the procurer
for less than seven years!

The only thing, at this point, I can [tie] to Georges' shepherd story is [me as a]
lamb being led to the slaughter . . .

The parable-like story that Blot told me may have sounded Charles Perrault–ish, but
it was a real case that had real bearing on our own mess here.

That case set precedence for France to overturn the Napoleonic law from which
the crime of "arson by communication" was derived—the charge being formally laid
on me.

The perfect analogy for the pretzel logic of arson by communication would be to
find someone guilty of premeditated murder by ricocheting bullet. Something like
this is either murder or it's an accident.

In Blot's legend and lore, there was this little knoll with a five-acre wooded lot on
the top. The shepherd at the center of the legal heat had set the field on fire to clear it,
making way for it to be green and lush the next year. It was standard agricultural
stuff, I guess. Anyway, all of a sudden, the wind came up and caught the whole forest
on fire, burning down a chalet and killing its two occupants in the process.

The authorities tried to charge this guy with murder—for killing these people with
his *arson*. But there was no intent; there was no motive.

The shepherd received a light sentence and France ended up ridding themselves of
the old precept. There was no more "arson by communication" charge in France.

That was twenty years before.

Monaco, well, they still had it on *their* books. Why rock any of Bonaparte's *bateaux*?

———————

My personal void and vacuum and dregs of downed-hope all came to a *tête géante*
when I met with Patricia Richet for the nineteenth—and final—time. We had a perfectly *merveilleux* chat.

It was Normandy Beach with words.

We started with talking about the empty surveillance tapes, again. Then it was
onward and upward: she picked at the issue of the "self-inflicted stab wounds" again.

As part of that, we wrestled with a bottle of lidocaine that would become a burning beacon of prosecution in this whole dim dance.

> Lidocaine is "a common local anesthetic and antiarrhythmic drug . . . used topically to relieve itching, burning, and pain from skin inflammations, injected as a dental anesthetic or as a local anesthetic for minor surgery."[101]

The police said that lidocaine had been found in my system and a bottle of it found among my possessions. I used it, they said, to numb the areas where I stabbed myself.

Lidocaine wasn't in *my* medicine cabinet, so here's where the tearing up of my hotel room (back when the cops nabbed and then rousted Heidi and her brother) comes in to big-time play. Here's where that CYA insurance of leaving a little something in my room was just more payments on that policy of burying the American.

When Patricia Richet held up the evidence bag with the lidocaine they'd "found" in my hotel room, I almost jumped out of my chair.

The only lidocaine *I* was ever around came in a plastic vial with a red plastic top that Edmond's dermatologist showed up with occasionally. Safra had some pre-cancerous lesions, some sun spots on his head, so the skin doc used lidocaine to clean up Safra's scalp.

But the bottle Richet was showing me had a rubber top and was completely different—I'd never seen it in my life. The *best* part about this bottle was that it had a *label*. And as nurse, I knew that the contents of that label could provide tracking as to its source.

This was it! The smoking gun!!

I faced the interpreter. "Tell her that bottle has ID numbers all over it! Lot numbers. Serial numbers. Manufacture date. Everything! It's easy to find out its origin and where—and whom—it was delivered to. Maybe we could find out it was sent to Princess Grace Hospital. Of course, *I* wouldn't have access to it there, but Monagasque authorities at the higher levels surely would!"

I was extremely agitated, standing and pointing at the vial. "Tell her to investigate *all* of that, because this bottle sure as hell didn't come from me, and wherever it did come from was way, way out of my reach!"

This was my nineteenth meeting with Patricia Richet. One hundred twenty-five hours of pissing in *le vent* with this woman. If I thought Griffith was frustrated, well, I was reinventing the term. I was losing it, and so was Richet.

She just went on and on, going over and over things we had gone *over and over* already, endlessly. I told her nothing was going to change.

She asked me questions this way and that way, upside down and backward and forward, trying to see if I was going to slip and make a mistake. She was playing such an obvious and marked courtroom card: When you think somebody is lying, catch them in a miscue and trip them up. But everything I told her for three years was the truth.

"You can ask me anything, Patricia Richet; ask me in any way you want and with any temperature of fire you care to breathe, but it's still going to come out as the truth.

"It's not going to change."

And anything that I had to answer in lockstep with the confession continued to be tagged with my "at this time" dig, always looking ahead to when the real truth would finally be known.

The one thing I was grateful for was that as time went on, it wasn't only me this magistrate investigated. She had taken my advice—*maybe*—and looked for "answers" in other places.

She didn't hide the fact that she had interviewed every policeman who was there, every fireman, the police chief, the fire chief, the butcher, the baker, the candlestick maker, and the guy who did the "remodeling" of La Belle Époque that resulted in the bolting shut of the fan housing. Richet's analysis of the failed security system was just as exhaustive.

She went even further with me and my activities apart from my job with Safra. She found out that I had things in place with the ABC school for my kids and a home for my family to live in over there. *Why would I do all that just to kill its potential at the source?*

More questions and some actual answers piled up.

If I were a numerologist, I'd have been a little freaked out, because for our nineteen times together, Richet had a total of nineteen boxes of paperwork and documents stacked high.

But in all her research, she *hadn't* investigated the origin of the lidocaine! For some reason, she never would. (Or if she did, *that* answer never saw the light of day.)

I was incensed. But I wouldn't give up. I challenged her on her interviews with the cops, again ripping at the interpreter while looking squarely at Richet.

"Did any two or three policemen corroborate one another's stories? Did they all say the same thing? No? Hell, they were all there. Did they tell you who was in charge or giving the orders; who was telling whom to do what? Did any two or three policemen or firemen tell the same story at all?!"

Richet looked down.

I told the interpreter to ask her again.

And again, I got one of those: "I'll be the one asking the questions here, Mr. Maher, not you!"

"Tell her I take that as a definite no," I practically spat at the interpreter.

Then Patricia Richet toughened her tactics, reloading with emotional hollow-points.

"Ah, Mr. Maher," she said through the translator, "I can see how frustrating this is for you. And I can see how I'm getting ready to break you. I *will* break you!"

No, you sure as hell won't!

"You're not breaking anything," I said. "But you *are* pushing me into a corner." I stood up and two of the policemen *sur la garde* grabbed me.

I kept talking.

"You're pushing me into a corner where I want to take this chair and throw it at your ass. But you know what? I'm not going to do it. And you know what else? I'm not coming back here to see you anymore.

"I've been here for almost three years. I've cooperated a hundred and ten percent. I've been called a liar, a thief, a murderer, everything. And then we leave, and then we come back; and invariably you admit, 'Mr. Maher, you're telling me the truth,' that you found out this was true and that was true. I've proven myself time and time again to you."

I always looked right into her eyes as I spoke—as I was telling the truth.

"But now, madame," I said, "I'm through."

I sat down. The room we were in held two attorneys; a total of three special police-men; the interpreter; Patricia Richet; and me. Things became very strained after I made my emancipation proclamation.

Richet ignored what I had said and simply continued on *comme d'habitude*. She would ask a question in French to me via the interpreter; the interpreter would then address me. But then you'd hear the theme song to Final *Jeopardy*. Because I wasn't saying anything. Two, three, four, five minutes would go by. Then finally the interpreter would look at Richet and state the silent obvious: *"Il ne dit pas n'importe quoi . . ."*

"Je suis conscient!" Richet would say through clenched teeth. *I am aware.*

This went on for three more hours.

Finally, everything quieted into a dead-zone where we just stared at one another. I turned to the interpreter and shattered the silence with one final statement: "Tell her I'll never see her ass again."

Somehow Richet caught the gist of *that* without the aid of literal translation.

"Quoi?!"

Richet started yelling and the interpreter got busy: "She says she'll order you back. She will forcibly bring you back."

No . . . she won't.

I returned to the prison, walked in, sat down, and said to the officials and to any-one else within range: "I'm not eating and I'm not drinking and now you have a problem. Mark my words: I'm a man of resolve. I don't care what it is, if I put my mind to something, it's done. You have a problem here."

I will not wait any longer, I thought. *I'm losing my family and my life. I've held on well into this third year. I've had it. It's become more than ominously obvious that I'm only decaying in this dark dungeon as a sacrifice to the "sunny place" of Monaco, so why not become a real sacrifice? I'll starve myself until I get a trial.*

Richet must have actually thought she was going to break me. *Never.* We had, however, reached a breaking point. And time would tell just who would break whom. The most high-profile inmate on the planet would make for an ugly media-attracting corpse rattling chains along *le golden rues de Monaco . . .*

CHAPTER 31

THE HUNGER STRIKE

May 2002

I wasn't eating.

I was in bed.

I had resolve, but they still needed to control me. They transferred me from the jail to Princess Grace Hospital. They kept my lights on all the time. I was handcuffed and my feet were shackled; no turning, no getting up, flat on my back.

Very eerily crucifixion-style.

Twenty-three and a half hours a day I was like this.

In the mornings, they'd take off my shirt and I could shed the bedpan and *really* go to the bathroom and clean up—whether I needed to or not. With the rest of my generous half-hour, I got on the bed and did jumping jacks. I was doing squatting exercises, getting my blood flowing, anything to keep things moving.

I wasn't eating, true, but nor was I suicidal. I was intent. I had to do *something.* The average person—and even the well-above-average person—could not go on like this.

After the fourth day, they got worried.

"He's really serious . . ."

Five days.

Six days.

Whatever I had to do, I knew I could do it.

The word got out; the hospital had leaks telling the whole world that the American was going through something.

"What the hell is going on here? You can't do this to an American citizen!"

I mean, Prince Albert—getting ready to succeed to his father, Prince Rainer's, "throne"—is half-American for god's sake! His mother is Grace Kelly! *America's* Grace Kelly! Entertaining the world with Hitchcock, Sinatra, Crosby, Cooper, Grant, Stewart, and Holden—*that* Grace Kelly!

But right now I wasn't feeling quite as hero-psyched or noble as Grace in *High Noon*:

> I don't care who's right or who's wrong.
> There's got to be some better way for people to live . . . [102]

Maybe, but right now I needed fluids to survive. I refused to get anything intravenously because I didn't trust those bastards, but I managed to get down a routine minimum of drinks with high sucrose, minerals, and vitamins.

Then came the injections. Since I was lying on my back for twenty-three and a half hours at a stretch, they shot me with Heparin, an anti-coagulant. They were worried I was going to throw a blood clot or get thrombosis because I wasn't moving—I couldn't move because they had me handcuffed and chained! I refused each shot, though, until I could see it in the vial. And I made sure it was sealed and contained and that I saw the nurse put the whole thing together before I got stuck with it. They could have been injecting me with Ebola for all I knew.

Again, I didn't trust them. And for good reason.

From the first day it was, "Oh, we'll show him. There's no way anybody's going to be able to stick this out."

Certainement . . . not with the full chaining down, the 24/7 lights, and all the rest.

But I am not just anybody.

What saved me was my training—my psychological training. I knew this was a waiting game, and I would win. They would lose. The end.

During my big half-hour of hygiene hijinks, they would bring me into the bathroom where a female guard would watch me, to try to psychologically break me down while I was completely naked. It was an old, old tactic.

I didn't break.

"Oh yeah, baby, you want some of this?!" I asked.

She was mortified. *There's* your breaking.

Then I started to shave. With a disposable razor.

A *weapon!*

"He's got a blade!" somebody yelled.

It was there for me to shave with, but now they were *afraid* of it! Law enforcement in Monaco never disappointed when it came to entertainment—if you liked slapstick.

They took away the little plastic Gillette and gave me a full-on electric job, complete with charging cord.

I unplugged the cord from the razor and threw the razor to one of the three guards now watching what was left of my thirty minutes of grooming. His hands went out and caught it, and when he looked up at me, I was holding both ends of the cord like a wild-eyed psycho-killer wielding his *garrote*.

"Look at what a nice tool this is, huh?" I said. "Lots better than that crappy little plastic thing. How fucking stupid are you guys, anyway?!"

The next day they gave me back my razors.

———

As I lay there in that bed for twenty-three-hour period after twenty-three-hour period, I thought about so many of the political prisoners I had heard and read about who suffered through incredibly long hunger strikes. And here I was, an American citizen, and I knew that I held the trump card. For good or ill, it made a difference. If something happened to me, there was much that Monaco would have to pay. We'd see how long they were willing to roll these deadly dice.

Their latest throw of the bones came up with a four—four psychiatrists. They came into my room with true *concern*: "Mr. Maher, Mr. Maher, are you okay?"

"Sure I am!" I said. "Gosh, there's no smoking allowed here like there is in the cell block. I love this."

"Well, you can't go on like this."

"Sure I can," I told them. "The only thing I need is the love of my family; and I already have that."

They all looked at each other. Then they signed their little forms, shuffled some paperwork, and quietly walked out. They knew right away I wasn't crazy. They also knew that I knew they were whores to the system. I was sure that at some stage of their growing up, they'd all read *The Emperor's New Clothes*, reaching out to touch and expose European monarchy. Now they were living it. Here they were in Monaco, working out of Princess Grace Hospital, being paid an exorbitant amount of money to take care of the few people in it and nothing more than that.

Why would they stick themselves in the limited confines of Monte Carlo instead of enjoying monster practices in France or Rome? Why would a prestigious psychiatric doctor be stabled into a corner of this holding company of a hospital if he wasn't just another of the Monaco spread-'em-for-cash street-team?

One especially gushing trans-Atlantic leak about what was going on was Manasse pouring out the saga to Griffith. That led to a visit—a visit that made the news in a detailed report by Court TV's John Springer:

> Heidi Maher recently returned from a rushed and hushed trip to Monaco with a lawyer [Michael Griffith] and Ted Maher's mother . . . to persuade her husband to end a hunger strike protesting harassing, closed-court interrogations by Richet.
>
> In early May, Ted stopped accepting food from his guards at the hilltop prison where he is being held . . . He was transferred to the psychiatric wing of Princess Grace Hospital, where he was kept under 24-hour guard as the protest continued.
>
> . . . Griffith learned of the hunger strike from Ted Maher's court-appointed Monegasque lawyer, who wanted it stopped . . .
>
> Heidi said she was strip-searched before being allowed to enter a small hospital room where her husband, dressed only in a hospital gown, was confined.
>
> She noticed that his 6-foot-1-inch frame appeared considerably lighter, and his blond hair had turned white. A guard pulled out his sidearm and stood between the couple after Heidi rushed forward to hug her husband for the first

time in 18 months. It took Heidi three more visits and a promise by the prison to deliver Ted's letter to Prince Rainier, to get Ted to end his 11-day hunger strike . . .

"I have collaborated to the full extent of my ability for more than 500 days. *I* will not be brought forth for interrogation by her for the sole purpose of being harassed, demeaned or ridiculed," the defendant wrote.

Toward the end of the letter the prisoner hinted that he might entertain a deal to lesser charges.

"I am not asking for any special treatment or favors. I am only asking for what is right: that the charges be reduced to their just proportion as Judge Richet knows they should be," Ted told Rainier. "I must ask you this for the sake of my wife and *my* three little children."

Ted's *wife* knew about the planned hunger strike and endorsed it, confident that Ted would make his point without harming himself.

"I supported his starting it and supported his ending it," Heidi said of the hunger strike. "He did it out of protest, not out of depression at all."

Griffith thought the hunger strike was a bad move . . . "I tried to impress upon him and stress that you don't want to piss off the person who controls the keys to the jailhouse door."[103]

—John Springer, Court TV

Two weeks in

Heidi, my mother, and Griffith are back in New York. Despite the media reports, they *didn't* convince me to stop the hunger strike.

Conversely, there was something I failed to convince Heidi of: staying away from my trial.

I already foresaw the event as a classic one-way inquisition, in which those administering the pain would get what they wanted, prevailing over any vestiges of the truth. I didn't want my wife to witness all the blood-letting and the lies.

I also didn't want her to be eaten by the media.

"If all this Monegasque manure gets smeared around a court of law," I explained, "shit's going to happen that I don't want you to hear."

Because if I didn't lie, if I didn't confess to the witchcraft that offed Edmond Safra and stained Monte Carlo, well, they'd toss away the key to this American pig's cell and throw me to the dogs in a French prison where my lineage might not make me Mr. Popular. Inside, I felt confident I could take out a few people, but let's be real: when ten militant Muslim brothers jump your ass, I don't care who you are or how good you are, you're going down. In a big way.

And I was *already* gonna go down at the trial.

I knew what this scene would be, and it sickened me. I knew the court would ask me if I stood by my signed "statements," and I knew I would have to say yes. And I'd be ready to throw up. I knew I would look out at the crowded courtroom, wanting people to know I had no choice in any of this, and that I had to go with what they were telling me to say.

But when I looked out, I *didn't* want to see Heidi.

"But I want to be there, Ted. I love you . . ."

She insisted on coming—assuming we finally went to trial, that is.

Despite knowing what could and would probably happen, I still had my resolve. Resolve that was now driving the Monegasque out of their minds—*hors de leur esprit* as I continued my hunger strike. It became a high part of the game to ask me again and again what I wanted, and then to just ignore me.

But I was getting harder and harder to ignore. One afternoon again I was asked what I wanted; this time they seemed to care *juste un peu*. Or maybe they were just sick to death of me.

"I want what I've always wanted," I told them. "To have this ended. I'm done with Richet and I want to be brought to trial. I want the free world to see just what went on so I can get back to my life and my family and pick up the pieces. I can't keep going on and on and on like this."

"Well, that's all you want?"

My god, could it be that I was actually getting closer?

"Yes!" I told them. "That's all I want! What part of this don't you understand?"

———

There was, however, something *I* didn't understand. Something I didn't know. Something neither Georges Blot nor Donald Manasse nor the cops nor Patricia Richet nor anyone else bothered to tell me. Something neither Michael Griffith nor I had uncovered in our research of the Monegasque way. Something I had no idea of as I was wasting and choking through yet another day of no food.

It was this: if I was not brought to trial within three years of my arrest, I walked. It was Monegasque law!

This tiny, overlooked chunk of *informations importantes* had just hit number one on my list of "Things I Don't Know!"

And here's how it factored in: While a trial would primarily be about me and the ramifications of my confession, Patricia Richet was inviting others to participate in the games at the party.

For all of her ass-reaming of me, Theodore the Accused, Richet was also sifting through the muck left behind by the Monegasque-inept. She was dissecting everyone that stepped in their own *selles* and had a hand in the death of Edmond Safra.

She may have been a pit-bull bitch, but at a diminutive hundred and five pounds, Richet had gotten especially tall and forceful in taking a stand against the police and fire departments—the entirety of the *force publique*. After she trod through the manure that made up all those interviews she did with the cops and firefighters, she refused to close the file (Monegasque legalese for sending a case to trial). I believed that by now, she smelled the shit-stench of a conspiracy. She got serious about just where the recordings of the communications between the emergency agencies for that day had landed. Why, indeed, had the tapes from the fire department and the different police agencies—the regular police, their SWAT-like bunch, their traffic cops, etc.—not yet been brought forward?

"I want those recordings on my desk now!"

"But, *nous excuser*, Mademoiselle Richet, we have the tapes from all the agencies for the day before and the day after, but for the date in question we have *rien . . .*"

Wow—what a fortuitous fluke. (My personal guess is that, by now, they're sitting in the casket with Prince Rainier.)

So Richet issued an ultimatum: "I will not close this file until there is a criminal indictment issued against the Monaco police and fire departments for their part in this travesty!"

Well, that wasn't going to happen. Monaco's authorities were not going to give her those indictments. But no way were they going to let me walk, either.

Something had to give.

And while all of this was going on, I was not-so-fat, dumb, and somewhat happy, figuring I was applying leverage to get the trial going.

I was.

But I was in the dark about the three-year rule *and* about the pressure Richet was applying. As far as I knew, my stay here in the bowels of Monaco's jail was open-ended. As far as I knew, this throw-away-the-key song and dance could linger on until "Every Little Breeze Seems to Whisper Louise" hit the top ten again.

CHAPTER 32
THE WAY WE DO IT IN MONACO

"That's the way we do it in Monaco."

I was told that over and over again.

"That's the Monaco way . . ."

It was just something else that made me want to heave every time I heard it. For months and months and months, I was hit with that phrase whenever the logic and truth in anything was skewed and twisted. It was getting really old.

I heard it from the prison *directeur*, Charlie Marson, every time life was made more difficult for me in there.

Team Blot-Manasse said it when they convinced me to stay with the guilty plea.

Things, however, had changed. The way things were being done now was that I wasn't eating. I was bringing pressure on these bastards as I was also slowly dying. Confession or no, I wanted that trial, I wanted the truth to be known, and I wanted to get the hell out of there and get back to my family.

The dynamic that Michael Griffith had brought may not have completely turned things around, but the slapstick was gone from the act. Hamlet was expounding that "there is nothing either good or bad, but thinking makes it so"; while Moe had put down the big wooden mallet and was no longer chasing Larry.

And I still wasn't eating.

At that point prison officials, including the director, were added to my list of visitors at Princess Grace. They arrived with a message: I would have my trial if I ended my hunger strike.

Hmmm . . .

Deal?

Now we were back to *High Noon*, with a who's-quickest-out-of-the-holster stand-off. Had I won or had I backed myself into a setup? The one hidden bullet I had was that everyone on the outside knew about this now. Nothing was being sliced off, burned, whipped, or maimed in some faceless dungeon.

They had to be telling me the truth, didn't they? This had been about PR since the beginning and nothing had changed in that shallow end of the give-us-your-money publicity pool.

"Get the key to these chains and get me some food."

"Yes, Mr. Maher . . ."

I stayed at the hospital another two days getting my system restarted after not eating. Then it was back to the layers of bars at Maison D'Arret. But this time I had something to wait for.

At last.

Working my way back to health, I readied for trial. The process was rolling. Patricia Richet would preside. Michael Griffith would be my reinforcement behind the sure-to-retreat Blot-Manasse, lobbing in whatever truth grenades and evidence bombs he could use to blow holes in the party line.

But somewhere in the midst of the ups and optimism and preparation, Donald Manasse made his way through the prison's eight levels of security to come a-calling.

"Ted!" he said to me. "Yes, yes they are closing the file, and this will all go to trial, but we have a little situation."

A situation?

"They got rid of her—Patricia Richet. They removed the senior magistrate."

What?!

And who the fuck is "they"?

"They" was apparently Prince Rainier, who could do whatever he wanted to. And *apparently* what he'd wanted to do was sign an executive order transferring Richet into a cushy judge job in Paris. If they couldn't muzzle the pugnacious mutt who wanted indictments of the Monaco police and fire departments, they sure as hell could remove her.

After three years of at least knowing this case *de l'intérieur et de l'extérieur*, after three years of depositions, investigations, contortions, and confrontations—Richet was simply gone.

I just stared at Manasse. Any optimism I had was being burned out of me like hot metal on my flesh. I could almost hear the hiss. I could almost smell my skin frying amid the white-hot emotional torture.

"They've elevated the junior magistrate, Jean-Christophe Hullin," Manasse went on, "and he's telling us they're now going to ask for twelve years."

I was still staring.

Twelve fucking years?

What the hell?!

All this shit about a shepherd in his fields and a token three-year sentence and my getting back with my family. Now, by the time I got out, I'd be ripe and ready for the Senior Soup & Salad menu at Denny's. It had all been a scam.

Twelve years?!

And just who the hell was this Jean-Christophe Hullin? We'd never seen each other or met or even screamed at one another in golden moments like those I'd shared with Patricia Richet.

Jean-Christophe Hullin?

No meeting?

No interviews?

Oh yeah, I could see it. I could feel it. Here you are, a junior magistrate, just becoming something in the Monte Carlo system. You're working on money-laundering and all these other cases that show the free world how straight-arrow you are when you really aren't doing anything. And now all of sudden, this career boost lands in your lap and you become the man in the biggest legal case in Monte Carlo history.

But, wait, the only requirement is that you play off the same sheet music as the rest of the band. You have to march in line.

Non?

Oui!

But of course.

Within two weeks of Hullin's appointment, we were indeed scheduled for trial. But I was being screwed at every turn.

Le pont a été empilé.

Although Prince Rainier was ill and dying, I knew he was tits-deep in this, along with the minister of justice, *and* the procurer, *and* the judge of instruction. This was all so planned out.

A few days later, amidst my pacing and pending apoplexy at all that was going down, Manasse waddled in again.

With even more tidings of comfort and joy.

"Ted," he started, nonchalant and easy, "you realize that there was a three-year statute of limitations on this matter, don't you?"

I was back to that now-familiar stare as—again—I just looked at him. It was becoming a terminal habit. This genius would show up like Cleopatra's messenger with all his toxic news tidbits, lay them on me, and then stand there looking like a wounded basset hound. It was all so hard to believe; it was so hard to get any kind of a hold on this.

"Uh, Donald," I said, trying to stay sane, "where did you get *this* bit of information?"

"Oh, I just learned about it," he told me.

"Donald," I started off slowly, "you're my defense attorney.

"And, Donald, *you* realize that I was just on a *two-week* hunger strike—not eating a thing!" I was losing it. "I could have thrown a blood clot and lost my life, just to get this thing moving! And you're just now telling me that there's a statute of limitations of three years!"

Blood boiling, I continued my rant. "Donald, maybe you could have said something like, 'Oh, hey, Ted old buddy, why don't you just hold off on that thought process and save yourself half a month of not eating, lying there in bed, chained up like Hannibal Lecter, because one way or another something is probably going to happen here soon.'

"What the hell, Donald?!" I spat. "'Oh, I just learned about it . . .' I'm so happy you're educating yourself at my expense, you asshole!

"And for god's sake, Donald, Georges *must* have known about this! Just what the fuck is going on here?!"

It wasn't the calmest of days in the annals of attorney-client rapport.

Would Patricia Richet have let me walk? Would she have directed her venom even further at the cops and fire department while I just drifted out the jailhouse door?

And what—if anything—would indicting them have ultimately solved? Making the authorities look like fools for "their part"? Cutting my sentence? Lengthening it? Conjuring up some kind of Lourdes-like miracle, in which the entire judiciary would suddenly be visited by apparitions and visions of who was really behind Safra's death? Or would my trial continue to be what I predicted from the start: a neatly calculated, minute-by-minute shredding of a scapegoat taking the fall for unnamed and unseen gods of gold?

November 7, 2002

A week before the trial was set to start, I was suddenly called in by Hullin—*oh joy, we would finally meet!* With him were two junior magistrates and three Monegasque jurors.

Hullin spoke: "Don't worry that none of your attorneys are here, Mr. Maher. This is just an informal thing."

Nothing *très important.*

"But, Mr. Maher, we do want you to know that Michael Griffith at this time will not be able to participate in the trial."

Excuse me?!

"Mr. Griffith," they reiterated, "will not be able to participate."

"Is this about language?" I said. "I know he doesn't speak French, but I also know that there'll be two interpreters in there. Look, Michael Griffith is my attorney and he will participate or I won't be participating!"

"Well, I'm sorry," said Hullin, "but you *will* participate, and Mr. Griffith will not. I won't tolerate Anglo-Saxon justice in my courtroom!

"That, Mr. Maher, is the way we do it in Monaco!"

CHAPTER 33

THE TRIAL: ACT ONE

MAHER TRIAL STARTS TODAY

The world's press is descending on Monaco as the trial of American nurse Ted Maher opens today in Monaco's criminal court. The court has only thirty spaces for press representatives and almost every major news organization wants a seat. International news crews have flown in to report every twist and turn in what promises to be the most sensational court case Monaco has ever seen.[104]

—Jenny Paul, *The Riviera Gazette*

November 21, 2002
Twelve days.

We all had an interesting twelve days in our futures. When it began, of course, none of us knew just how long this trial would take. But from the splashy and flashy trailers I surmised just how this *cinéma* would turn out. For the next twelve days, or twelve minutes, or however long we would be in our officially assigned seats, the gilded moments ahead of us would provide a glittering stage for the glory that is the Principality of Monaco.

The proceedings were not merely the "Trial of the Century" [105]—*non, monsieur!*—these proceedings would be the formal Proscenium Opening from which Monaco could demonstrate to the rest of planet Earth the slick truth behind their claims at being a nation-Nirvana, the perfect corner of the civilized world.

But, yes, of course!

I could already smell the greasepaint and I would soon hear the roar of the crowd. *I knew.*

But I also knew that if any hard evidence was allowed to come out, even slightly, the whole trial would go belly-up. There would have to be an acquittal, and I would walk. Real evidence would boomerang on the fire department and the Keystone Cops, and this whole steaming mess would be poured down their shorts.

But like so much else that hadn't gone my way, I knew it was a long shot. Patricia Richet had been exiled, and my *real* attorney might not even be able to get a loge ticket to the show.

I could see so much. In my mind I saw Monaco's law enforcers constructing the gallows and rolling in the guillotine.

The media was right on the money with their prediction of a sensational show; it would be worth the price of admission. However, there would be *some* surprises.

One of the first of the "twists and turns in what promises to be the most sensational court case Monaco has ever seen" screeched around the bend when Michael Griffith was suddenly reinstated and permitted to dance in the chorus line of my defense team.

Public relations concerns, my bitching, and maybe some behind-the-scenes direction and strategy sessions probably all had something to do with it. But Hullin was not going to fully bend to "Anglo-Saxon justice" in *his* courtroom.

Michael Griffith was still reeled in on several levels.

First, he had to wear the traditional French judicial *vêtements*, wrapped in the regalia of a flowing robe. This was obviously just cosmetic, but also a bit psychological.

Viva le différence!

No.

However, the meat of the Monegasque manipulation was the second stipulation: that Griffith was not permitted to speak openly in the courtroom. He could not cross-examine directly. He had to present questions to the controlling attorney, the illustrious Donald Manasse. And *if* Manasse thought that what Griffith was posing was pertinent and valid, Manasse could then allow it.

Plus, everything was being buffered through the court translators.

Still, having even a harnessed-back Michael Griffith on my team provided at least something in the way of hope for me. I had told Blot and Manasse that Griffith would use the media to our benefit. I had begun to know him. He was not Jacques Vergès. He was not a media *hound*, but he knows people all over the world. He would take chunks of this case and chew on them. He'd bring in expert witnesses.

The biggest fish on the expert-witness plate prepared by Griffith was Dr. Michael M. Baden, the number one forensic pathologist in the world; then-host for HBO's show *Autopsy* and the Forensic Science Contributor for Fox News.

Baden had a few things he wanted to say about Safra's and Vivian's autopsies and, in particular, the way Vivian had died.

Griffith also had witnesses lined up from the fire department in New York City. He pulled in police presence and statements from Scotland Yard. He had experts take the stand to explain that oxygen is the number one priority in safe house design—and that whoever designed this area of La Belle Époque had messed up big time.

Within the context of my clung-to confession about purposely laying out this ludicrous scheme, everything Michael Griffith had assembled was designed to show my limited liability in its effects.

Griffith presented his work to Blot and Manasse. "Here's the report from the police department . . . here's this . . . here's that . . . this is what we're going to show. This is going to be one heck of a trial, boy!"—but he was danced around and shrugged off.

The rest of the team had their own super-case to prep for.

"What will we have for lunch today, Georges?"

"I don't know, Donald . . . how about the duck?"

Yessiree . . . one heck of a trial . . .

The physical setting of the courtroom and the tribunal acrobatics were different from in the United States—as different as Coney Island hot dogs and *Escargot de Bourgogne*.

First, in the United States, a testifying defendant is called up to the stand. Not here. In the Monegasque playbook, the defendant is always under oath, always seated in a special "box" and always available to be questioned by any of the attorneys, *whenever*. It was very oppressive.

I say attorneys, plural, because there were nineteen of them in the room! And only four were on my side—and only *one* of them was actually working to help me. Besides Griffith, I had the impatient-to-get-me-declared-guilty-and-go-to-dinner set, aided by Sandrine Setton who fit like Mickey Mouse's glove into the "sidekick" caricature category . They were quite the cavalry. In addition to my team, the courtroom was filled with lawyers for every party present: fire department party lawyers, cop party lawyers, Vivian Torrente's party lawyers, and Lily Safra's party lawyers (one of whom was the former justice minister of France). These were civil lawyers, as the entire spectrum of injured people in a criminal trial could each be represented by their own attorney.

It was like a bar convention, or a hospital waiting room after a train wreck. These lawyers added to the crowd scene and each of the nineteen was distractingly involved. Some were merely there to make their presence known; quietly observing, though on a constant lookout for anything that might in any way impugn their clients.

Lily Safra's attorney, Marc Bonnant, was not one of those. Bonnant was ever on-the-move, speaking and steering everything that was even remotely *implicating* away from his beloved and regal client.

Oppressive.

Now, any and all of those attorneys and any and all people called up to the Monaco court's version of an actual witness stand could theoretically put in their two euro-cents about me. But they couldn't say anything *directly* to me; they had to channel through my attorney. And then the attorney had to address me through an interpreter. They would say to Blot or Manasse, "Monsieur this, Monsieur that . . ." and I would answer the question, going back through that long linguistic pipeline. All with the stenographer typing away in triple time.

This was nothing like *Perry Mason*. It was *un cirque!*

And, as with any circus, you had your three rings, your animal cages, and your clowns.

There were the three main judges, including Hullin, and the Monegasque jury box with the three puppets who rounded out the total of six "jurors."

Then there was me, the lamb exposing his throat to the knife; and over there was the procurer general—the top banana prosecutor, Daniel Serdet—and then there was the altar and the crucifix.

Yes, a crucifix.

A courtroom totem of Jesus Christ on the cross—the biggest I've ever seen—hung above the judges.

Father, forgive them; for they know not what they do . . .

When someone was being questioned, they would come right up to the middle of the courtroom, facing this *altar*, where the respective attorneys, procurers, and judges would administer their prophecy and sermons. I didn't, however, see anyone bless themselves at the foot of the shrine.

The circus then spread to the carnival midway. Out there in the gallery-audience sat reps from every international newspaper. They were elbow-to-elbow with Dominick Dunne, movie producers, and everyone else from all corners of the media.

Fine.

Bienvenue!

But few of those people could speak French. They each needed an interpreter in their ear telling them what was going on.

Come one, come all!

Now, let's get started!

Ladies, gentlemen, boys and girls of all ages, welcome to the Greatest Show on Earth!

Step right this way!

The procurer opened the gate by reading the charges against me, mainly their weird semantic-twist on "arson by communication" translated into "arson to lived-in premises resulting in the death of two persons found there,"[106] which they backed up with a couple of their confusing (especially in translation) articles of law:

Article 372: Any one spreading the fire to one of the properties listed in the previous articles, by willfully setting fire to any properties, belonging to himself or to others, and placed in such a way as to spread the said fire, shall be punished with the same penalty as if he had directly set fire to one of the said properties.

Article 373: In all these cases, the penalty shall be life imprisonment if the fire, for anyone being in the premises, resulted in death, injuries or invalidity defined in the second paragraph of Article 236.[107]

Of course, that part about "life imprisonment" was not confusing in the least.

It was an incentive to stay focused and alert.

I made myself a pain in everyone's *judiciaire arrière* from the start. I immediately stood up in the box after the charges were read. Speaking through the interpreter, with everybody staring at me—including my wife, who I'd been unable to convince not to attend—I asked the procurer how they could charge me with this when they knew there wasn't any actual arson involved.

I remember their response well: It was *my* act of lighting the fire that led to the tragic blaze that killed Mr. Safra.

But what about the law's stipulation of the fire being "placed in such a way as to spread the said fire"?

Let's see . . . I placed the trashcan in the center of the room, away from curtains or other flammables. In fact, it took three hours for that flame to spread.

Plus, if I had intended to torch the place, why would I have positioned it directly under the smoke detector? Wouldn't I in fact have disabled the alarm somehow?

By no stretch of the imagination could any claim that spreading the fire was my goal.

I wanted to get clarification on that; I wanted everybody to understand that crucial fact!

Years later, when I appeared on *Dateline*, statements made on the show indicated that I at one point denied lighting the fire.[108] That, like so much else involved in the media swirl, wasn't true. I have *never* denied lighting the fire in the *poubelle*. I *did* light the fire—for one purpose: to set off the alarm! Which it did!

The cavalry was supposed to come and *put it out.*

I mean, hell, what if the blaze had spread two days after I lit the tiny flame, and no one had put it out in all that time?

When were the people who did nothing going to be implicated?

I went further, again expounding with my analogy of "arson by communication" being like "premeditated murder via ricocheting bullet."

The procurer then advanced from the charges to noting the little matter of the confession: "Mr. Maher, do you agree with the body of admissions you have made within the confession you signed?"

Here it was.

L'heure de vérité.

I had to hesitate. I knew what people were saying about me. I *wanted* to come out with something like, "Is everybody in this fucking courtroom crazy?! Don't you see all the bullshit that they're slinging?!"

That is what I *wanted* to say, but nope. I wasn't going to make myself look like a raving lunatic, so I had to do things in a very *laissez-faire* way; the French way.

I had to be very straight.

I stood there, knowing that I couldn't answer "no."

Body language kicked in. I was method acting, playing things out like I had with Patricia Richet. I internalized, developing the sensory, the psychological, and the emotional.

I will never forget my response. It hadn't changed over the course of three years: "I stand by this confession . . . [Pause: slowly look around at the courtroom and the audience] . . . *at this time.*"

My words had to go through an interpreter, but the English speakers there were a step ahead with their raised eyebrows.

My actions spoke loudly, to ensure that my intent could not be missed in *any* language. I was sending a message to anybody and everybody out there, just begging the question: "What is he saying that for, 'at this time'?"

"Sounds like maybe he's being blackmailed or some other shit's going on that we're not aware of . . ."

"Maybe we don't know everything . . ."

The procurer asked me again.

My answer remained, with even more emphasis: *"At. This. Time."*

I would make this first day in court *très memorable*. After the reading of the charges—and my commentary—I had a few questions about the selection of the three civilian jurors.

The exchange went something like this:

"We are clearly playing a game here and I must know the rules; beginning with the jurors. How are they chosen?" I asked.

"Random selection," I was quickly told.

"What does that mean?" I pushed. "Did you guys use like a voting pool, or was it like a lottery? Did you stick their names in a hat and pull them out?"

The translator sort of smiled. "Do you really want me to say this?" she asked me.

"Yes, I want you to say it just like that."

There may have been a cultural disconnect when it came to the names-in-a-hat stuff, but the slightly muted conversation the translator and I were having wasn't going to be tolerated. That led to a ban on my speaking directly to her during the in-session proceedings.

That would not last long.

Then, after the final "random selection" answer to my continued annoying questions about the jury pool, Donald and I had our first *debate*.

"What the hell are you doing?!" he screamed at me.

"I want to find out what's going on here! You're not doing anything and I'm really not up to being that sacrificial lamb without some kind of a fight—some kind of a statement or two! 'Random selection'—what the hell does that mean?"

"Ted," he said, "just sit down!"

"No, I'm not going to sit down, Donald. I want to know how they picked those damned jurors. Who are they? Everyone should know whose pocket they're in! Are they going to have a cruise after this is over with? Or are they going to count the millions in their secret bank accounts? I want to know how they picked these people and telling me *random selection* doesn't tell me shit!"

Yep, we started off just like that. And as things got going, it didn't seem like any cohesive plan was in place to coordinate this Trial of the Century. It looked like it was all about high hopes that this would be a low-volume expository-only prelude into who, how, why, when, and where.

"Prosecution, call a witness."

The introductory witness was fittingly one of the first cops—*policies*—to have arrived on the scene on that December 3 morning. My guess is that he was designated to go first in bringing this drama to life because he was dull and dour and simply offered an exposition. He made for the perfect nondescript, non-distracting narrator who could get the audience involved in clear journalistic facts right away—and make sure that Ted Maher was at the center of everything.

Speaking through Manasse and the interpreter, Griffith jumped on the guy, seeing him as red meat in the hungry circle of what he hoped would be conciliar carnage.

Griffith didn't let the guy tell his basic story. Michael questioned and shook the cop into bumbling through a nervous tale that exposed Monaco's finest as a headless band running back and forth, getting in each other's way as they scrambled for armored vests, guns, and helmets. The cop tried his stammering best to present a slick and professional police operation, but the bright lights and Griffith's hot questioning melted his story. Their cop-op came off as the "What the hell do we do?" mess that it was.

The kicker came when the guy-with-a-badge noted that when I stumbled downstairs and collapsed, the Belle Époque's concierge told police there was a "hostage situation: man shot and wounded."[109] Griffith smelled blood. Because, of course, I was knifed, not shot. Again, having to use the prescribed, long-way-around method of questioning, their dialogue went something like this:

"Have you ever seen a gunshot wound before?"

"No."

"Have you ever seen a knife wound before?"

"No."

"How long have you been on the Monaco police force?"

"Twenty-two years."

"Hmmm, interesting . . . what's the worst injury you've ever seen in those twenty-two years?"

"Well, one time one guy hit another guy over the head with a champagne bottle."[110]

If I didn't want to cry, I would have laughed.

Was that a low-brow Don Perignon, or a vintage magnum of Rotheschild's Opus One?
I wanted to ask. *Cause that's the way we do it in Monaco!*

Griffith just rolled his eyes.

The witness pool got deeper but stayed with the straight-ahead read-the-reports, lay-out-the-story kind of theme. Monaco's police chief took the stand and coldly related what he saw. Griffith jumped in again, searching for some type of recognition of negligence within the emergency personnel. Surely this chief had looked into the biggest atrocity ever to occur on his watch. Everyone else saw it.

Griffith's questioning went along these lines:

"Was there an investigation into the actions—or non-actions—of the police?"

"No."

"Was anybody reprimanded?"

"No."

"Has anyone been demoted?"

"No."

Griffith shook his head and looked down.[111]

Next was the electrifying performance of the two Monegasque investigators whom I woke up to in the hospital: Captain "I speak English" Oliver Jude and the ever-gloom-and-doom low-budget gendarme, Gerard Tiberti. They were the architects of *la confession*.

Griffith was more than disgusted, and I was getting dangerously edgy.

And this was just day one.

Because Jude and Tiberti were each being questioned about the same matter, they had been separated. Jude appeared first, then Tiberti. Their stories conflicted and I was losing it. Listening through the interpreters, I was thinking, *Time-out!*

"They're lying!" I said to Griffith. "Do you see this?!" I was going crazy!

Now, Griffith told me to calm down.

Calm down? With my life on the line?!

Life imprisonment . . .

I was flaming mad! Manasse and Blot were doing nothing, and Griffith looked like he was about to throw in the towel out of frustration. We were back to Moe and Larry pushing pies in their faces, and now even Hamlet was contemplating Yorick's skull.

Calm down?

FUCK calming down!

I disobeyed my communication ban and screamed at one of the interpreters (there were two because of the mountain of material being shot out every second): I asked her to read to us again how these two detectives had contradicted each other's stories; how they had lied!

Despite my passionate outbursts and demeanor, one interpreter and I had developed a good rapport. She had been a part of each and every one of Richet's interrogations, and she was French, not Monegasque.

While meeting with Richet, I noticed the interpreter was having trouble with one of her eyes. I recognized conjunctivitis just by looking at her. "You definitely have a bacterial infection," I told her. "It can cause a lot of serious damage real quick."

She followed up by seeing a doctor and got the potentially bad swelling and infection taken care of. That helped her to see the human side of me, apart from the "criminal" and "murderer" labels. Later, this interpreter helped me translate some of the more difficult documents I had to deal with. And she helped me pro bono, because I had absolutely no money.

So now, surrounded by *le cirque*, that interpreter was basically telling Griffith, "Yes, the two stories, they conflicted."

Donald was losing it again. He was like a raging bull, running back and forth screaming at me, "What the fuck are you doing?!"

"What I'm doing is trying to get at the truth here! Look at these guys: they're the two main pieces to this confession I was forced to sign, and they're perjuring themselves! When did Heidi come into the picture? Then? No, *then*. Was there a passport? There *wasn't* a passport. There *was* a passport. Was Ted shown a passport? *No.* Was he shown a passport? *Yes.* This is bullshit! One says yes, one says no. And they were in the same room—with me! This is crucial, Donald! This shows not only perjury but blackmail! This should blow their whole case right here! Doesn't anyone care that this whole police force hasn't even been well-trained in the fine art of complicity?!"

I guess I'd been wrong about the trial going belly-up if any evidence was allowed to come out. I guess I'd forgotten about the unwritten law so diligently applied to this case: *l'evidence, quelle evidence?*

Manasse took Griffith aside and told him, "You've got to understand the system in Monaco. If we persist like this, it will get really nasty. Ted will be in prison for life. You need to get him to sit down!"

Sure thing, because that's the way we do it in Monaco. They had the right to take away your judge and they had the right to deny your attorney. And it was obvious we weren't looking at a sentence for me of *only* four or five years. We never were.

We were looking at much more and headed for bigger and bigger hoopla under this shredded big top. Wonderful. The show must go on, and each time I tried to emote with the truth, Donald came up and said, "Ted, sit down! Every time you do that I have to try and fix what you said."

"What I said, Donald, was the truth! *You're* not doing that! You're not bringing up evidence! You're not doing *anything*! You have a report here that says the alarm went off for three hours! At what point did the fire chief realize there was a fire? Don't you think you should ask, do, or say something about slightly troubling things like that? And then, nearly two hours into things, you have a fireman who actually sees a small fire. Why don't you plan on getting that fireman up here and ask him why he didn't put that fire out? Richet did, but she's been kicked out of here; just in time for the hardcore stuff. She knew that fires usually get bigger not smaller. Why didn't you put out *le match* before it became *le torch*, Monsieur Fireman?

"Why the fuck *anything*, Donald?!"

CHAPTER 34

THE TRIAL: ACT TWO

November 22, 2002

Trials are like the tough-yet-tender pineapple: they have a rough and ripping outside and a vulnerable-when-exposed inside.

On a trial's outside are the observers, and that includes the jury and courtroom personnel. They are the ones who can go home after the judge says *ajournée*—in any language—or simply turn off their television sets or change the channel.

Only one person is truly on the inside of a trial, and that is the defendant. The defendant is the sole keeper of one hundred percent of what is going on one hundred percent of the time. The defendant is the only one directly in the slow swaying shadow of the noose.

In his or her soul, the defendant is the one who knows the truth. The truth—beyond the closest witnesses, beyond psychosis, beyond sociopathy, beyond anything.

And in a case like mine, the defendant is the one not going home. The defendant is the one who may never go home. The defendant is the one who is shuffled in restraints from where the authorities want him or her to be; not where he or she freely chooses to be, like those on the outside.

The defendant thinks about nothing else but the proceedings and what the future will be for him or her. It's incessant—there is no network to change or door to reach out and open.

Or close.

Being a defendant accused of a capital crime provides a unique perspective; it's one of those positions you have to endure to genuinely understand.

It radically alters the feeling of each new sunrise and morning.

It can turn twelve ordinary days into the tied-down horror of being buried alive.

And that's exactly what it felt like. The flow of the trial was dammed up quickly. What happened on the first day wouldn't happen again. It started off with such a bang: my *defining* of the charges; the stink and challenge I made about the jurors; then the whole ricocheted bullet thing. Then that first cop came to the stand, and Griffith made an ass of him; and then the chief, and the perjury of Jude and Tiberti; and—

But wait, Michael and I could not be the stars of this show! No Anglo-Saxon justice here!

Cut!

Manasse and Blot started pushing Michael further and further into the background.

After the initial ineptitude-injuries and truth-traumas of that opening day, the trial atmosphere slipped rapidly into a coma, and I was the one who was "under." It was like a tortuous plot in a dark and disturbing movie, I felt anesthetized but still aware of everything going on around me, trapped in a maddening inability to act.

With Griffith and me under control, the force of the trial's flow was now back to being tight and predictable.

Keep all of this simple.

Keep Maher in his box.

This part of the show intensified the basic how, why, when, and where scenes without input from Griffith or me.

Let's further examine what Mr. Maher did.

And the ramifications . . .

Safra's head of security, Samuel Cohen, took the stand. Even without Griffith's prodding, the throwing of the police and firefighters under *le autobus* continued, but by now it was obligatory—and of no real help to me. It was merely something that couldn't be swept away.

Facts were facts and the timeline was the timeline, and no one could dispute that Monaco's protectors of the peace didn't do their jobs. But the spin always came back to me. If it wasn't for what this man in the box did, the police and firefighters wouldn't have even been involved. That damn ricocheting bullet was blamed every time!

I clearly recall the security chief's testimony. Funneled through the translators, it went along these lines:

> I arrived quickly and I knew how to get into the penthouse. But when I got to Belle Époque, the police grabbed me. I told them I was the head of Mr. Safra's security, but they didn't believe me. They grabbed me, handcuffed me, and put me into a corner. I was kept there for about twenty minutes or so. Of course, at this time, the fire's getting bigger and bigger.
>
> Then, when they finally realized I was telling the truth, they let me go and I ran upstairs to the sixth floor, but the police once again screwed up. The police downstairs didn't tell the police upstairs that I was coming, so when I came—and I was willing to give my life for Edmond Safra—when I got upstairs, the police didn't know who I was, and they tackled me. They handcuffed me again and took me back out. It was a complete fiasco![112]

Accounts like this wove through the court room, filling the first couple of those twelve extraordinary days.

But so what? What was it doing for me?

The exposition phase of the show continued.

Discussions of architecture were constructed. Yves Lagrula, Henri Vieillard, and Ghislaine Reiss were among experts brought in by Griffith, and they were reluctantly allowed to testify. They "appraised operations" and "deplored the absence of a smoke removal system connected to the fire detectors."[113]

Yep, the place was a fire trap. But again, so what?

It was discovered that even the valance—yes, *that* valance—had a safety feature that in case of fire, it was supposed to automatically close to prevent air from coming in to feed the flames. But it didn't; one more thunder cell in this perfect storm. And more fatal fallout from the open valance.

The interior of the Safras' flat entered into the "safe house" discussions, and the man in charge of security and telecommunications for the entire building was brought in for another exciting episode of *Surveillance Soliloquy.*

But saying that the place should or shouldn't have been able to flare up like a two-dollar Te-Amo cigar really wasn't doing much to help out the lone defendant on the inside.

Michael Griffith, however, kept trying. He tried so hard to steer the subject back to my culpability, or rather my lack of it. But the frustration was getting thick as *garbure* stew.

Once again, Griffith attempted to make some kind of impact with his findings to Manasse and Blot. This time what he exhumed—or constructed—were careful architectural analyses concerning the accessibility to the Safras' residence quarters in La Belle Époque. Details I wasn't aware of back on the morning of December 3, 1999, were now about to be exposed. Griffith's homework as a surveyor could have my two assailants practically shaking hands with everyone in the court. But the optimistic and key words here were "could have . . ."

"Hey, guys—get this!" said Griffith to Manasse and Blot. "I figured out how someone could enter the Safras' flat from the outside! Isn't that great?"

Without waiting for an answer, Griffith pressed on. "Did you know that the Hermitage next door has a restaurant deck, which is right next to the fourth floor of the La Belle Époque building? That's just one floor down from the Safra residence on the fifth and sixth floors."

Griffith went on to explain how, on the wall rising up from the Hermitage deck, there was a big lattice covered in flowers and stuff, and how next to that lattice was a large protrusion; an air-conditioner housing or something. It was about three feet high and a person could easily stand on it. So, if a person stood on the protrusion, they could put their foot into the lattice and it essentially became a ladder.

"Are you with me here, guys? Are you following here?"

He further described how above the lattice was a three-foot overhang running along the entire fifth floor of the Safra apartment. Stepping up from the deck onto the protrusion and then climbing the lattice-ladder, a person could get on to the overhang with little problem. And if there were two people, one could help the other one up. Then that person—or persons—could walk along this overhang around the side of the building to the French doors.

"Of course, the Safras had cameras, but the cameras were facing toward the harbor. The glass doors were *behind* the camera. There was another camera on the other side of the building, but—*apparently*—it wasn't working that night.

"Now here's the key to the whole thing," Griffith went on. "The Hermitage has a hallway that leads from a restaurant and bar area out to the fourth-floor deck. The hotel keeps that hallway and the adjacent door open twenty-four hours a day. Therefore, anybody can come into the Hermitage at four in the morning, walk through the restaurant area, and then head down this hallway out to the deck. And hey! There's nobody around at that hour, so they can step on the things and hoist themselves up."[114]

Of course, the other key to this whole thing went back to the valance protecting those French doors.

The valance the kidnappers wanted me to leave open.

The valance Lily *did* leave open.

"Do you understand what I'm saying here?"

Donald and Georges couldn't have cared less; this information was irrelevant to my "guilt." Griffith's findings were never aired in that court of suffocation.

Instead, one by one, the main points concerning the deaths of Edmond Safra and Vivian Torrente and all the dawn-break events of December 3, 1999, were tenderized but never cooked.

Everything always came back to aim at the easiest target.

How, why, when, where? Look at Ted Maher. Everything pointed back to me.

The prosecution turned yet another expository corner in my direction when they brought up the time I spent working in Las Vegas as a surveillance and gaming expert. Their implication was that I could have easily disabled a surveillance system such as the one in La Belle Époque. *Non?*

Sure, and I could also flap my arms and fly to the moon. Lily Safra was the only one with a key to that system and I had no clue where the controls were anyway.

Maybe that person with the key was the one who shut it all down . . .

A video expert testified, providing more remarkable insights that "the magnetic signal that is supposed to go through the videotape . . . didn't happen because the signal was erased either accidently or someone did it, because everything [that] was supposed [to be] on that tape was gone . . . and . . . the video couldn't be erased by the fire . . . someone had to do it. Someone who knows exactly how it works, how to dismantle it that way, because the fire couldn't do it by itself."[115]

But *then* it came out that the system may not have been working for months; even before I arrived. It was on a network that included cameras on all entrance points of the bank, cameras left, right, upside down, every which way, everywhere. And there were also the cameras at the flat itself, as Griffith had noted. Theoretically, the whole thing was a huge big-bucks communication system, recorded as digital files—not onto videotapes—that were safe and preserved for a year. *But not working? How does that happen? How does one of the world's richest men have swap-meet grade electronics to protect himself?*

Lily fulfilled the judge of instruction's demand for all existing surveillance video by giving him an old VHS tape of a dinner party that had occurred seven months prior. That was claimed to be the extent of Edmond Safra's library from his high-tech cloaking and protection.

I could have been a veritable wizard with this stuff in Vegas, but how could I have orchestrated the total disappearance of all of the Safras' and the emergency services' communications recordings for the day of the murder—the final *paille* that brought down Patricia Richet's fury on the cops and firefighters?

Again, we had a barrel of ifs. If the surveillance recordings had been made and preserved, they would have shown a couple of masked men coming and going. On the "going" side, one would have been carrying or dragging the other because I had cracked his skull with the 10-kg barbell I was swinging. That footage would have been my proof, because his blood was not. With the temperatures that were reached in that room, no blood or DNA could survive.

Circle Ks, 7-Elevens, and mom-and-pop convenience stores on every corner in the civilized world have high and wide surveillance systems that help to ward off thefts of forty bucks and twelve-packs of Budweiser. But keeping an electric eye on the "the world's costliest flat"[116] on the night that the 199th richest man in the world was killed, well, that was another story.

CHAPTER 35

THE TRIAL: ACT THREE

The twelve days were reaching midpoint. There was no calm "eye" in the center of the convicting swirl. The winds were getting even dirtier, picking up more and more debris and shrapnel. And my wife was hanging in there, witnessing each and every grimy gust.

With the exposition of setting the stage complete, the trial became routine and chronic. On each of the first few new mornings, I once again rubbed my eyes, trying to get in touch with some kind of reality.

Unfortunately, the reality we were getting into now was the tense and ugly part where all dialogue was a study in tearing down the character of the real villain. The theory of my ability to disable all the surveillance systems was a nice lead-in.

Team Serdet and the rest of the prosecution began *this* episode by citing my first interrogations and how my story changed in the days following December 3, 1999. They said I finally admitted to stabbing myself and fabricating the story about the intruders during my fifth interrogation.[117]

Maybe, Mr. Serdet, the reason for that sudden change goes back to the lies, the black-mailing, the abuse, and the coercion that spewed from Jude, Tiberti, and the rest of the scum in Monaco's police department when they—with the help of Lily Safra and her staff—kidnapped my wife!

Maybe!

This change in my story was the perfect primer for a dramatic accusatory romp through a character assassination of me, accompanied by what the Serdet prosecution pack was absolutely sure had happened that night. That fell back into the risky realm of those on the outside versus those on the inside of all this.

Only five people on Earth could possibly have known what really happened that morning, and four of *them* experienced only half of it. Two were in a room completely apart from *the action*, and they were both dead. Two others made a quick exit after getting bloodied in a battle they hadn't planned on—at least one of them might be dead now, too.

The prosecution was not among that fate-bound quintet, living or deceased. The prosecution was not possessed of *any* firsthand knowledge, but Serdet was certainly gifted with an overflowing ooze of imagination. Why not plunge right in, keying off that damned bottle of lidocaine again?

This is what Maher did . . . He opened a container of lidocaine. He opened his shirt and *[gave]* himself a shot four times . . . Then he went back into the room of Edmond Safra after Vivian called him to help her take Mr. Safra to the bathroom . . . And then he went back again in the nursery to look for his black bag. Then he took the bag and then he took out his knife and went back at that time to the bathroom again . . . after he took out his knife . . . he *[took a]* paper cup and he started to scratch himself in the face . . . He leaned over, he took the knife and he bent down and he cut himself with the knife . . . [118]

—Prosecutor's Report

Someone must have had a very high-def crystal ball to see all of that!

Then one last exposition was thrown in, designed to head off what I had been saying about Lily's changing of the schedule at the last minute, placing me in the flat on that specific ominous night.

Did it have something to do with my kidnapping?

Did outsiders cause that change?

Two of Safra's assistants, were the ones who planned the nurses' schedules. The schedules are always prepared two weeks in advance and then are given to Lily Safra for approval . . . But the schedule always can be modified at anytime of the day, anytime even at the last minute. An example of that was seen on December 2/3, 1999, when the schedule was changed by Lily Safra to accommodate [another] nurse . . . because she had been promised a night off.[119]

—Prosecutor's Report

The vicious gang of facts on my side was never really a match for the Monegasque machine. They were running this show. *Open this obvious murderer up to a public exam. Dissect him. Skin him alive.*

Some of the most hurtful probes came from the constant stab of the "I wanted to be a hero in Safra's eyes" push. It popped up hard and often. One incident in particular was said to have torn my self-respect down and set me on a reckless path of having to come up with *something* to save face with the staff.

The prosecution really got into character as they related this particular story of embarrassment and shame. Though maybe they should have asked *me* what really happened one quiet afternoon when one of Safra's physical therapists suggested that I go to Italy for a daytrip.

"Like France the other way, Italy is so close," he said. "There's this neat little town just across the border. It's full of shops that seem to specialize in kids' clothes. I'm sure you could pick up some holiday things for your children."

Why not? I planned it. The therapist gave me directions and distance. Not many kilometers, so I figured I'd walk.

I started out at seven in the morning; comfortable in walking shorts. Almost five hours later, I realized I wasn't even *halfway* there. Evidently his directions were in miles rather than kilometers!

Then, *bang!*, the weather changed. I was freezing my ass off, so I slipped into one of the many typical, famed Italian bicycle shops and bought myself a logo jacket that made me feel like I should be spinning around in a velodrome somewhere.

Next I went into a coffee shop.

Posso aiutarti?

I did my best to order a regular cup of coffee.

Certamente!

What the hell was this? I ask for coffee and this guy gave me schnapps! I wanted coffee!

Well, it wasn't schnapps; it was espresso. And I didn't know what espresso was at that point. But after a few sips, it wasn't bad; and it was warming me up, so I had two more shots dumped in. The guy behind the counter was freaking out!

I didn't know what espresso was and I sure as hell didn't know the effects of having a triple. I left the shop walking and about fifteen minutes later, *whooooo,* I was flying! My heart was racing!

I rode the caffeine the rest of the way into the town and my shopping spree *Italiana* went *perfettamente.* I got a cute yellow dress for my daughter, some pants for my son, and gifts for my wife.

By that point it was late; no more walking. I jumped on a train bound for Monte Carlo. Eight and a half hours to get there, forty-five minutes back.

After I returned and the staff found out what had happened, my odyssey struck Anthony Brittain as especially strange. He started making jokes: "Oh my god, we've hired Forrest Gump!"

Safra had a different take: "Somebody who could walk that far and for that long has to be in good shape! He's the kind of person I'm proud to have working for me!"

But the media and Serdet kept milking Brittain's comments as a slam that haunted me. Nobody seemed to realize that what that episode actually showed was that I had to do nothing other than be myself to be a "hero" in the eyes of Edmond Safra.

And while Brittain may have thought I had the mental chops of Forrest Gump, the professional shrinks who examined me in the hospital disagreed. Their findings were a mixed bag of reviews, but none had me stumbling and ruminating over chocolates. Of course, what they said was introduced into this phase of the trial to show just how competent I *was*—to make me appear even more conscienceless. The worst villains are those who know exactly what they are doing:

Enjoying a good physical health, Theodore Maher . . . does not show any alienating mental abnormality . . . the offense chargeable to him is not related to any major mental pathology; Theodore Maher does not display any dangerous condition in the psychiatric sense, he is open to a criminal sanction, inasmuch as he can understand its meaning, he can be readapted socially, and at the time he acted he did not show any condition of dementia in the sense of Article 44 of the code of criminal law . . .

Theodore Maher [is] an intelligent subject, observant, with an excellent memory and a very good capacity of reasoning and argumentation."[120]

—Prosecutor's Report

The experts be damned, though. The *real* juicy stuff must come from the trenches—no reason to throw in any neutrality or objectivism. Let's just paint a big picture about my alleged drinking and insomnia and any other issues that those guys with the psych degrees probably missed. Let's go again to the dramatic and imaginative findings of the prosecution:

Sonia Herkrath always caused a problem for Ted . . . he was afraid of losing his job because of Sonia . . . He criticized her because of what she did to him each time she worked with the schedule, changing it, giving him hours when he wouldn't be able to sleep . . . but Sonia would tell him that it was Lily, not her doing it . . . but by working and alternating days and nights he is not able to sleep and that is what causes his bad moods . . .

To take some stress off, at night he would go to a bar at the hotel and he would ask the bartender for double whiskey and he would drink that one after another . . . On the night of November 30/December 1, 1999, he drank with gym instructor George Maranjo . . . Ted drank 12–14 glasses of red wine and he drank so much that he was throwing up and his head was hurting him badly . . .[121]

—Prosecutor's Report

Really? Double-whiskeys night after night? Throwing up and headaches? With all this bodily abuse, how on earth did I maintain my physique and my employment as a nurse with one of the richest men in the world? How did I *always* manage to stay awake all night (*not* puking my guts up) under the steamy, stressful conditions with Safra? How did I *never* get reprimanded or even fired? How come *no* complaints were ever issued?

None of it made sense.

It was one of Safra's limo drivers who testified as to the wine binge. The truth was that I indeed got sick one night on some wine—bad wine; bad shit that made me sick long before I could even think about two glasses of it, let alone fourteen!

Speaking of inventiveness, when Ms. Sonia Casiano Herkrath took the stand, here was the pulse of the play when it came to the Ted-Maher-is-a-bad-guy readings of the script:

> Ted was always sure of himself. Everybody was afraid of Ted because he was a lunatic. He was very hyper and sometimes would do bizarre things. He would always try to do something better than you . . . in the beginning I always wanted to be nice to Ted . . . I never said anything bad about him in front of my employer . . . [122]

> —Sonia Herkrath's statement,
> Prosecutor's Report

There I was watching my life melt into the Mediterranean in an acid bath of lies and conjectures.

But at one point in Sonia's testimony, she came out with a real zinger; something that veered from the Ted's-a-bad-guy theme. Really, it was the one and only time when that ricocheting bullet was parried and *someone* in this courtroom—other than me and Griffith—blamed Monegasque ineptitude for this needless tragedy!

Sonia happened to mention that her boss, the now-widowed Lily Safra, had said that because of negligence, "It was the Monaco police that killed my husband!"[123]

Those were powerful words to relate from a tearful and still-in-public-mourning billionairess. Sonia confirmed that she heard those words directly from Lily Safra's impeccably shaded lips immediately after Edmond was discovered dead.

Of course, three years later, Lily was fully backing the extremely convenient Let's-Blame-Ted-for-Everything party line, but that comment clearly pointed some well-manicured fingers at the Monegasque as well.

But it pointed *away* from something, too.

Forget about those niggling questions that might have arisen about *Lily's* involvement: about that night's schedule change, about the open valance, about the missing surveillance tapes, about the entire security team getting the night off, about Safra's will change . . .

Why should any of *that* matter?

As I sat there in my "box" reflecting on Lily's statement of nearly three years prior, I realized that few paid much attention then, and fewer would pay attention now.

Why should they?

They had their man.

CHAPTER 36
THE TRIAL: ACT FOUR

It was another morning in court, with yet more sermons before the bleeding Jesus and prosecutors taking their final bows in the defame-Maher portion of this play.

Following up what the prosecution speculated earlier about the lidocaine, we now heard proselytizing proof that I injected the drug into myself to kill the pain that would come when I—yes—stabbed myself.

Can we hear an "Amen"?!

The holy prosecutor put a Dr. Pepin on the stand.

The good doc testified that in a small sample of blood they took from me as I was soaked in the mess of my own gore, they noted a small trace of lidocaine. He reemphasized that it was a very tiny amount. "It's not really enough [to do anything] . . . it was very little."[124]

More mixed emotions. Basically, the doctor was supposed to be on their side, but his testimony wilted the more he talked. So, I jumped into the semantic gymnastics and started to forward some questions of my own. I remember my back-and-forth with the doctor went something like this:

"Doctor, how would you describe lidocaine when you get an injection of it?"

"It burns like hell."

"Now, on injuries such as mine, if one were to know they were about to occur, it would take quite a few injections to numb and prepare, correct?"

"Yes, a lot!"

"The injections would be far more painful than the cuts or even the resulting stitches—isn't that correct?"

"Yes."

"So, once more, to be perfectly clear, if I were to take a very sharp knife to myself, it would be easier, pain-wise, to make a quick cut than it would be to endure many lidocaine shots, correct?"

"Oh yes, absolutely."

The more I spoke, the redder I could see Donald getting out of the corner of my eye. I ignored him.

"So, what we're saying here is that getting lidocaine is like pouring salt into an open wound. In order for me to have self-inflicted these cuts, anesthetizing the area beforehand, I would have had to have stuck myself with several vials of it. That would bring me to choosing between being shot with a needle twenty or thirty times versus having a razor-sharp knife and just making one cut. If I were going to do this, I guess we all now understand which would be quicker, neater, and a hell of a lot less painful!"

The judge did his own interjecting, *reminding* me that they had found this vial of lidocaine in *my* hotel room.

I responded that with a 142 IQ, it seemed bizarre that if I'd planned to orchestrate this scheme, I would have left such obvious evidence behind.

Looking at the "exhibit" of Monaco's CYA vial I also reiterated what I had screamed at Patricia Richet. "That has all kinds of identification numbers all over it," I said, now begging the same thing of Hullin I had begged of Richet. "Please—I haven't asked you to do anything for me up until now, but *please* investigate where this came from and to whom it was delivered."

He said that wasn't necessary, given that the drug was found in my system, per the police report and Dr. Pepin's testimony.

Their whole claim was like the "Immaculate Injection"! That drug was *not* in my system. And that police report was more from the creative-writing class of the cover-up.

I shared my convictions and begged the judge to investigate that report along with the origin of the lidocaine!

My logic about the shots made sense and by pushing for a real investigation, I was winning the joust, but Donald was now *rouge vif* and going nuts. It was raging-bull time again. He came up to me shouting a now-familiar but tired line, "How am I supposed to fix this?!"

"Fix what?" I yelled. "The truth?!"

"How can I make you look guilty if you keep making yourself look innocent?!" he asked. I was slack-jawed at that one. "Just sit there, shut up, and let me do my job!"

"You're not doing anything!" I countered. "They're building those French gallows right outside in the courtyard, and you're supplying them with the nails! Can I see you grow a set of balls here?! The whole point I've made with all this," I continued, "is why shoot myself up with something that hurts worse than the injury itself? What is wrong with you? I want you to start working on the truth!" I continued to try to persuade him. "They're scared, Donald; they're scared! This is their worst nightmare. I walk, and you'll hear the citizenry, 'I guess we'll be moving to Liechtenstein or Switzerland or someplace that's *really* safe and honest!' People will pull their money out of this 'safest country in the world' quicker than you can spin that wheel at the casino."

Again, Donald told me to sit there, shut up, and let him do his job.

Everything was always back to square one. *Always.* Time and time again, even the little truths that hinted strongly at my innocence were washed away, tweaked, or changed. It made no difference if things were planted. The framing around me got thicker and heavier.

Manasse and Blot were furious; and Michael, wrapped in that robe, was back to shaking his head and looking down.

The easily discovered origin of the lidocaine was never investigated. Instead, something like ten thousand euros was spent by the court to surgically remove the bullet-proof, bombproof, rocket-proof door from Mr. Safra's room. It was then sent to some conflagration expert in Paris where it was microscopically examined to see if the locks matched keys that I may have had, to determine if I actually locked Safra and Vivian in the room to die!

As the day ended, moving into the last half of the trial, I was slammed back into being that defendant. Reminded that I was sole keeper of one hundred percent of what was going on one hundred percent of the time. Back to being the one with the truth. Back to wishing I could just reach out and change the damn channel.

November 28, 2002

Another sunrise. Another morning of late-season magnificence along the Côte d'Azur. Another day of being placed and shuffled where they wanted me.

The Grand Rabbi of France was the next to speak. The trial had long left the here's-what-happened beginning; they had meandered through the anatomy of a villain. We came to the final phase where the world would be told over and over what a wonderful human being Edmond Safra was.

Lily had gone to rather great lengths to fly this illustrious rabbi in from Paris on a private plane and have one of her drivers deliver him to the Monte Carlo courthouse.[125]

The good rabbi warmed up the house with a homily about the upstanding and righteousness of Edmond, truly one of the *Tzadikim*. Rabbi Sitruk was praying away all theories about Mr. Safra being bad or corrupt in any way. There was still a downer air in the wings, though, as Donald kept firing his "sit down and shut up" volleys at me. But by law, I remained gifted with that annoying right of being allowed to question all witnesses.

"Mr. Maher," the judge obligatorily asked, "do you have anything to ask Rabbi Sitruk?"

"Yes, I do."

Right on cue, Donald told me to shut up and not say anything.

I ignored him.

"I'm not Jewish," I remember telling the judge, "but I would like to ask the rabbi if he could say a prayer in his native language for those deceased in this terrible thing that has happened in Monte Carlo."

News outlets later called my request "bizarre"[126] and "an astonishing and surreal moment."[127] They also conjectured that "people began to wonder if he was all there."[128]

But when that rabbi started chanting in Hebrew, someone next to the rabbi stood up, then someone else, then Lily Safra, then the prosecution, until everyone in the courtroom was standing. And three-quarters of the people were crying:

The presiding judge asked the accused whether he had any questions for the rabbi . . . Maher requested that the rabbi say a prayer for the deceased. The rabbi replaced his wide-brimmed hat with a yarmulke and began to pray in Hebrew on the witness stand. It was at this moment that Edmond Safra's wife, Lily . . . broke down in public for the first time in her life.[129]

—Isabel Vincent, *Gilded Lily:*
Lily Safra: The Making of One of the World's Wealthiest Widows

The most jarring juxtaposition came when the rabbi started *davening* as he faced the six judges. The rabbi rocked back and forth, praying, and all the while, on the wall behind the judges was the crying Christ on a cross.

Yehei shmëh rabba mevarakh lealam ulalmey almaya . . .

Jurors, witnesses, and visitors; everyone was caught up in the *hitrag'shut*. The newspapers reported that Safra's two brothers "appeared visibly moved" along with Lily, who had been recently elevated on the rich-rankings leader board as "Britain's eighth-richest woman."[130]

In the end, my request—that recess of prayer—may have been a "surreal" juxtaposition of Judaism and Jesus, but I wanted everyone in that courtroom to know that *they* weren't going to destroy me. And that I was still a caring human being.

There's a character study.

My character.

November 29, 2002
Good morning.

Bonjour!

We're all back; those on the outside and those—*me*—on the inside. Back to those *études de caractère*.

One of Edmond's brothers took the stand:

Edmond was a real brother and a father to us because our parents died very young. . . . We miss him very much. We worked together, and for forty-five years, every day I spoke to him on the phone. . . . We weren't so close in the time just before he died, but I am sure we will meet again with the same love and affection. [131]

Everyone in the courtroom knew of the family struggles that had torn apart their relationship *and* who was responsible for those struggles. Which segued perfectly into the *main* event in the "show."

Lily took the stand.

She continued Rabbi Sitruk's homily. Once again, let's forget any facts about this case; let's just kibitz about the wonder of Edmond Safra and the disdain for the disturbed American, Ted Maher. *That*, after all, was what everyone had come for, no?

With tears in her eyes and biting irony in her purpose, Lily laid it on the court: "On the evening of the fire, Ted told me, 'Tonight you will have a good sleep.'" [132]

They should have lowered the lights in the courtroom as she went further into dramatic horror-movie foreshadowing, murmuring about how she nervously mulled over my remark as she headed to her room in the night. How she believed it had "ominous overtones." [133]

"Maybe,"—her voice tied and tripped with emotion—"he wanted to kill us all!"

Lily began weeping, describing seeing Edmond's body.

"It was very hard for me to go in and see him. He was covered with soot," she said. "I looked at his eyes and I could tell that he was dead." [134]

They were using all their big *armes à feu*, but I had one silver bullet of my own left—with blast potential that just might upstage Lily's touching showstopper.

The final Friday in November was also the day when Michael Griffith would present forensic pathologist Dr. Michael Baden. This was the day when Baden would unleash some facts about the way Vivian died, based on the evidence found in the autopsy reports.

It was to fit perfectly alongside Lily's recollections of seeing Edmond's body.

Blot smelled like a rutted rained-on vineyard; Manasse was angry at me as usual; and Sandrine Setton seemed baffled by the complexity of it all. But Griffith had his plan wired.

"With the autopsy report, we have some very solid claims," Griffith reassured me. "We have the combat-like blow to Vivian Torrente's thorax, her DNA under Mr. Safra's fingernails, Mr. Safra's DNA under her fingernails, hematomas on her legs, Mr. Safra's blood on her undergarments, another mortal combat-type blow to Vivian's trachea—all of which were reported by the Monaco autopsy doctor. It's obvious something was going on. It seems there was a struggle or fight."[135]

Enter Baden, forensic pathologist, contributor to Fox News, former chief medical examiner of New York City and with experience in over forty thousand autopsies. He was prepared to provide his interpretation of these autopsy findings in court.

Marc Bonnant, Lily's lawyer, had tried to claim that Mr. Safra was like an invalid, that he was in no way strong enough to have struggled with Vivian. He suggested that she might have just fallen down.

Yeah, she fell down on her thorax. Who's kidding whom? And I can tell you that, per my recommendation, Mr. Safra was working out with weights every day and that even with his disease, he was strong for his age.

As for motive, I had already surmised that the likely reason for the fight was Safra's acute anxiety. And Griffith concurred. It was yet another way in which their deaths could have been avoided, if Safra had allowed Vivian to exit the room and get help.

And when all that occurred, I was at the hospital!

Griffith's research into the timeline showed phone calls between Vivian and Sonia, during which Vivian, coughing from the smoke, was told to come out—the police were outside.[136]

At that point, Griffith and I reasoned, Vivian Torrente probably said to herself, *Hey look, I'm out of here. Even if it's a terrorist out there, I didn't do anything that the PLO's going to hate me for—the Russians have to know I wasn't laundering their money. And Sonia says our cops are outside, and if I stay in here, I'm going to die! So, I'm out of here! Bye!*

But Safra being Safra, he wasn't buying it. He was still thinking that the police outside were really the so-called attackers.

According to the timeline, the last phone call was made at about 6:30 a.m. Vivian and Safra were found dead at 7:45 a.m.[137] So during that period was obviously when the struggle—a fight—occurred. According to reports, when Vivian's body was discovered, Mr. Safra was sitting in an armchair and Vivian was lying on the floor behind him.[138]

So, it all fit together quite logically, and we had the entire scenario lined up and ready to go. Griffith was sure that Dr. Baden's testimony would exculpate me from at least Vivian's death, because if the intervening incident with Mr. Safra prevented Vivian from leaving and being saved, then Safra was responsible for her death—not the fire.

But . . .

Ten minutes before Dr. Baden was scheduled to take the stand, Michael Griffith was handed a letter there in the courtroom.

Handed a letter!

By Donald.

It's a letter from Donald to Michael regarding Dr. Baden's testimony.

Donald handed me a copy, too.

Donald Manasse

Avocat au Bureau de Nice

Avocat aux Burreaux de New-York et du Connecticut

29 November 2002

Muchael Griffith, Esq.

Hotel Hermitage

Square Beaumarchais

Monaco

Re: Ted Maher—Testimony of Dr. Michael Baden

Dear Michael:

This will confirm that we co-counsel with you of Theodore Maher strongly object to the presentation of the testimony of Dr. Michael Baden at this point in the criminal proceedings in Monaco.

Dr. Baden's testimony, as brilliant a man as he is and as respected an expert as he may be, is in our view not only irrelevant but harmful, and clearly against our mutual client's best interests. It will only serve to remind the Tribunal of the death throes of the victims, and will not in any way serve to exculpate Ted Maher, whose best interests are our only concern.

Sincerely yours,
Donald Manasse
Sandrine Setton
Georges Blot

cc: Ted Maher
  Mrs. Heidi Maher
  Dr. Michael Baden[139]

What?!

I looked at the paper in my hand, and then I looked back at Donald. Griffith did the same.

"What are you doing?!" I screamed at Manasse. "Who the hell are you representing?!"

Unfortunately, I knew the answer.

Manasse had the power to approve (or, more importantly, deny) any question to be asked by my defense team, so he completely controlled the situation.

In the end, Dr. Michael Baden *did* testify, but his expertise was figuratively bound and gagged by Donald's duct-tape of a decision not to utter *le peep* about Vivian's injuries. Donald only allowed Griffith to ask about the smoke inhalation and its results—effectively returning the court's focus to the fire, which kept the court's focus squarely on *me*.

So again, evidence that Michael Griffith had exhumed was forced down, ground up, and reburied.

And worse, Daniel Serdet and his prosecution posse took Vivian's death into even farther depths. According to them, Safra had nothing to do with it. In fact, her death could actually have been the reason for this entire ordeal.

(Key the surprise "ah-ha moment" organ music from the soap operas . . .) "Why, Mr. Maher was actually having an affair with Vivian Torrente. She was going to tell the truth about their tawdry dalliances, ruining Mr. Maher's marriage and his job and his life and his entire universe."

My God!

The energy and time required to project that strange, way-out-of-bounds fantasy of Serdet's was evidently more important than looking closer into the real clockwork of the last fifteen minutes of Vivian Torrente's life. It seemed like everyone there just wanted to ensure that Edmond's lasting legacy would shine, untarnished in any way by the truth.

The truth that *could* give me my life back.

CHAPTER 37
THE VERDICT

. . . it must be noted that the conditions of intervention of the fire and police department during the fire resulting in the death of Edmond Safra and Vivian Torrente, contrary to the schemes chargeable to Theodore Maher, do not have any criminal character . . . Therefore, the investigation is complete as to these events and no other measure of investigation is necessary for the demonstration of truth.[140]

—The official word from the court
rejecting Ted Maher's pleas for further investigations
into the fire and police departments' involvements
in the events of December 3, 1999

December 2, 2002

One of the many rules for effective courtroom closing arguments is this: *Use a pound of logic for every ounce of emotion.* Not bad advice when trying to save someone's life. Not bad advice when you want to show that, in a tangible and real sense, what your client is accused of simply couldn't have occurred.

Brilliant closing arguments have won cases, set precedent, and have become immortal within journals of jurisprudence. From Clarence Darrow to Vincent Bugliosi, from Johnnie Cochran to Thurgood Marshall and the ACLU attorneys involved in the landmark Ernesto Miranda trial—you can't argue that the drama in closing arguments often provides the most potent punch in court contests.

"Justice is the great interest of man on Earth. It is the ligament which holds civilized beings and civilized nations together."[141]

—Daniel Webster

I, on the other hand, had Donald Manasse's minion, Sandrine Setton, delivering a big part of this proceeding's unforgettable keynote address. She wanted to bend what I had done, just a bit, to the six jurors.

Her message: Stupidity is reprehensible, but it is not a crime.

Well, there's a dump truck's worth of logic poured into a carload of emotion! Lock up the elephants and the tigers, tuck in the clowns, call it a day—I'm home free now!

Hail me a cab!

No?

Setton's passion-dripped performance was still holding everyone in a breathless trance when the jury adjourned for deliberation. I was taken to a holding cell through a small door in the courtroom. It was really more of a closet than a cell—just three feet by three feet. I was no stranger to its confines. I was brought there during every recess, every lunch, every break.

The area around the cell had big "NO SMOKING" signs posted, but all the cops would smoke right there anyway, and I hated it. I hated the ever-present and ever-stale smoke.

But I was back here; maybe for the last time.

I had my closet in which to move and pace. And think.

Am I going to be in here for days-long deliberations?

Probably not.

I had already built *le mur*. I tried to be hopeful, but I knew in my heart what was going to happen. I paced and I thought some more. I thought about Patricia Richet's huge stack of nineteen boxes of investigative paperwork being completely ignored by Serdet. They were part of the overall file and Serdet, as the procurer, could ask for anything he wanted.

But he asked for nothing.

I thought about the lack of any kind of spotlight on Lily despite her mighty inheritance and her incriminating behavior before and after the fact.

No one was interested in all that . . .

I thought about the autopsies and examinations and testimonies by the pathologists and biologists and blood experts that showed the fight between Safra and Vivian and the sick twist on her death.

No one seemed interested in any of it . . .

I knew.

I was certain they had all huddled up.

"Here's the game plan, guys: We're down on the four-yard line, you're the minister of justice, and Prince Rainer has already signed the executive order. He's already been told through his attaché what he has to do. He's going to remove Richet, we're going to give this to Hullin, he's closing the file, he won't even see Ted Maher, and then Daniel Serdet, as prosecutor, you're going to ask for twelve years, but we'll give him ten, and that will show some compassion as far as this being Monaco, and Maher being an American citizen and all, and we'll go through twelve days of an emotional trial and we'll suppress as much crap as we can and just gloss over the rest, just go with the flow and make him look as guilty as possible . . . BREAK!"

The one thing that team didn't consider was my resolve. To me, this was no game. I had a playbook of my own.

———————

"Le jury a rendu un verdict!"

After deliberating long and hard for a full forty-five minutes—yes, forty-five minutes!—all the players were reassembled. Really, I was surprised that it took them that long. The reading of the jury statement was awe-strikingly official and solemnly stern.

It was also ridiculous.

It went on and on and on. It was the courtroom equivalent of a Marcel Proust novel. Oh yeah, baby, that statement was something just casually jotted down in three-quarters of an hour.

The climax to the epic was what I knew: Convicted. *Condemned.*

It was done.

But here is where there should have been a bit more hard drama than Griffith escorting my teary wife from the courtroom. Here is where there should have been gasps, cries, and tears from me and the spectators. But no. No one needed a spoiler alert for this verdict. Just like we all know mid-movie the *Titanic* is gonna sink, Amelia isn't flying back, and that Old Yeller is gonna die.

I just stood there.

And, yes, as planned, with their immediate sentencing, I was to spend ten years in prison. I showed no emotion. Nothing. They were going to get none of that satisfaction.

I had satisfaction. *I* had the comfort of knowing that a Plan B was already in the works.

Ten years, twelve, life . . . now it was all the same. I was there and I was condemned.

But I wasn't going to live with it. *Any of it.*

Their strange wishy-washy "arson by communication" law wasn't actually a murder conviction. Nowhere on any paperwork did it say that I was convicted of murder; nowhere was that indelible stigma that brands and burns for life—but it may as well have been there. That had already been done before the trial by the media: Ted Maher the murderer, Ted Maher the assassin, all the conspiracy theories involving me.

But I wasn't going to just lie down and take it.

I opened *my* playbook. My next move had already been planned. I am very good at planning.

And I am even better at making plans work.

CHAPTER 38
THE GREEN LIGHT

After the verdict and the sentencing, I went directly back to the jail in a front-page flurry of worldwide news. My old friend, Ellen Thorburn from the US State Department, paid me an immediate visit.

No small talk.

I had one question. It was a question I already knew the answer to.

"What happens if I'm on American soil?" I asked. "Like the consulate in Marseilles, France, or the embassy in Rome? What then?"

"What are you asking, Ted?" was her obligatory, diplomatic response.

But she knew.

"What's the position of the United States if I'm in either of those places?" I pushed.

"I can't answer that."

"Well, I want an answer and I want it quick! Because this trial is over and I'm going away for a long time and I'm sure they're making preparations here to get my ass to a real prison in France. If I go there, I'm a dead man."

This was back in the very-still-high-on-everyone's-mind post-9/11 era—where Muslims' hatred for Americans had been slammed into the American psyche as hard as those Boeing jetliners slammed into the World Trade Center. In this climate, I believed—I *knew*—that as an American in a majority-Muslim-population prison I would be a prime terrorist-target.

"I'll be knifed in the courtyard by a lifer who will be paid and given anything he needs for the rest of his days to do me in," I pleaded. "My death will be an 'accident' or just one of those sad happenings that goes on in the sewer of inmate existence. But any way you look at it, I'll be dead! That's the way this shit works!"

I knew . . .

I knew from the beginning what the outcome of all this was going to be and there was no way I was going to sit there and tolerate it; especially after what I had gone through in a court with zero appreciation for logic or justice! I knew what I had and hadn't done. The window for my statement about sticking by my confession "at this time" had slammed and shattered shut. There was no way I was going to rot away any longer, and there was no way I would wind up sliced to pieces in a French prison.

No way.

―――――――――――

My playbook was opened; I had Plan B all mapped out.

I was ready to step on *le gaz,* but I still had to wait semi-patiently for the real answer to arrive from Colin Powell's State Department before putting the pedal to the metal.

Twelve days later, I got another visit from Ms. Thorburn.

Another response.

A different response.

"Ted," she speculated, "let's just say that if you were in either of those places you mentioned—the US Consulate in Marseille or our embassy in Rome—well, we could give you safe passage back to the United States. Further, we would not extradite you back to Monte Carlo, because we know what has happened to you and what has occurred throughout all of this. This is not justice."

The green light was on.

I'd always been pretty certain that a Special Forces team wouldn't be assembled to extract me in the dead of night and put me on a nuclear submarine with a nonstop ride to Kings Bay, Georgia.

What I needed was a guarantee that if I could *in some way* get to Marseille or Rome—if I could make myself available—that I'd have the backing of our government. Without it, what was I going to do? I couldn't do the dog paddle across the Atlantic Ocean. I didn't speak French very well, and no sort of asylum was going to

be granted to this murderer. I'd be a political albatross heading for sure death in captivity—and I would have worked real damn hard to get there.

———————

For the next step, I wrote a letter to my sister and gave it to Griffith. He was not to
read it—just get it to my sister immediately.

That in itself was risky. Another of my psychological torments was the hit-and-miss
of my communications. Most had to go through the US consulate. Some made it to
the consulate; some didn't. Even Michael had some legal papers taken from him at the
prison, and he was livid!

But this letter *had* to get through.

It must.

Naturally, Michael asked what was in it. I told him it was private and personal—
addressed to one of just a very few people whom I now trusted. In the letter, I explained
to my sister something I wanted done.

My sister didn't need an incentive to help me, but I did tell her in the letter that
the only way the truth about me and what went on in the trial was ever going to
surface was if I came out alive. If I wound up six feet under, no one was going to
investigate the case further and come up with the answers that I *knew* and had lived.
I again laid out the chilly fact that if I were to land in a terrorist-infested French
dungeon, it was over.

"Do this thing for me and I have a chance," I wrote.

———————

That "thing" revolved around an idea I'd had leading up to the trial. Already realizing
how it would likely end, I knew what I'd have to do next.

I could see it . . . I could feel it . . .

Once the early "ups and optimism" went down *les toilettes*, I had to make sure I
wouldn't join them.

It had taken me a while to formulate my Plan B, but I'd had plenty of time to
think.

And plenty of time to get to know my small room in the jail.

My aunt who had added her twenty-five grand to the Michael Griffith expense-fund had sent me a note of support: "I know this is going to be a difficult thing for you to swallow, Ted; but just remember: you can eat an elephant if you take it slow and take it one bite at a time. One day you'll look around and it'll be gone. You will get through this . . ."

I had mulled over her words as my thought became a plan, and in harmony with my aunt's message, I believed there was a perfect plan for everything, given enough time.

"You will get through this . . ."

So my plan was in place before the verdict even came in, but I only took action after getting the green light from Ellen Thornburn; that's when I had Griffith send the letter to my sister, telling her what I needed.

My sister's husband was a professional welder. Working on nuclear submarines, he was one with metal. He used mirrors to weld parts that were behind other parts, and his work had to be flawless, subject to x-rays. The man was an artist. I knew a little about metal work, too; enough to know that I wanted to have my sister and her husband get me some high-quality 32-TPI (teeth-per-inch) hacksaw blades. I wanted four of them, carbide, cut down to about eight inches.

I then asked my sister to go to a bookstore and get me a neonatal book. Christmas was about a month out and it was the kind of thing that would make a great gift for a favorite brother locked up in a far-off land. The jail officials knew I was a nurse in neonatology, so a present like that, well, hell—that would make a guy feel better, reading about babies surviving and miracles in new young lives; all while he was decaying behind bars. Perfect escapist and hyper-hopeful stuff.

I told my sister to take the book's binding apart, put the blades in it, and then carefully reseal it. That was why the blades needed to be trimmed to eight inches: a book large enough to accommodate full-sized blades would attract too much suspicion. We didn't have coffee tables as part of our accommodations and décor—let alone coffee-table books.

But how would the doctored-up book get inside? Every item and every person who entered the jail went through a metal detector.

Well, almost every person.

I had been getting regular visits from a seventy-eight-year-old retired priest named Father Ball—Father Peter Cannon Ball, an English, multilingual, former Anglican cleric for the British Navy. He'd perform fill-in services for the Episcopals and Anglicans in Monte Carlo.

Father Peter "Cannon Ball"? Too bad I didn't foresee the devastation he'd blast into this venture . . .

Father Ball would routinely drop in on me because of Donald Manasse. Years ago, Donald's wife was found dead from asphyxiation in their home, a victim of a faulty heater. Manasse was the one who discovered her body. Ball went to their home shortly after the incident to console Manasse.

Now—in a show of humanism—seeing the hard time I was having in jail, Manasse shepherded the father my way.

The priest would serve me communion and we would talk. It was great speaking English, and Ball would keep my brain working. He'd come maybe once a week, walking—teetering—around with his cane. He became the neutral conduit for the funds that my family would send from America; a small bank so I could buy extra toilet paper, stamps, and just a few beyond-prison-issue luxuries.

So, what could be better than for my loving sister to send her gift for me via this priest? For him to look at the book first and share in the joy of saving and helping new infants to live and to grow? And then to hand-deliver the book (and unwittingly, the blades) to me with an inspired passion?

He could also deliver this gift to me without the burden of having to pass through the metal detector. You see, the good father had a heart condition that required a pacemaker. The risk of fouling up the rhythmic beat of the life of a man of God was never a question. I noticed that they *always* let in this saint—and his possessions—unchecked.

But if for any reason they decided to wave that wand this time, we were all fucked. Implicated and impaled.

My plan also included where to hide the blades once—*if*—they got in. Plan B had to include that kind of foresight because of the daily searches. Given the slim hiding foliage of this jail, I had to take the unrelenting searches seriously—I needed to find a way to make this place a rainforest.

Where could I hide the blades?

My bed was nothing more than a piece of foam on a thin, fully sealed bunk-bed frame. I had a toilet and a little sink, but the plumbing, too, was completely sealed. So far, this jungle remained barren.

There was no safe place to hide anything up or around in the ventilation system, either; they searched all the time throughout the ducts with mirrors.

And then there was the all-powerful long arm of the metal detector wands, just in case any of the other safeguards were somehow breached.

So how could I do it?

How?

I was lying there in bed when it came to me; an idea just came to me. Amid the plague of blood and frogs, I did feel some divine intervention.

The cell had a little tiny refrigerator; you could stock it up by buying food with whatever money you might be able to get into your prison account.

I looked at the refrigerator. Nothing could be hidden in the metal framework because, like everything else industrial and utilitarian, it was all sealed.

But the refrigerator door . . .

First of all, it was held closed by magnets. Oh my god, how sweet was that?!

Second, the rubber sealing strip around the door was just as wide as a hacksaw blade!

But were the magnets strong enough to hold the door shut *and* hold the blades? We would see.

———

Griffith and my sister both came through for me. My letter made it quickly across the Atlantic and what I asked of my sister and her metal-master husband was followed explicitly and in record time. The priest arrived with the book.

"Welcome, Father Ball! Right this way . . . through this door . . .

"Happy Holidays.

"Bonnes fêtes!

"Ho, ho, ho!"

Father Ball had no idea what he was carrying.

What a wonderful early Christmas gift!

I steered the visit short; no long talks or communion this time. As soon as the father left, I went to work. I took the book apart. The blades, as prescribed, were in the binding. It felt like the end trail of a long, involved treasure map where you could finally start digging over the "X." You felt the shovel make that first contact with the top of the chest.

My God . . .

You knew you had *something*, but was it what you were expecting?

This was. There were the blades, cut exactly as I'd requested. This was business. Cold business. But I couldn't get giddy and I couldn't go the other way and drip sweat. I had to forget all the emotions and just do the job.

I made a little slit in the refrigerator door sealing, using one of the blades from the plastic disposables we were given to shave with. (I had to laugh—after that big scene in the hospital bathroom where the little razors were branded as lethal weapons, as soon as I got back to the prison, I again had access to all I needed. They were standard grooming fare here, and no one counted them or kept real track of their use. I guess in jail they weren't considered in the same league as a machete. So one day, I just broke the head of one in half and smuggled out one of the two mini razor blades.)

Relying on my suturing ability, I then tied dental floss to each saw blade and eased it into the recess between the seal and the door frame. Then I sealed the crack with butter.

Time to test the strength of the magnets—and my future.

I shut the door. Everything held in place.

I breathed quietly but deeply.

I lay down on the bed to think. And I smiled. *What are the odds in all this? Those guards are going to open that refrigerator door dozens of times in their upcoming searches; but will they find these blades? The metal detector isn't going to show anything, and even if I tell them exactly where these things are, they'll still have to rip all that sealing off to find them!*

But those odds reached way, way beyond just finding the hardware. If I did escape, I'd be an easy-to-spot American fugitive on foreign soil. I hardly spoke the country's language and my features and bearing were as American as apple pie.

Are my chances really this slim? I pondered. *Nothing is guaranteed.*

I knew my room and I knew the only way out; but I knew, too, that I had layer upon layer of metal to get through! Would the blades hold up?

God, it was such a long shot!

But I had to get home. Heidi was slipping from me; I'd picked up on that. The pressure was crushing us both. The stress was hurting us both, and it was pushing us both. So, I told myself I could do this.

I *could* do this.

I'd been conditioned for certain things. As a young man, I didn't go through all that intense military training—dragging sand bags around and jumping out of planes—to become a Green Beret, and not keep that fortitude with me. I didn't have to think about this; I knew I could still claw past any supposed limits of what my body and mind could do.

Never quit!

Never quit!

Never quit!

That was part of the training. They ground you and ground you and spat on you and threw mud on you to try and make you quit. To try and get you to say "I'm outta here."

I'd never been the "outta here" kind.

Until that jail cell. That was a whole different story.

I *would* be out of there.

CHAPTER 39
PLAN B

Nothing moved fast in the soothing and brooding Mediterranean sun, regardless of the season; so I was hung out amidst Monaco's pending transfer of me to a long-term French prison.

Perfect.

I was involved and so was the US State Department. Neither of us wanted me to be thrown into a mainline French facility. Back then, in the early 2000s, they were recognized as the bottom of *le canon* in Western Europe, with the worst violence and suicide rates amongst the fifteen European Union countries.[142] We all knew I wouldn't last.

Yeah, there was the odd institution or two where I might have had a prayer of safer housing in the form of isolation and solitary, but it was a prayer I couldn't bank on having answered by the saints in charge.

I had my *own* answered prayer within cold steel in that refrigerator. I was anxious to start, but I knew I had plenty of time with the two governments jumping rope with their red tape as to where to stick me.

And I also knew that I couldn't do this totally by myself. That meant I had to bring someone else into my plan; someone I could trust.

That would take some doing.

Nothing ever changed in the overall personality of the prison population. Those soft-sinners were seldom if ever from your hardened criminal pool.

When we could wrestle down the language barrier, I'd talk with some of them on the promenade.

"Oh, what are you in here for?"

"Drunk driving."

"You're going to get four weeks."

"How do you know that?"

"I've seen a hundred of you since I've been here. If you don't have a connection to the procurer, you're going to do four weeks. I don't care if you're a banker or what, four weeks. So, settle in . . . get comfortable . . ."

Then I met Luigi Ciardelli. He was one year older than me, and *un autentico criminale*. Luigi was a bad guy, but I thought I could trust a bad guy, because he had nothing to lose and everything to gain.

This was business. Cold business . . .

Ciardelli had been condemned for armed robbery. He'd done that all his life, along with dealing and using cocaine. When he needed more money, he'd do another robbery; simple demand and supply.

But Luigi always wore a mask while doing his "jobs," so even though he'd been nailed for a series of *armé vols* in Italy, a couple in Monte Carlo, and some in France, there was never any hard and complete proof that it was him. But that didn't matter much. He was condemned in France based on authorities finding a DNA-matched cigarette that he had supposedly smoked at the scene of one of the crimes. The bogus-quotient hit me like a planted bottle of lidocaine: how many pros rob someplace in a mask, smoking a cigarette, and then carelessly throw it down? But that's how justice smelled in Monaco. If they couldn't prove it, they *would* prove it. Somehow.

Ciardelli got seven and a half years in a French prison, served his time, and then they simply "dropped him off" in Monaco. He was to stay in jail here while another of those eternal "investigations" was ground out, looking into the Monaco *vols* he allegedly pulled off.

No warrant.

No extradition paperwork.

Just a drive-by drop-off from the French frying pan into the Monegasque fire.

That's the way we do it in Monaco . . .

Actually, France was happy to be rid of Ciardelli. In his quality time spent with them, he performed two evasions—escapes—gone once for a couple weeks and once for a couple of days.

Again, perfect.

Good credentials.

Here, I thought, *we have the makings of an all-star team.*

Maybe.

Luigi had the expertise as far as evasions went, but he was a very frail man. Even though I was lighter than I used to be, I was still in shape; running, exercising, doing push-ups. I was also in good mental shape.

I talked to Luigi. I dug around, found out about his background.

He wasn't stupid. He was articulate, wrote poems, and he spoke Italian, French, and English fluently.

Could I bring this guy in with me?

Would this guy come in with me?

Be a part of those long odds?

In the nine months Luigi had been in the jail, overlapping sentences with me—overlapping my trial and all of my discomfort—he'd had a Monegasque adventure of his own.

With Luigi's drug addiction, his teeth were shot to hell. The Monegasque jail dentist looked at his mouth-mess and proposed to Luigi that he pull out all of his remaining teeth and make a full set of dentures. Luigi agreed.

Start pulling . . .

There went the last of the teeth.

Then the dentist submitted his package for Luigi's dentures to the director—officially the *governor* of the prison—my old buddy Charlie Marson. And Marson denied payment! So now Luigi went crazy hearing about his false-teeth plan being chomped! He got tossed into solitary confinement for two weeks to calm down. But he managed to take all his writing stuff in with him and was writing "Marson is a bastard" everywhere in the cell.

He even got agonizingly biological and smeared his feelings about Charlie on the wall in excrement.

Then he started his letter-writing campaign. He got through to the Italian consulate.

They're pulling my teeth and here's Monte Carlo, with the self-proclaimed best jail and best everything else in the world, and they don't even have medical treatment in here for inmate dental work?!

He sank his fangs—or lack of them—into a scandal. Within a very short period of time, all of a sudden, the jail had a fifty-grand-per-year budget for dentistry and Luigi got his teeth!

Every time after that at meals, when he was eating something hard, he'd make this incredible noise with his crunching.

"Damn, Luigi," we'd say, "why are you making all that noise?!"

"Because I can!"

Whether it was his length of time there or maybe just a move to keep him—and his teeth—quietly busy and out of everyone's way, my potential partner was made a prison trustee. That meant he was kind of a penal teacher's pet, and he was given a "job" in the library.

The move paid off for the jail. Because of his multilingual and organizational skills, Luigi was able to chronologically sort the French and the Italian books by author, subcategories, fiction, nonfiction, drama, you name it.

I needed this trustee-librarian even more now; he had ins that could pay off in much bigger ways than just a fine appreciation of the Euro version of the Dewey Decimal System.

At certain parts of the day, all the cells were open. We could congregate—*socialize* —with the other prisoners. I went to Luigi's. I brought the blades.

We exchanged a few pleasantries. I sat on his lower bunk, he sat in a chair.

"Look," I calmly instructed him, laying out the four blades on the bed.

"Oh my god!" he said.

But right then we both heard something. I froze. Luigi stood up. The bunk had a pillow, and the blades were lying just in front of it. Like a specter in smoke, there's Marson, along with his chief of security, a guy named Zabaldano. They were on a quickie unannounced tour with a director from another prison.

Luigi was a special prize in the zoo. All the directors knew he had escaped in France twice before.

But not here!

"No, sir!"

"Cela n'arrivera pas à nouveau!"

"He's reformed. He's running our *bibliothèque!*"

"And we're sure you've heard of Mr. Maher . . ."

I was still frozen. Holding my breath. *Holy fuck!* All they had to do was to step a couple of feet into that cell and two inmates chatting about the weather became a conspiracy to evade. The damaging evidence was lying right there on the bed, just below the sight line obscured by that pillow.

Thankfully, their little tour moved along.

Bonne journée, Messieurs . . .

Once my blood pressure got back to normal and my heart eased into low gear, it was back to business. I was there to show Luigi that what I had in mind was no bullshit.

I had to tell him about—*show him*—the blades. Trust was thin on both sides of our honor among thieves, but so was credibility. It was an easy thing to say, "I'm getting out of here! I'm blowing this joint!"

"That so? You gonna put on a cape and rip the bars open with your bare hands?"

No.

I was *really* getting out of there and those blades were my ticket.

"Want to go?

"Want to join me?"

He accepted.

Why the hell not?

Good.

I went back to my cell. The blades went back in the folds of the fridge. But then it was time for more of those plan-in-motion questions: I asked myself how Luigi and I could get him bunked in the cell with me. Especially since the "NO VACANCY" sign seldom got turned on at *Hôtel La Maison d'Arrêt.*

Not only were overcrowding issues rare in this hole, but the Monegasque wanted to keep me alone because they were afraid someone would want to kill me. So I guess it was low-risk for me to chat with check-kiters on the promenade or in open cells in the noon-day light, but in the dark, watch out! You never knew where the reach of the Russians or the Palestinians or any other enemy might stretch!

Another actor added his thespian skills to this cast. Luigi approached Marson. Charlie may have been Luigi's old nemesis and the anti–tooth fairy, but Marson had the power. Luckily, their teeth-and-graffiti feud had healed with time; and besides, Luigi had become a superstar and a model citizen between the library stacks.

"Ted is getting all these bad letters from his wife," Luigi lamented to Marson. "He's so depressed. I think he will not last much longer. If you want him to survive at least long enough to get to France and be out of your hair, then you better put me in his cell with him. He needs some company. He plays a mean game of chess; we play together, and it keeps him busy. The social worker can't be with him twenty-four hours a day, but I can.

"Look, I'm just letting you know that if you don't do something, on one of your guard's visits to his cell you're going to find Maher face-down in a pool of blood. Ted's smart enough to figure out a way to do it and then you'll have some explaining to do."

The next day Luigi was my roommate.

We got locked in every evening around 8:30 or 9:00 p.m. The television would go off at twelve straight-up, and that was it for the night.

Every hour, the guards came by. They were like Swiss watches, always within three minutes of their expected time. They reminded me of German Gestapo.

Are you ready for me?

Ready to try and break me again?!

Ready to tear my room up again?!

Ready with your jack boots?!

That was okay; just fine. I'd be cutting many strings soon. But just as when my trial began and none of us had a clue how long it would take, I really needed to define "soon."

This scenario had a difference, though; a big difference. I had been fairly certain how that trial would play out, but I had no solid idea how this next act, Plan B, would progress.

One thing, however, was absolute: the time ahead of us would in no way "provide a glittering stage for the glory that is the Principality of Monaco."

Not *this* time.

CHAPTER 40

FIVE AND A HALF WEEKS

I had assessed the escape route long ago. It wasn't hard to choose; we had one window to the outside. And I knew what was in that "window"—hence the blades.

Later, I would read media accounts that made this vantage point to the Mediterranean sound like the perfect photo setting for a *National Geographic* panorama. Even the fair and balanced Dominick Dunne pushed the hype just a bit:

> As prisons go, the one in Monaco is pretty deluxe, from what I hear. I was not allowed to visit Ted Maher . . . but I was told he has a nice view. He can watch the boat traffic on the Mediterranean, and on clear nights the reflection of the moon ripples on the water. Below him are well-tended gardens.[143]
>
> —Dominick Dunne, "Death in Monaco,"
> *Vanity Fair,* December 2000

My window with what Dunne called the "nice view" was really a narrow, yards-long tunnel through thick fortified walls. Maybe some cells in the jail overlooked the water, but I sure hadn't been graced with that kind of "penthouse suite." So to see Dunne and others write about the boats and yachts going by was maddening! I was looking through a square black tube, and if I was aesthetically lucky, I'd see a sailboat every now and then in the flicker of light at the end. And gardens? I never saw a tree. I never saw anything green. Occasionally, I saw the sky and sun during certain periods of the year, but essentially I saw shit.

My "window," my view, was a hole in the wall that served double-duty as an obstacle course for anyone crazy enough to try and escape. The first layer was an actual window that slid open. But after that, it all went to metal hell. There was wire mesh, then this paradoxical German-looking decorative metal Iron Cross, then a set of bars. Then another. Then more wire mesh and a final set of bars after that.

Counting the window, I had seven layers of barricades that dampened the lovely "reflection of the moon ripples on the water."[144]

Seven layers to break through.

Seven layers to freedom.

Time to prepare.

Time to move.

Luigi and I had been stockpiling "makeup" and cosmetic supplies that were a big part of this plan. We made craft-supply visits to our social worker—a woman who had the happy-face job of keeping us sane through the creative use of our minds and hands.

Every Wednesday, we could get this galaxy of glue sticks and construction paper and all kinds of wondrous things to allow us to express ourselves through the outlet of art!

And why stop there? We started to ask other, less creative prisoners to get us their allotment of *fournitures* too—more glue sticks, tape, and marker pens. We traded our Sunday pastries for fun tools of therapy.

My trustee partner could supplement even more from his library stock. Luigi's loot included old model-making stuff they were getting rid of, like half-used jars of paints that were never quite used up when some poor, hardened credit card convict failed to finish his perfect replica of the Spanish Armada or a Renault Spyder.

Black-and-white hobby enamel mixed with some cigarette ashes gave us the perfect shades of "Prison Bar Silver Swirl" and even variations on "Broken Weld Gray." Just the right *cosmétiques* to camouflage our work-in-progress when the regular inspections hit.

Our stuff rivaled *L'Oréal*.

Soon we were ready for our initial night of work.

It was finally the end of a long day of waiting.

I was moving.

Luigi was staring.

I went to the fridge, and for the second time since Father Ball had raised the healing staff of these clandestine blades, I delicately broke that cover-up of butter, gently pulled back a portion of the rubber seal, got a light grip on the thread of floss, and resurrected one of my four toothy saviors.

Luigi just stared.

We were really getting out of here . . .

The guards had passed minutes ago, so we had our first hour; the first hour of how many? Would we even do this? Or would we be found out and hung up to dry on this *tout premier* night?

The first layer

Open the window.

I slid it and smiled at Luigi.

That was easy! Phew!

One down, six to go . . .

A journey of a thousand miles begins with a single step . . .

Fuck all that—let's go!

The second layer

The first real cuts sliced into that web of mesh; and immediately we had answers to some of those questions about how long this would take.

The wire mesh was a screen of tight one-inch squares of galvanized metal about an eighth of an inch thick. And the damn galvanizing was eating the shit out of the blades right away.

Damn it!

This cannot fail!

We're just starting here!

Relax.

Analyze.

Okay, what that told me *wasn't* that we had to ditch the whole plan; what it told me was that we had *no* room for leeway. I had to cut only what I needed in order to squeeze myself through. The project was definitely not building for comfort, only speed.

Analyze . . .

I measured myself: from my sternum to my spine it was twenty-two and a half centimeters. I measured the mesh. I looked at the math and saw that I had to cut forty-six of those wires to make a loop that would pull back into an opening that was, yes, *exactly twenty-two and a half centimeters wide*; just enough for me to get through there.

If I exhaled.

And I would have to go through it sideways.

I shared my numbers with Luigi. He looked dubious.

We peered down the tunnel at the bars and the other mesh layers. I did more measurements. The reality of just how small that opening was began to set in, and we could see that our path wasn't going to be as tidy as it might have been if I'd had stronger tools.

Like a jackhammer and some dynamite.

I noticed our bunk beds. The steel ladder along the side was made of half-inch round stock. I measured the openings on that ladder from rung to rung and from side pole to side pole. It matched the 22.5-centimeter clearance exactly.

Luigi looked at me, and then at that ladder. He knew what I was thinking.

He shook his head. "It can't be done, my friend . . ."

"Don't tell me it can't be done!" I told him in a whisper-yell. "I'm going through that ladder and I'm going through that window. I weigh twenty-five pounds more than you do and you're going through, too! Watch!"

With the help of Luigi's boost, I went parallel to the floor and slipped—*squeezed*—through that ladder.

Don't tell me it can't be done . . .

Don't tell me anything can't be done . . .

The squeeze-through became a nightly practice routine. We morphed and wiggled like a crossbreed of cats and jellyfish.

Back to work . . .

The first cuts were some of the most difficult from a logistical standpoint. Down in the "tunnel" things would get tighter and more complex, but now, in this beginning step, we were more exposed. The tunnel would make moving around difficult, but it would also provide cover.

But not yet.

Watch the clock!

Every hour we had to pull back!

More trial and error.

It was also our first dial-in of the audio.

How loud would it be?

How much noise would we make in the dark, echoing silence of this mausoleum-like prison?

That was answered quickly, too. You couldn't dig right in. Everything had to be done surgically, a tiny bit at a time. We couldn't afford the noise; we couldn't afford any noise. No sense in disturbing our neighbors; wouldn't want them complaining to the landlady. If I got through four or five of those wires in three hours, hooray for me.

My aunt's words rang in my mind: "Ted, just remember: you can eat an elephant if you take it slow and take it one bite at a time. One day you'll look around and it'll be gone. You will get through this . . ."

After I cut the wire of the mesh, the Cover Girl processes kicked in. They were processes that would make even a bomb defuser want to scream; it was tedium times ten.

I'd take out one of the glue sticks, fill in the cut, and then get out the paint and cover it up. Every night. For every three hours work, it took me one hour of makeup.

Front, back, side.

Inspect it.

I'd have Luigi look at it and tell me what it needed.

"Oh, it needs a little of this or that . . ."

It had to be one hundred percent perfect every night.

Every night of every week that was passing on by.

We'd work several days and then sometimes take a day off. And there were times the frail Luigi would get sick, as the clock kept ticking.

The third layer
Three weeks in.

It had taken three whole weeks just to cut the galvanized mesh to the point where the loop could be pulled back, allowing me to go on to the next level. Six inches past the mesh was that big Iron Cross.

Iron irony.

The cross was evidently part of the original garrison bars. Its bars were 1 to 1.25 inches thick, but made of relatively soft steel, cast in the 1860s. But I was still looking at all those layers and I had only four blades; and not full-size blades at that. Two of them had already been all but used up on that damned screen, and I had all those levels to go.

I don't know if I'm going to make it.

I have to make it!

Think!

A cutting agent! That would help. Yes! And I knew where we can get plenty of it. Olive oil! We were in the South of France!

Bon appétit!

Inmates Maher and Ciardelli are suddenly cholesterol-conscious. Keep those heavy salads coming!

Let's keep those bad numbers down!

Little things like that really should have tipped off those prison idiots, but then again we were playing it to the hilt. I had time to think this all through a hundred and ten percent. If I'm going to play a game, I'm going to do it right.

We'd eat the salads and talk about our health.

We'd be so "crafty." We would make tons of stuff from the construction paper. Oh yes, stuff for the wife and kids. We'd leave these little hearts and crap with the glue sticks all around them on the floor and table. It was penal-preschool but, hell, at least that Maher guy wasn't slitting his wrists.

"Hey Luigi, next let's make a cardboard pony and mouse ears!

"Hey Luigi, next let's get the fuck out of here . . ."

I was almost through that cross, but I needed to get something that would hold it into place. The thing was heavy, maybe twenty-five pounds or so, so it couldn't just be bent or "pulled back." This one had to be cut clean through and would have to be moved each night as we went forward.

Think . . .

Within our regular food allotments, we had access to those round Babybel cheeses in the thick red and yellow packaging. If you pulled the plastic off the package, it opened up to wax. *Eat the cheese, put the wax shell in your hand, squeeze it, maul it, and it all turns into a one-centimeter-by-one-centimeter cube that's like heavy clay.* I used that "clay" to wedge into the cut bars on the cross, creating enough pressure to hold it steady. Then we'd clean up the clay, glue around it, paint it, and it was as clean as when it was set in there in the late 1800s.

That took care of the third layer.

So we'd started eating a lot of cheese along with the salads. Our crafts had become masterpieces rivaling Auguste Rodin; the peppiness of that paper pony could've easily challenged the angst of *The Vanquished*!

But we were always aware that *we* could become "vanquished" at any time, too. All a guard had to do on one of his inspections was to get a little over-*curieux* and walk up to that window, slide it back, push on the mesh and that would hit the cross and the whole works would spring and pop, then collapse like an *accordéon*.

It could have happened. One reason they would sometimes take a closer look down into the window chasm was to see if an inmate was storing any contraband in there; something attached to a line that could be reeled in like a fish.

But psychologically, a guard, or anyone, couldn't imagine somebody going through all those barriers and in any way slipping out that tunnel. If a prisoner's going out, he's going out the front door, with a hostage, taking someone's car, and probably not getting very far before he and his commandeered Peugeot are shot to pieces.

Out that window?

Out that tunnel?

Hacking through all that metal?

Pas question!

Throughout our five and a half weeks of work, we would undergo a total of nineteen individual daytime room inspections to go along with my still-daily strip searches.

(There's that number again—nineteen. It seems to haunt me. I was married to Minnie for nineteen months, I was in charge of nineteen nurses at Columbia-Presbyterian Hospital, and there were nineteen bedrooms at La Leopolda. I was brought in front of Patricia Richet nineteen times and she stacked up nineteen boxes of documents about Safra's death. Nineteen attorneys crowded my trial, and I dodged nineteen attempts to dig into what Luigi and I were doing in our cell. I've also learned that some religions believe nineteen is the number of angels guarding hell!)

In those nineteen inspections, as the guards poked around, I was tickled pink. I had more swagger than sweat.

I knew it was a waiting game, and that I would win. They would lose.

Even though we were playing very little chess, Luigi and I always made sure that the game was changing on the board. We were always in that middlegame joust.

As far as our little workspace went, well, it was business as usual. Sometimes they would just come up to the sliding window and look through it. Or they'd slide it back in a quest for bad-stuff-on-a-string. Either way, they'd be looking at my mesh-masterpiece of disguise and deception.

Nothing to see here . . .

Solide comme un roc . . .

No one's leaving this way . . .

No one . . .

The fourth layer

Close to a month had passed.

The next barrier was a series of three-quarter-inch-thick vertical steel bars, about six inches apart, over a yard in, past the window and the galvanized mesh and the Iron Cross bars. At that point, I had to go well into the tunnel.

And I had to stay there.

I couldn't extricate myself at each hourly passing of the guard. So Luigi would form a phony lump of "me" beneath the bed covers. My arms and legs were shaped out of the big quart Evian bottles we were given to drink. After drinking the water, we'd fill them back up with regular tap water and put the cap back on so the guards wouldn't take the bottles. There I was night after night, in bed, all comfy, asleep to the drone of the TV or, after midnight, just sleeping away.

Sometimes the guards would ask why I was going to sleep so early.

"Oh, Ted's been really stressed out," Luigi would explain with a near break to his voice. "The whole trial outcome has been really getting to him."

And as far as the window went, all Luigi had to do was shut the damn thing to block out any view down that dark shaft.

It worked.

All of it was working.

I was a machine.

I was pushed.

Getting out of there was my only chance to expose the truth, and my brain was in overdrive for every little thing.

In the fourth layer, I was able to cut just the bottom of the middle bar and then bend the relatively soft metal back. That gave me just enough room to get through sideways, and I didn't have to lay on too many cosmetics, either, because it was at least two meters hidden down into the hole.

At that point, I was working with just the light that reflected from the outside; the cell light was now mostly blocked by my body and the down-tube distance.

But someone had been watching me as I cut through that deep fourth layer. Watching me *closely*, as I applied the olive oil to the bar with toilet paper, laying it aside to continue the cutting.

That someone would dash out from the shadows and eat the oil-soaked wads. Extra-virgin olive oil was a pretty good treat for a jail-bound mouse with a limited menu; the tissue itself probably provided good roughage.

So there I was in a tunnel, in the dark, with a mouse.

I loved the scene.

I loved it because everything has been taken away from me but I had a pet mouse that I was feeding olive oil, and we were sharing the view.

And it was quite a view of life for us both.

From that quiet vista point, we could see the courtyard, and we could see the people walking around, and all the lights; but they couldn't see us.

They had no idea what a strange pair lurked in the walls.

They couldn't fathom the thoughts and emotions and angst and fear and anticipation and the power of survival that was cutting through the aura and the air just above their heads.

They had no idea of what the future might bring for a man and a mouse reflecting down on them in the aura and the air just above their heads.

Neither, of course, did we.

———

By that point it was getting tougher and tighter to physically jockey in and out and in and out of the tunnel. I'd go in, and come out scratched, cut, and bruised. Guards would see me in the shower and wonder if I'd been fighting.

"Oh no, just a rough workout . . ."

One day in particular, I had bigger and more numerous bruises than usual all over my chest. Another inmate looked me over. "What the hell happened to you?!"

"Oh, man," I said, "I fell down in the shower and I'm taking all this aspirin as part of the low-cholesterol stuff and now I bruise real easy."

"Man, it's kind of weird; you fell on your chest? And you got *all* those bruises?"

"Yep . . ."

Yeah, right.

My battered shape was yet another red flag in our clandestine caper, but my quick excuses kept it at half-staff. No one ever investigated beyond grimacing looks at my black-and-blue body; and no one ever did connect *les points*.

Like the crafts and the salads and Luigi's near-OCD penchant for neatness, they bought it all: *crochet, ligne, et platine.*

Les fous!

Through all of this, while my olive oil–addicted pet gave me a slice of cheesy company and comfort, my guardian angel was still my *real* rock when it came to keeping my spirits up and juiced.

Yes, I was focused on this évasion.

Yes, I would make it happen.

No, I never quit or backed off of anything.

But I *am* human.

I was more than aware that I'd lost everything. I was more than aware of the frustration that I was one of the few who knew the truth about what happened that night when Safra and Vivian died. I was strong in my commitment to get the hell out of there but that didn't change the fact that I was at the lowest, lowest point in my life.

In the middle of this post-trial trauma and jailbreak jumpiness, my intern-friend Kate caught up with me at one of our collective événements.

"I've been talking with my mother and I know what happened," she whispered. "I know you were screwed in that trial!"

Holy shit! I realized. *Somebody other than me* does *know that I've been the Tituba in this witch-hunt. And this angel is Monegasque, at that!*

I slipped Kate all of my contact information and then I quietly spoke with her. "I can't go into a whole lot of detail right now, but in the near future I may need to get in touch with you. You know what happened to me; you know that I'm innocent. I'll need a contact number for yo—"

She didn't hesitate a millisecond.

She gave me her number and I hid it right away. I knew that if they found Kate's number in my cell during one of their more extensive ransackings, it would be game, set, match. Not only did I hide her number, but I put it into code. If they found anything at all, they'd see gibberish; the formula for the area of a trapezoid—not the phone number of a *sympathizer*.

Damn, somebody else fucking knew what had been done to me!

I was pumped.

I was ready.

I felt like I could have *bitten* my way through the rest of those bars and spat ripped metal right into the face of all of those who had conspired to lock me inside them.

The fifth layer

Close to a yard beyond the three-quarter-inch bars was a set of half-inch bars; closer together than the last set. I had to cut two of them in the center of the set to be able to bend them and keep up with my continued contortionist success.

Fine.

I still had some teeth on my blades, plenty of olive oil, and my rodent roommate was getting fatter.

But looking ahead at the next layer—more mesh—I knew it was time to think about adding to our supplies.

The jail did have a very small gym (nothing to compare to Safra's!) where they had a few free weights and some other assorted exercise gear. Along with the handful of equipment were some carabiners; those "D"-shaped, snap-link hooks used by rappellers for their lines—and by everyone else for just holding things together.

I needed them to round out our expedition's outfitting.

And, like our crafts and new-enlightenment diet, spending more time in that closet of a gym so I could get my hands on the carabiners attracted no attention at all. For a long time, the guards and everyone else had seen my regimen of running and exercising in my cell and in the "dog run," so they'd already dubbed me as a health-nut.

I easily pilfered a couple of carabiners, but they were only half of what I needed to work the next layer of mesh. I also needed some of the "rope" I was weaving for our final descent into what was really a park at the base of the prison, two stories below.

Even before I started cutting through the bars, Luigi had been collecting plastic trash bags as he diligently emptied the garbage in our cell, in the library, and everywhere else he made sanitary-conscious rounds in his role as trustee.

He'd go to the central supply part of the jail: "We need more trash bags for the library . . ."

No problem.

Then a few of what they'd give him would go to us.

He'd actually store them right there in the library; in a dead space between two book shelves that butted up against each other at an angle in a corner. They would be our literal lifeline.

Luigi would sneak a few at a time into our cell, where I would take each one and fold it and fold it and fold it until I got it down to one inch wide. Then I'd affix tape from our craft stash on each end and along the middle to keep it at that width.

Afterward I'd braid three of them together at a time, always leaving one loose end to weave in another three. Luigi would then mix the growing rope in with another load of trash and smuggle it back into the corner "hole" in the library.

With some more math work, I calculated we'd need just under fifty bags to comfortably get us to the ground.

In the beginning, though, Luigi wasn't onboard this Hefty train at all. After my first loom job, he freaked: "There's no way these plastic bags are going to hold us! We'll die going out that window!"

"Luigi," I tried to settle him down, "I'm telling you, this is how we're getting down that wall."

But he was rattled. He had visions of us splattered and squashed headfirst into the ground, all wrapped up in a shroud of shredded polyethylene thermoplastic while the Man from Glad flew above us laughing like an evil angel in his smarmy white suit.

I had to prove to Luigi that this would work. I wove a length of six of them together and tied them to the steel rail at the top of the bunk bed. With my feet on the side supports, I leaned back at a forty-five-degree angle, hanging and swaying and tugging and pulling like the highest flying tail-spinner in Cirque du Soleil.

"How much more proof do you want, Luigi?" I asked, still dangling from my perch.

"Oh my god!" he exclaimed. "You are right!"

My point was well made, but right now, as I looked at the last two layers of heavy hurdles down that window, I had another use for a short length of that bag-rope.

The sixth layer

Right up against the final bars was a second layer of wire mesh. It was gauge steel, not galvanized, and it was a double mat. Again, it was a huge pain because *again* it was one-quarter to three-eighths-inch wire mesh that I had to cut on the side and the bottom in order to pull it back, just like the first mesh layer. But the problem was that the blades were getting down to nothing and I still had one more bar on the outside to cut.

And, unlike the first mesh that we could bend up, crawl through, and let bend back down; I knew this one would have to be propped up while I cut through that final outside-facing bar.

Here's where a length of our rope and the carabiners came into play. I cut through the sides and bottom of the steel mesh, lifted it up, and hooked a carabiner tied to some of our rope onto it. There was another carabiner tied to the other end and I hooked that end onto a bar from layer five. That held the mesh up and allowed me to go to work on the final bars.

Paralleling this project was a little something that, in the overall scheme of things, I didn't necessarily *need* but it was damn sure something I wanted. And it led me to stumble on another crucial piece of information.

It was Luigi's dental *crociata* that had got me thinking.

Back in New York, before I went to work for Safra, I had a tooth that developed an infection. My dentist gave me antibiotics. Fine. But it kept happening. It turned into an apical abscess so he had to do the old drill-and-drain.

More antibiotics.

More reoccurrence of the infection.

Back to the dentist and he redrilled the tooth; but he was in a hurry, halfway out the door on vacation, and he drilled a larger hole than necessary. That made the tooth weak, and that caused a hairline crack on the enamel down to the root. The bacteria would follow the crack right down to the blood and gum line and become, yes, another infection!

When my dentist finally returned from whatever exotic getaway my money helped him hit, he gave me some options. I settled on an implant. The long procedure was midstream, and we were waiting for my mouth to heal and be ready for the new tooth when I found the Slatkins' camera.

Suddenly I was in Monte Carlo, but I figured I could slip into the dentist on one of my New York swings and it would all be good. That never happened.

Years later, there I was in a Monaco jail, still with a titanium steel pin sticking out of my jaw with a little aging cap on it, waiting like a stood-up date for a never-to-arrive part.

It wasn't the disaster Luigi was trying to chew with, but I'd been babying that painful half-done hole for years, and it was annoying as hell! Plus, I'd decided I wanted to exit that land of the luxurious lost with one climaxing silent smile and a closing "fuck you very much."

And thanks to Luigi Ciardelli, our caring home away from home had a recently acquired a budget to fix teeth.

The doctor is in . . .

The procedure was major. It wasn't a cleaning while you listened to Kenny G from invisible speakers. They were going for a crown. But first, a root canal. I knew the bucks were piling up. *Great! I have a tab. I'm on the dole!* But the glue on the crown didn't take.

They tried again.

Same results.

During that back-and-forth incisor-insanity, I had to make regular visits to the medical offices for pain pills. And one visit offered considerable comfort. A male nurse manned the pharmacy, such as it was. And he was chatty—especially on that day.

"You know," he told me, "your buddy Luigi still kind of bothers the heads of the prison, what with his escapes in France and all.

"So, because of him they just installed this new camera system."

"*Really?*" I asked. I was *very* interested.

"Yep," he continued, "they sure don't want an evasion here, so they put in this ten-thousand-dollar panoramic camera setup. Come here and take a look."

"Sure . . ."

"It's over there," he told me, pointing out the medical office window.

"Where?"

"There." He pointed again.

I finally focused in.

"Now watch," he told me. "See it pan across the whole prison?"

I saw it and I timed the pan: forty-five seconds.

I had just learned exactly how long we had for one of us to get down that plastic-bag rope before the other could follow. I trusted my bags, but both of us weren't going to be on that rope at once; our plan was about escape—not research and development for Hefty.

The one risk would be in hoping that the camera pan—or whatever genius might be watching it—would miss the dangling rope. It was a pretty safe bet that it wouldn't be seen in the shadows and darkness, and it was a bet we'd have to make. There just wouldn't be time to get a body down that rope, reel in the rope, drop it back, and then get a second body to climb down in three-quarters of a minute. So, after the first drop, the rope would just have to dangle.

My next visit to *la clinique de la prison* was equally cheery.

"We'll try to permanently attach that tooth again in about a week, Mr. Maher," I was told. "We've ordered this special glue, and it will be here on Friday."

I wasn't necessarily nervous, but I *was* anxious. I wanted the tooth fixed, but even more so I wanted to stick it to these bastards on my way home. And Friday was the day I was figuring on getting through that last barricade.

Friday. The *super* super glue arrived!

And I was back to the dentist. Third time's the charm and everything held tight. *Maybe this is an omen!*

My whole package cost thousands. *Thanks, Prince! I'll think of you every time I eat a steak, Monaco. You can shove those salads and that cheese.*

Bon *fucking* appetite!

The seventh layer
The last layer.

We'd held our breath for five and a half weeks.

We'd walked a tightrope for five and a half weeks.

This would be it. The final set of half-inch bars was mainly cosmetic and, as with the third layer, I only had to cut the middle one. But there would be no bending at that spot. That one had to be taken clear through at the bottom and partially at the top so we could easily and quickly snap it out when we made our big move—our *grand déménagement.*

The mesh layer I had just cut through was right against the outer set of bars to prevent anyone from throwing anything into any cell from the outside—an idea that seemed pretty academic right now.

The mesh seems to be holding up just fine, I thought as I was making the last few cuts.

I need more olive oil! Don't spill it! How much is left?

Damn, that mouse is getting fat!

There should be just enough "cut" left in this last blade . . . just enough teeth left . . .

What time is it? Do you hear anything? The guards? Is Sergeant Schultz bumbling around?

This is working!

It *had* worked.

I thought back to that first cut on that first night of our undertaking. I thought about how Luigi and I had learned so much and had eventually done everything so right.

Discipline makes for victory.

I'd always put the blades—dull or not—back into the seal of that fridge every night, with the care that any workman, or surgeon, or soldier, would afford his finest tools. The work became reverential. It was what would save a life. Or two.

I would work.

I would clean and prepare and disguise and camouflage.

Then I would sleep.

And I would dream.

I wasn't dreaming on this last night of work, though. I was at the very real end. I was so close. There I was, on the literal physical edge. I was looking down, looking down at freedom.

Finally I saw the view that Dominick Dunne had so poetically described. And I felt the breeze. It felt wonderful.

It was a free breeze, but it was a strong breeze.

Then I snapped back; my excitement had worked against me. I'd gotten overzealous, and in the murky light and thoughts, I had sawed almost completely through the top of the bar, too.

No!

I needed to solidly anchor this thing back in place, against the wind and weather and against any settling and creaking that this old garrison might do. And that piece was so light; it wasn't that Iron Cross. As much of a pain as *that* was, it was at least heavy enough to stay in place inside the tunnel. The final layer, though, was hanging by a thread on the edge and I had no desire to watch it tumble with loud clanks and thuds to the quiet ground.

Not after five and a half weeks.

I did what I could with the glue and the clay and the Babybel muck and everything else I could come up with but for once, after working, I didn't sleep at all. I could hear the December wind whistling through every crevice in that jail. It was dark but there were enough reflections for me to look out the window—down the tunnel—and see that big bar shaking against its temporary spit-and-gum moorings.

Hang on!

Please!

The morning after the final cut

The house of cards was finished. Most of it was stable and complete, just waiting for that push.

But not yet.

Luigi was back in the same manic mode as when he was on his dentures crusade and worried about the bag-rope. He was antsy and getting extreme.

"We have to do this! We have to do this! Jesus, you even got your tooth fixed! We need to go!"

Then he pushed me; and I pushed back. I could have killed him in a heartbeat, and he knew it.

He froze and stared at me.

"Calm the fuck down!" I spat. "We're not leaving. Not yet. We've got one shot and one shot only. This all has to be right!"

When I cut that final bar and felt that breeze, I knew that we had to wait for one more thing: even worse weather. The cameras, the cops—none of that would be on their best game at eleven o'clock at night in the rain and the dark and the wind. We needed every bit of help for a head start that we could get.

"We have to wait," I said very, very quietly. "Judging by the weather forecast, maybe just a couple of days."

Luigi just turned and paced.

I didn't say anything else. I didn't have to. I looked out the window at that damned last bar; still shaking, still there.

Hold on . . .

CHAPTER 41

THE SMELL OF FREEDOM

Tuesday, January 21, 2003

A weekend of torn emotions had engulfed me. Each time the sea wind rose up I'd look *up* in hopes of rain; each time the sea wind rose up I'd look *down* the tunnel to see just how badly the big bar in that last metal layer was shaking and rattling.

I knew it was still there; it had a built-in wake-up call. If the bar dropped, it would be only minutes before the guards were at our cell.

Game over.

The only question was: would the bar drop before our evasion? A quality-control check wasn't possible. I wasn't going back into that tunnel and risking everything we'd labored five and a half weeks to set up. We had to gamble on that last layer holding. The ship had been launched, sink or swim.

As the day progressed, I kept running my tongue over my smooth and shiny new tooth, courtesy of Monaco's new dental plan for prisoners.

Luigi just kept pacing.

And the weather kept turning colder. Soon it started to rain. By evening I knew this was it. We would move.

"Here's the deal . . .

"We'll go out of the window and down the bag-rope as close together as possible, but keeping in mind that forty-five-second camera scan."

Luigi would go down the ladder and drop first. He was lighter and smaller, and frankly, I just wanted him to get through the tunnel as quickly as possible so I wouldn't have anything to worry about except squeezing myself through. If I was ahead of him and he started having a problem behind me, there would be no way I could turn around and help him. I didn't want him having any kind of issue and making any noise. With Luigi ahead of me, I could at least push his ass.

One thing I had no worries about was his resolve. He had done this shit twice before. *Niente di nuovo.* Nothing new.

And we would go to Italy, not France. Luigi spoke both French and Italian, but I felt more comfortable with him operating in his home *territorio.* Besides, he had his own special connections there to get him to wherever he was headed. He just needed to get me to the US embassy in Rome and then *arrivederci.*

No problem.

We settled in to wait.

11:00 p.m.

The guards strolled by.

Nothing to see here.

Just two hapless prisoners getting drowsy in their cell while life-giving rain fell outside, bestowing natural nourishment on the bountiful coast of Southern France.

Everyone was yawning and easy.

The guards moved on down the line.

Now!

Get up!

This is business. Cold business . . .

Gather up what we need.

I had two sets of clothing layered on.

Monaco's pride ran deep, even into this jail—appearance-wise at least. No orange jumpsuits here. No tacky, unflattering stripes. We had to live up to *l'image!* We had to be *sportif!* We roamed the halls of our *maison d'arrêt* garbed in Pierre Cardin and Nike gym-wear.

For us, that pretentious shit would pay off.

I had made friends with another inmate, a behind-bars businessman of sorts called "Gambler." On Friday night he scored me some brand-new sneakers: bright-white leather but still fashion-forward, in a travel-casual mode.

My appearance was that of a tourist. I fit right in, bottom-lining as the most typical of typical Americans cruising Europe. Clad in expensive new tennies, I looked runway-ready and poised to spend some serious US currency. Where did anything about me say escaped criminal?

Next we readied the bag-rope and the carabiners Luigi had brought in with the trash shuffle from the library.

We pulled on it like a tug-o'-war.

And pulled again.

Tight.

Strong.

We looked at each other and then back at the rope. We had tested and retested my weave-work. *But still . . .*

This couldn't come loose. It was like we were mooring the *QE2*; Cub Scouts don't tie these kinds of knots.

The last thing we wanted or needed was to be in one of those "world's dumbest criminals" shows, having suffered the excruciation of sawing through those bars only to have our lifeline to the ground snap with the first weight and deposit one idiot with broken legs in the laps of the even more idiotic Monaco police, while his dazed and confused accomplice looked down from two stories up.

Hell, no.

We were not idiots and this wasn't a low-rent robbery or dime drug deal. We were performing an international evasion that will save our lives.

We pulled one last time at the dropline of plastic trash bags that we'd crafted together like the strands of an old French *tapisserie*.

This *would* hold.

We assembled our decoy selves in our bunks. The Luigi lump was made of bunched up clothes and Evian bottles we'd leave behind. His topside was not in plain view so the details could be a little less exacting.

My lump on the bottom was in fairly plain sight. *That* needed to be detailed. There would be no television or Luigi sitting in a chair or anything to distract a guard's view as he passed by from this point until whenever it is we were discovered missing.

And the longer before that happened, the better. I needed to look pretty damned good on that mattress. Clint Eastwood had his papier-mâché dummy in *Escape from Alcatraz,* but it didn't compare to the Madame Tussauds–inspired masterpiece that I came up with.

The *coiffure* used to come once a month to cut my hair.

"Don't bother to clean it up," I'd tell him, looking at the sheerings on the floor. "I'll take care of it."

I "took care of it" by saving the pieces of hair in my pockets for my clone.

The lump in that lower bunk had a fine head formed from dampened and molded cardboard, with nice, full, glued-on hair sticking out of the covers to impress and *divert* any guard that stopped to take a look.

Pleasant dreams . . .

———————————

Before we jumped into our tunnel, I grabbed my one personal possession.

Three or so years ago I had everything. I had elite international employment, I had a family that was about to enjoy a world-class education and experience, I was zeroing out the last of my bills, and I had an overflowing bank account to work with.

Now I had this: A cigar in its container. I looked at it. Held it up. This is what I had. I got it as a little gift to myself. During the holiday season, the jail allowed inmates to order special treats: caviar, high-end cheeses, Italian panettone bread, select liverwurst, different salamis, things like that. Or you could order choice cigars. I don't smoke, but one of the stogies on the menu had the name "Freedom." It caught my eye.

Later it *really* caught my eye.

I saw one of the other guys get the cigar and I noticed it came in a metal container with a screw top. So I ordered one.

Now, as we were about to bail, I looked at the cigar again. Held it up again. It was all I had, but inside of it was what I *really* had. Inside of it was all that was left of my life. As this day, this evasion, approached, I'd put my life onto a poor man's micro-fiche—a microscopic documentation of all the precious phone numbers and contact info of people who could help me. Though I wasn't allowed to journal after my arrest, during my trial the reins had been loosened; I had twelve pages of notes I'd taken over the years, which I'd condensed down to half a page. It looked like a mouse—or maybe a pro forger/engraver—had written it.

I had rolled up the half-page and fit it inside the container around the cigar. That's the purpose of cigar containers, isn't it? To be waterproof!

I screwed the top back on and took the cheese wrapper wax and put it around the seal, just in case I had to jump into water someplace for some reason.

And I kept that cigar, too—that "Freedom"—because I knew I was going to be free. And when I escaped from this place, I was going take that son of a bitch and smoke it.

I had everything I needed.

Midnight

I slid the window open. I dove into the metal layers.

You can't be giddy and you can't go the other way and drip sweat. Forget all the emotions and just do the job . . .

I pulled back the mesh, I dislodged the Iron Cross and left it lying flat down in the tunnel. I get back in the cell and lift Luigi into the tunnel along with the rope. With the cuts in the remaining bars, Luigi could easily push or pull them back or away, giving us both a clear shot. Just don't let anything drop to the outside!

Luigi anchored the carabiner on the end of the rope to one of the three-quarter-inch steel bars that hadn't been cut through in that fourth layer.

Now he was at the end of the tunnel; I was at the front.

I climbed in.

I pulled the mesh in after me and snaked my arm and hand under it to slide the window shut behind us. For the foreseeable future, the guards walking by every hour would see inmates Maher and Ciardelli asleep in their bunks, with their one window to the outside snugly closed.

What *I* saw was my partner easing out of the window.

This was really it!

And, my God, this was working!

The bag-rope held, and Luigi monkeyed down the twenty-six feet to the ground in the dark and the rain.

He hit the ground and I had forty-five seconds.

Please . . . don't let that camera catch a shot of Luigi as he hides and waits for me!

Don't let that camera see the rope whipping in the wind!

It was time!

Down!

I made it!

The camera turned.

I ran.

Luigi?!

Luigi?!

Where is he?!

I was close to being physically sick. I realized that Luigi Ciardelli had used his forty-five seconds to take off like a rabbit scampering into the night.

Gone!

Just like that!

Rapido!

And now I was alone.

Motherfucker!

That was my *arrivederci*.

I stood there in shock for a second. *What the fuck?!* But just for a second; maybe less. I wasn't gonna stand long enough for the camera to pan over me. I had to go.

For just one short burst of quick-time, though, I actually thought about what might happen if I said "Screw it," and went back up that bag-rope and back into that cell.

Cut my losses since my Euro-link into Italy was now broken.

God! Where had *that* come from?!

There was no going back! Luigi or no Luigi! I knew this. Not now! Not ever! This deal was done. This was that time when reality has you by the neck and it's shaking you loose from any stray thoughts and daydreams.

This was happening!

You are here. Now all alone. In a foreign country under the gray-night shadows of a prison you've just escaped from. These are the facts. All the "chase" dreams anyone has ever had and all the classic escape-pursuit movies from The Defiant Ones *to* Cool Hand Luke *have just been shot into your veins like the hottest mainline heroin and you're being kicked square in the teeth by what you have to do. You are not going to wake up from this and have everything be hunky-dory. A cold, sleep-shock dream-sweat and some hyperventilating is small shit when sided up against where you are now: you're a single scared animal soon to be hunted and run down to the death by a pack!*

This is happening . . .

I started moving.

We'd dropped into the park. A promenade extended from there that led to the bay, then the gulf, with only one locked gate at the end. I climbed over it and that was that.

Ciardelli was gone; I changed my plan.

Okay, they'll probably figure that fucker will head to Italy, so I'll make the run to France.

How?

By the coast?

No.

That was the obvious way in. The easy way in. The last thing they'd think about is my going up over the mountains and through the woods to Grandmother's house we go; to Nice. At Nice, I could regroup and make my calls and contacts. Then it'd be 125 miles to Marseille and the warm open arms of Colin Powell's staff and buddies. Then home.

3:00 a.m.

It was January in the mountains, and the rain had turned to a steady chilled drizzle. It was fucking cold and I was basically running a marathon. My double set of clothes was soaked completely through. I was shivering uncontrollably and I knew hyperthermia was setting in.

I thought about what might be going on at the prison. It was close to three in the morning. Had they noticed us gone? Had an alarm been sounded? A bulletin issued?

I focused on my thoughts, trying not to let the cold get to me. I thought of my kids and I thought of Heidi. And I thought of how I was losing her with the pressure of this.

I cried and my tears nearly froze.

I will do this.

I made it to La Provençale, the French "interstate." It was a good and quick route to follow, but at this time in the morning, my "typical tourist" persona had switched to "Who the hell is this guy walking along the autobahn at this hour?"

I continued pushing, though. I walked through a couple of the long tunnels. I walked the opposite direction of the cars, knowing that if any authorities were traveling toward me and noticed me, they couldn't readily turn around. If that happened, I'll at least have time to get out of the tunnel and go back down into the hills. It was the best decision to go this way; around the coast I'd be trapped. Screwed.

4:30 a.m.

Nice, France.

I made it.

Four and half hours.

Four and a half hours of fighting the hyperthermia.

Four and a half hours of pushing my training and will.

My first social street encounter was enjoying dawn with a cop! I tipped my hand to him.

Bonjour!

Beau matin, même avec la pluie . . .

Oui!

My French had improved *beaucoup!* Luigi and I would practice for hours. Since I was condemned, the prison system was not obliged to give me any kind of education, so again, I worked things out myself.

Like I would now.

5:00 a.m.

Murky sunlight was coming up over the Mediterranean in a soup of clouds. I was drying *un peu*, shivering slightly less, and back to looking a little more like an American tourist—though my new tennis shoes had taken a beating during their break-in jaunt.

I found a hotel and knocked on the door.

"Hello, sir. I'm an American. Can you help me?"

Thanks to my tourist persona, they opened the door even at this unconventional hour.

"Yeah, you see, my rental car broke down over there and, damn, I left my wallet and passport with it. Yes, sir, it's raining out. Whooeee, I'm freezing! Can you let me use a phone to call a family member? Come on in? Why, sure, if you don't mind. I really appreciate this, sir!"

The innkeeper gave me his phone. Call number one: Heidi.

Her voice. A connection outside those bars! My wife! Finally!

"Baby, I'm free! I need some help! I need a credit card number. I'll be home soon!"

But, no! No! I knew she was slipping, but no! Not like this! First, Luigi ran from me, now Heidi was running, too; to join his disloyal exodus.

"You've escaped?! No! No! We have no credit cards . . . they've all been canceled long ago. You're on your own! You're not going to pull me into this!"

Click . . .

I took a minute. I showed no emotion in front of the innkeeper, watching me from across the room. Just a smile, a shiver, and call number two.

My sister.

And it was her birthday.

"Ted?! You're able to call me?!"

"Yes, I made special arrangements!"

"How are you doing?"

"Fine . . . happy birthday! Hey, what do you want more than anything for your birthday?"

"Oh, mother of god, I want more than anything for you to be free!"

"Congratulations, you got your wish! Now, give me your credit card number. I'm in a hotel in France. I've been given permission by the State Department to . . . uh . . . find my way to our embassy!"

She was screaming at the other end of the phone.

She choked and cried through her information as I took it down. I also took on the name of her husband. How could anybody find me in a population of millions with a simple American name? The innkeeper was more than *heureux* to take my money via the card numbers.

Approuvé!

Voici votre clé . . .

5:30 a.m.

I went into my room and right into the bedroom, into a real bed for the first time in three and a half years. *God, is this what it feels like?!*

I lay there, opened my cigar container, took out my half-page of hope, and picked up the phone on the stand next to me.

Call number three was to Father Ball. I knew that from here on, I would need shepherding from Nice to Marseille. I planned on taking the train. I'd need some cash, some physical help exiting this city, and a hand with the logistics. He was the man. And I knew he got up very early in the morning for prayer.

I could use some of that, too.

I called him and laid out the situation.

"Call me back in a few hours or so at around 9:30," he said. "We'll make this work! I'll get to the bank and then rendezvous with you. They can't touch me there. I'll meet you wherever you say and we'll go!"

This was all working.

But Father Ball was not the last person I spoke to during my "intelligence briefing" from that hotel room; Kate was. I needed to hedge my bet with Father Ball, just in case something funny happened on his way to the fugitive. Besides, it couldn't hurt to have *two* locals on the outside holding lifelines.

I could get Ball to bring me the money and then use Kate to guide me to Marseilles. Really, with Kate and her car, I could even reverse course and go into Rome.

I made call number four and gave Kate a quick *carnet de bord* of what my easygoing, quiet evening had consisted of.

She was not *that* surprised.

"Do you know where the War Memorial is?" she asked.

"That's near to where I am," I said.

"Good, Ted! I'll meet you there!"

But because of her being in Monte Carlo and what she had to do to finish her work and leave without raising any *concern*, it would be close to eleven in the morning before we could meet.

Father Ball would make it first; *then* I'd assess what came next and make a field decision.

My thoughts drifted into mental juggling and second-guessing, though; maybe I should have called Kate first. If she'd jumped into her car before dawn and headed directly to my hotel, this current scene and timeline would be very, very different.

But then again, there were a fistful of fucking ifs in this whole ordeal. Hell, what if I'd never found that damn camera . . .

I didn't tell Father Ball or Heidi or Kate or even my sister exactly where I was. I couldn't risk that, with all the possibilities for eavesdropping or interception, electronic or otherwise. I told the good reverend that I would get down to the specifics when I called him back.

I finally hung up the phone, knowing that what all this represented was another level. I was going to rise to another level that I'd never reached before in my life. I felt it! This just had to be a test to see if I could handle what was being prepared for me, somewhere, someplace. Hell, maybe I'd run for governor or something!

I got up from the bed, went into *la salle de bain* and eased into a hotter-than-hot bath. Even though I had drip-dried somewhat, I was still feeling hypothermic and shivering my ass off.

When I got into the bath, I also grabbed my cigar.

I set one foot in, and then the other, and then the rest of my tired and cold body sank into that steaming water.

Finally!

Comfortable and safe!

I finally allowed myself to be excited and I lit that son of a bitch up.

Fuckin-A!

I did it!

I smoked half the cigar with my eyes half-shut, relaxing in that tub. I turned a few shades of green, but I smoked it! I didn't have a clue what an expensive, good cigar really smelled like—I was no *aficionado*—but the soupy smoke drifting around that bathroom had the sweetest scent I could ever imagine: *Freedom!*

CHAPTER 42
THE BETRAYAL

9:30 a.m.

I made that follow-up call to Father Ball. I was thinking that if he could make it there with no problems, I'd rely on him. I hated to stand up Kate, but I couldn't wait another hour and a half. I couldn't give up a sure *oiseau* in the hand and risk something happening on her end. Even the delay of a flat tire could do me in. I knew she'd understand. She would want me to do what was best, safest, quickest.

Just do this!

Ball answered.

I jumped right in.

"Father, we have things to discuss . . . It's a hundred and eighty-five miles to the embassy in Marseille. Just two hours on the train! But I can't go that far alone without being noticed. I'm whiter than white, an obvious American, and soon there's going to be bulletins everywhere about the escape . . . I need you with me, Father Ball! And yes, the money, take whatever's in the bank for me. There's what, like a couple hundred? Great! Bring it! Are we good? When can you be here?

"Father Ball?

"Father Ball?"

I heard him turn away from the receiver and say to someone, "The man you want is on the phone . . ."

What?!

I sank. I just stared at the receiver. It was 9:30 a.m., just nine and a half hours since my feet landed in freedom. I was just two hours away from *complete and permanent* freedom.

And now, once again, for some reason, I'd been fucked over.

I'd been free for nine and a half hours.

I sank lower.

I was sure the hounds were already thundering toward the door. All they needed was this confirmation; this electronic phone-trace pin in a map. Hell, maybe there were gunmen in the lobby already and that poor innkeeper was stuck under his desk, shaking.

I looked at what was left of my cigar in the ashtray. I looked at what was left of my freedom.

The Not So Great Escape

American Ted Maher and Italian Luigi Ciardelli sawed through prison bars and lowered themselves to freedom on a rope made from plastic bags last Tuesday night. Maher was re-captured the next day at the Apogia hotel in Nice after making phone calls to wife Heidi and other family members in the US. He also called a friend in Monaco . . . Monaco authorities are thought to have alerted the French police, who swooped at 10:30 on Wednesday morning . . . [145]

—Jenny Paul, *The Riviera Gazette*,

Thursday, 30 January 2003

The article says the police "swooped" in at 10:30. Let me tell you, I barely had time to throw on my Nike sweat suit and run downstairs, and they were already waiting for me. A nearby police station had gotten the call.

Although I was compliant, one of the brave members of this crack "strike force" grabbed me in an agitated frenzy, breaking the ring finger of my left hand. If I'd truly wanted to resist, broken bones would have been the least of anyone's worries.

I was brought to the local Nice jail, with sights on getting this *dangereux fugitif* to the prison at Aix-en-Provence *dès que possible*.

Once I was returned to lockup, my finger was *pointedly* ignored. I suffered in pain for over two weeks with no medical care, and as a result, the injury hinders me to this day.

While I was physically back in my cell, mentally I wandered back to that morning after the fire when I woke up in the hospital—that morning of ignorance and slashing secrets: *I didn't know Safra was dead. I didn't know Vivian was dead. I didn't know the small signal fire was allowed to grow lethal.*

I didn't know!

This was no different. Just like all the shit that occurred behind the smoke of that blaze, truths would explode *here* that would make me sick, angry, hurt, and more jaggedly scarred than ever.

And it started with Heidi.

The slipping away was obvious. The pressure and the stress. Okay, fine. But our calls lately had dredged up the specter of Minnie.

"Do you know what Minnie sent me?" she'd ask.

"No . . ."

"Yes, you do!"

"I don't know what you're talking about," I'd tell her.

Then she'd get mad and hang up, leaving me to wonder—unable to defend something I had no idea about.

It was just another part of the rabid rainbow of whats and whys I could lose myself in while I was processed into fucking jail. I'd add the Minnie mystery to the charm of being burned by Heidi's refusal to help me when I called—it was all just more rancid food for thought.

I also had to think about survival once I was transferred to the big house; the deepest level of my nightmare come true. This white-bread American would quickly be on the lunch menu for the bands of pissed-off Islamic insurgents behind those walls. The only question was, how long would it take?

The first abundance of revelation and answers arrived in the form of Donald Manasse.

A dismal déjà vu.

Manasse's Nice office just happened to be within *cracher* distance of the city's jail.

"Ted . . ."

"Donald . . ."

Revelations and answers . . .

Manasse began to lay out the timeline after I had called Heidi. He might as well have been cutting me in two; watching my guts spill out onto the fucking French jail floor. It was like being coldly told at sixteen years old, "Oh, by the way, you were actually adopted, and we've decided to send you back!" It was a truth that gagged with emotional nausea.

He spoke.

And he spoke.

My jaw dropped and my eyes couldn't open any wider. I was shaking and nearly shutting down as he spat out all that had happened. Like when a body goes into physical shock after trauma; an instinctive and involuntary fight-back.

My shock was disbelief.

My shock was anger.

I couldn't be hearing what he was saying.

I couldn't believe it.

It was a truth that bred hate.

"Ted, you have to understand . . . this is really very simple . . . . Heidi didn't want to be a part of this . . . she panicked and called me . . . 'Ted has escaped!' I, well, I simply had to call the authorities at the prison . . . uh, yes, three times I called them . . . they didn't believe me at first, of course . . . they said they had checked on your cell several times on their rounds . . . he's in there . . . yes, with Luigi . . . yes, we're certain . . . no, it must be just a rumor . . . but his wife said he has escaped . . . he called her! No . . . no . . . maybe she's deranged or drunk . . . and Ted, naturally I had to call Father Ball, too . . . I figured he would have heard from you. Ted, we were all concerned for your safety . . . we were afraid you'd be shot! We absolutely had to call the authorities . . ."

I had to breathe.

I had to absorb this.

I had to accept that another part of this horror had snapped a whip around my neck, making me bleed, and was wrenching me down.

Again.

Christ, I just couldn't take this

"You don't represent me!" I told Manasse. "You don't represent shit!"

I was bouncing off the walls in that cell.

"Get the fuck out of my face!" I went on. "*You* called them? Concerned for my safety?! *You're* concerned for my safety?! Why aren't you concerned for my fucking freedom?! Why aren't you concerned for the fucking truth?! Fuck you!"

Manasse turned around and walked out. Evidently it was *temps de l'apéritif* somewhere.

It sure wasn't happy hour in my cell.

I could only sit and wait and think. It was a flat and familiar feeling. I could only think about the trifecta of betrayals I'd just experienced:

My wife.

My attorney.

My priest.

An unholy trinity that might have just stolen whatever life I had left.

True torture transcends physical pain. True torture comes when your mind is bent and twisted and cut. True shackles are not just restraints on your hands and feet, but it is this: prison. Where your whole being, your entire life is put on hold and thrown into a cage and ripped away from you. And there is nothing you can do except pace and scream and wait for papers to be shuffled and motions to be made that may or may not ever help you at all.

It is here, where if the possibility of imminent freedom is just not on the table, well, then never a good or positive thought comes in.

That is torture.

When no sunrise means anything. When no breath of clean air means anything. When even waking up with reasonably good health means absolutely nothing.

That is torture.

The beauty of Southern France was outside. Inside I was thinking of the betrayal from Heidi. Heidi, whom I'd done everything for. All I ever did, I did for my family.

From taking the job with Safra, to acquiescing to kidnappers, to signing a bogus confession, to breaking out of prison.

So to be betrayed after all that was just soul-slicing.

And lurking within this betrayal was the specter of *Minnie*.

"Do you know what Minnie sent me?"

I didn't have the answer to that. But I knew Minnie and I knew Heidi, so I had an idea of the issue.

People get to be close, to really know one another in their souls, and to see who they are as human beings by living together. You don't get that from just going out on a date. Living with somebody lets you know when that person is sick, when that person is in a bad mood, when that person is *anything*. You just know it.

One fact never in question was whether Minnie would ever lose her jealousy of Heidi or her bitterness over losing Matthew. Even with me in prison, I knew Minnie's feelings festered. Maybe *especially* with me in prison, Minnie could lock onto an opportunity for revenge.

She was obviously in contact with Heidi, and it was a contact that Heidi didn't need.

I'd known my wife was suffering and that she was close to snapping. She'd lived through the media camping out around our home and their telling our eleven-year-old son that his dad was a murderer. She had lived through the police bringing Matthew to school because he couldn't wade through the paparazzi. I knew little was left of her tolerance.

And so, after teetering on the edge of nerves, stress, and waning patience for years, she obviously didn't need proof or truth of anything anymore; she just needed a reason to fully escape and disavow everything about me so she could have an excuse to go on with her life.

I didn't know how—*yet*—but I was sure Minnie had found a way to give that to her.

But like I knew Minnie and Heidi, they knew me. They both knew that I was no murderer. I would always say to Heidi when we discussed anything: "I'm telling the truth. Just look into my eyes and you can see that I'm telling the truth." Even on the phone from prison I would tell her, "I just wish you could look into my eyes; you'd see I'm telling the truth."

She had already encountered me turning down an opportunity to be unfaithful. At Columbia, I got propositioned by an attractive neonatologist; Heidi came up on us just as I was letting her down with a comment about my loyalty and love for my wife.

Heidi never forgot that—until now.

It looks like Minnie and Monaco and misleading had finally given Heidi her reason: a reason to forget everything.

CHAPTER 43

THIRTEEN MONTHS

Late January into February 2003

As prescribed, I was housed at *La Maison d'Arrêt d'Aix-Luynes* in Aix-en-Provence. And I was in minority survival mode; I really, *really* don't want to be road-kill for the Muslim Brotherhood here.

The only question is, how long would it take?

I'd already lasted two weeks. Two weeks of trying hard to lie low, but the act was wearing thin. They knew I was there and they weren't happy with George W. Bush's America or any of its spawn. They had little appreciation of Western cowboy dynamics.

Two weeks of trying to acclimate to the miserable pre-spring heat. We were allowed three and a half hours of daily outside activity; or we could decay in our cells. Not me. I tore up my bed sheet and made myself a *Lawrence of Arabia* head cover. I could exercise more and fry to a crisp less.

One afternoon in that open prison yard, I noticed a young Muslim guy who was obviously high on something; and he started to choke.

Really choke.

Everyone was watching this kid turn blue! I don't just watch things like that; I jump in and help. I turned this kid on his side, opened his airway, cleared out the vomit, and with a few back slaps, he was breathing again. I told the crowd watching to get a guard, *now!* Maybe fifteen minutes later, some kind of *personnel médical* finally came out and picked the guy up.

I saved that young man's life and that, in turn, saved mine. My fellow prisoners may not have liked me, but I had preserved and respected the life of a brother of Mohammed. For the duration of my gala getaway in *Aix-en-Provence*, just twenty miles north of the freedom I could have claimed in Marseille, the other prisoners left me alone.

Now the wait was all about extradition back to Monaco. I began to see that I could milk it if I'd wanted to. I could spend another three or four years in France without having to return to my "county jail."

It was a conflicting choice. The sickening heat, rats the size of cats, the potentially shaky truce with the brotherhood; versus doing my remaining years of hard prison time in the *petit* hometown slammer.

I signed the waivers and the extradition papers as soon as they were given to me but, as always, nothing was immediate here.

My gala getaway would last one year and one month.

I settled in.

My goal never changed: to get home and to shout the truth about every part of this to the world. But the everyday flow *had* taken a turn. The curtain was rung down on the evasion act to a chorus of boos and failure. The performance had closed and would not reopen.

My relationship with Heidi had not only slipped; it was plunged into a hole far too deep and narrow for a climb or struggle back up.

Michael Griffith would visit me as regularly as he could, still trying to help as much as he could.

So, there I was. Hollowed out but not defeated. That, strangely enough, was the time to be the strongest. I had needed unbending nerves to saw centimeter by centimeter through those bars, but now I would need even more. This was marooned-on-a-desert-island time; always looking out at the horizon with hope. Yet wondering how good of an idea it might be just to jump into that rough tide and swim for it—maybe die trying. Or pull up even more strength and simply wait.

———

One familiar shadow that did rise up over that horizon was Kate. She dealt with the hundred miles of travel and the craters of political and bureaucratic potholes to get in to see me.

As always, she—and her knowledge of the truth—were like a shot of steroids to my resolve.

My marooning was also interrupted with a fair amount of regularity by another blast from the past, Ellen Thorburn from the State Department. Hell, we were neighbors now. Marseille was a lot closer to my current prison.

Yeah, but you still can't do a damn thing for me, right?

Right.

Have a nice day . . .

Another familiar voice echoing over the gossip fence was that of the slippery Luigi Ciardelli.

Luigi never forgot how both France and Monaco screwed him over in their little shell game that landed him back in jail, waiting on another of Monaco's open-ended eternal investigations.

He wanted to make a fuck-you statement, so he called the press from parts unknown. He unloaded on what France had done, kidnapping him and tossing him into the waiting and equally corrupt arms of Monaco. Then he took the credit, along with the blame, for our entire evasion.

I guess maybe he was feeling *un po' colpevole*, just a little guilty, for running out on me, so he said he was the brains behind things, figuring he could take the heat. Well, maybe he had two evasions of his own on his résumé, but I had to laugh. He had no idea what to do about anything connected with our complex plan until I told him. But he gallantly committed to being the brains behind the op.

I thought of our final drop down that bag-rope; the only thing Luigi had ever repelled off of was his bed, high on cocaine or drunk! He never repelled out of helicopters, climbed up or down mountains, or anything like that. *He* was terrified that the chain of plastic bags was going to break.

"I did it all!" he told the world. "Ted just provided me with some help!"

A few months later, Luigi was pan-handling near the Leaning Tower of Pisa when he was picked up by the Italian police. He had gone back to his old occupation, but the prison-time rust on his skills showed. He was sentenced to twelve years in a prison somewhere in Italy for armed robbery.

If I had actually been stranded on a desert island, I might have been able to scrounge up a coconut or pineapple or two. But during my latest internment we had beets: sliced beets, cooked beats, raw beets, cubed beets, shredded beets. At this prison, we had carrots: baby carrots, straight carrots, shredded carrots, rippled carrots, uncooked carrots. The protein was also big-time: dark-meat turkey with the bones still in, never white meat. For variety they would sometimes toss in some nasty calamari stuff. Every time they brought it in to me, I'd flush it down the toilet, quick, to avoid the smell. I couldn't even have it in the room.

It was all cheap and it was all we had, all the time. If an inmate had a money source, he could go to the food canteen where they had bread, real meat, and fruit. Compared to our little shopping plaza at the jail in Monaco, this joint was Wal-Mart. If you had three hundred bucks or so, you could eat like a king.

Not me.

I could buy nothing.

I had to make do with what they gave me. Cheap shitty food, and cheap shitty toiletries. I lost twenty pounds.

And that was pretty much all I had to lose.

It's a stark feeling to genuinely have nothing.

Nothing.

Hollow but not defeated . . .

Eventually the Catholic priests who made their rounds of the prison donated fifty euros to an account for me (for more-than-obvious reasons, my old buddy Father Ball was no longer my bank manager!). I went all out and bought three avocados, a couple of candy bars, and a couple of stamps. That was it. But at least it was mine. And I wanted it to last. I wanted what I had to grow—literally.

I took one of the avocado seeds and I germinated it. I grabbed some dirt on the promenade, brought it into my cell, got an old container, and planted my avocado.

Within a couple months the damn thing was actually growing! It felt good. It was life. I felt just slightly bad, though, giving birth to something behind bars.

But it wouldn't have to endure that for long.

I began to play chess with a guy who had a serious brain, a man by the name of Kamel. He was in there for some kind of complex business scam.

In the French system, inmates are allowed to have their wife or girlfriend come in for a "visit" twice a week. The couple is given their own special little room for about two hours so the prisoner can continue the humanistic process of keeping things together until the incarceration ends. The process worked; Mrs. Kamel became pregnant shortly after I arrived.

When I heard that my chess buddy's wife was getting ready to give birth and that the end of his sentence was nearing, I told him, "I have nothing to give you as a gift except this."

I handed him the tree.

"I don't want them to kill it," I said, "and I know you have a house over here. Please, plant it, free it, let it grow."

He was so touched that somebody would be willing to give like that—from the heart.

"Ted," he asked me, "do you ever get the chance to speak to your family?"

"Kamel," I said, "you know they're in America; I don't have any money to call them."

Like the food, if you had cash or connections you could get anything you wanted in there. It was nuts. You'd go out on the promenade on weekend afternoons, and even though the guards were watching, it was like AT&T out there. Everybody had a phone to their ear.

"How are you doing? Good . . . good . . . oh, hey, hold on a second—I have another call coming in . . ."

Phones, heroin, cocaine, alcohol, porn—more than you could ever have in your dreams on the outside—what you wanted, when you wanted it. If you had the funds, it was there in your cell. The guards who were making maybe the equivalent of a thousand dollars a month were more than happy to help you acquire the necessities. For a price.

Naturally, Kamel had a cell phone with unlimited minutes. His thanks for what I did for him now made *me* connected, at least for one time; one precious moment before Kamel left. Because of him, I was able to join the cell pirates on the promenade one afternoon and I was able to join my family. Or what was left of it. It was the first time in so long that I could freely talk to my children.

"Never forget I love you guys . . ."

And yes, I spoke with Heidi. I told her that I knew she had reached the breaking point. I knew she wanted a divorce. "Fine, we'll both see the children. I'll do what I can for you when I get out. Just don't sell our house! Don't sell that vacant land we have," I pleaded. "I'll build a house on it when I get back and we'll split the profit. Yes. Thank you."

"I'll talk to you all soon . . ."

It would be seven and a half years before I would speak with my Matthew again.

And as far as what I had asked—*begged*—of Heidi:

She sold the house. She sold the land. She put all the money in a secret account.

She took complete custody of the kids. She changed their names.

Fuck Ted!

I got nothing.

Nothing.

Nothing.

May 2003

On the promenade.

No phone.

No chess with Kamel.

Hotter than hell.

Trying to exercise.

I heard something. After 325 parachute jumps out of a helicopter, I knew this sound. I knew the sound of choppers and I knew the sound of them coming in low. But I also knew that this prison yard was 'copter-proof. It was covered, spider-web-style, by these rubber band–type nets, wall-to-wall over the grounds. If a helicopter tried to drop in there, this shit would wrap in the rotor and that would be that. Mop up the mess and bury the bodies.

But still, I knew that sound.

Within seconds we had our own episode of *Mission Impossible*. In came a chopper that had been hijacked. It was obvious. Someone clearly had a gun pointed at the pilot's head. The bird hovered just meters over the web. They weren't stupid: they know what that mesh would do. A rope was lowered . . .

The guards in the towers couldn't shoot. Eight hundred-plus inmates were standing within sixty feet of that threshing machine in the yard below. That 'copter would make hamburger of a big chunk of them if the guards' guns dropped it. It would be one thing if the web snagged the craft and—*bang!*—unplanned and instant carnage, but the prison wasn't about to *cause* that kind of scene.

I had my own thoughts. Was this the Russians? Were these the bastards who roughed me up in that van? The ones who attacked me at La Belle Époque? Were these "employees" of Lily's?

Who the fuck is this and is it me they want?! Somebody wants something!

I hid behind a building. How many were going to drop down that rope? How many inmates and guards were going to be killed before they got to me? The Russians weren't going to be too concerned with collateral blood.

It took my mind off the heat and the beets for a few moments, that's for sure, but it turned out that the helicopter was brought in by a mob member who had actually escaped from our little home here. He'd sworn to come back for his brother and he was making good on his promise in a big way. Within three minutes, the brother was up the rope and the show was over.

A few weeks later, they were all recaptured trying to rob a bank in Switzerland and were separated into different facilities.

But this stuck with me. This prison had been breached. People not only had *escaped* from here, but people could get *in* here, too. I never stopped listening for that sound again.

CHAPTER 44

FOUR AND A HALF YEARS

February 2004

After thirteen months spent in the swelter and vermin nest of *La Maison d'Arrêt d'Aix-Luynes*, it was time. I was uprooted and transferred to another prison, one that doubled as a central transporting station.

Twenty-four hours later, I was jammed into a little Ford Escort wagon with three cops, returning to the magnificence of Monaco. I quietly noticed that they were not armed. I knew I could easily overpower them. I could do something here. But I didn't. I just wanted this all to be over and for the truth to blossom, like I knew my avocado tree was doing in Kamel's yard.

Freedom and life . . .

But that life was now in a danger I never banked on. Helicopters, fire, guns, the Green Berets . . . I had never been so full of pure abject fear as right in that minute! Those Frenchmen were driving that cheese-box of a car at ninety to ninety-five miles per hour all the way to Monaco, 120 miles away.

"Slow down!" I kept yelling at them. But all the while, they were receiving these frantic phone calls asking them where the fuck they were.

"Où es-tu?!"

"Où es-tu maintenant?!"

"Mr. Maher," they said with a smile as they pressed on the gas, "there is a party waiting for you!"

When we rolled into Monte Carlo, it looked like there'd been a massive traffic accident. Three huge van-trucks had emergency lights spinning. Motorcycle cops were everywhere with all their lights blazing.

Special police.

Pistols.

Rifles.

Uzis.

We pulled into an entourage of about twenty-five policemen. As I was being hustled through the crowd, I recognized one of the interrogators who'd brought me to some of the soirees with Patricia Richet.

"Francis!" I asked him. "What the hell's going on?!"

"Monsieur Maher," he replied, "you know, the show must go on!"

"You need all these people for *me*?!" I asked.

"The show," he just repeated, "it must go on!"

I was brought immediately to the minister of justice and a judge of instruction. I was slapped with the information that it was indeed showtime: "We'll be doing another investigation and we don't know how long this one is going to take. You're being charged with *s'évader de prison*."

This was going to be fun.

We don't know how long this will take?

I knew. I knew I was going to be sitting there for a while.

That "while" ended up being four and a half fucking years.

Maison d'Arrêt, The Remand Prison, 4 Avenue Saint-Martin, 98000 Monaco
Home sweet home away from home.

I was back.

Another trial loomed and that meant lawyers. Donald Manasse made his well-worn way through all the levels of security to my cell.

Just like the good ol' days.

"Ted . . ."

But it wasn't a warm, long-lost-buddy welcome.

"Fuck off, Donald!" I screamed. "You're the last person on God's green earth that I need to be talking to! I'm in this shit now *because* of you! But things have a way of turning. The truth will come out. You can mark my words, Donald: the truth will come out one day!"

Manasse tried to shrug me off and turn the "conversation" toward staid legal matters. "Ted, I have exchanged some letters with Mr. Griffith. I understand he is to be a part of this second trial. I strongly urge you not to use him. I will handle all of this."

"So, Donald," I asked, "you're suggesting that I should *fire* Michael Griffith?"

"You don't need him, Ted," Manasse said.

"I agree about some housecleaning," I shot back. "But I'm not firing Michael, Donald—I'm firing *you!*"

Manasse just looked at me.

It would be the last professional or personal dealing I would ever have with Donald Manasse; but not before he gave me one more thing to think about in that fucking cell.

"As you wish, Ted, but I'll have you know that you're dismissing royalty."

Royalty?

"What the fuck are you talking about?" I asked.

The grim tale that unfolded should have begun with "It was a dark and stormy knight . . ."

It seems that not long after the Trial of the Century climaxed, Donald Manasse, Esq., was rewarded by Monaco for his uncompromising and sterling defense of me.

On November 18, 2003, in the Monegasque Throne Room, "Mr. Donald Manasse, legal, commercial, and fiscal council" was awarded Monegasque knighthood! He was elevated to "a Chevalier de l'Ordre de St. Charles in the Principality of Monaco."[146] His elite status was bestowed "to reward merit and recognize the services rendered to the State or the person of the Prince."[147]

As Manasse talked, I sat slack-jawed and ready to heave. But I couldn't deny the truth in it: *Sir* Donald Manasse had definitely "serviced" his State and his Prince.

Pour récompenser le mérite et reconnaître les services rendus à l'Etat ou à la Personne du Prince!

Not long after I suffered through the glad tidings of Sir Donald, Michael Griffith showed up on *Avenue Saint-Martin* for his part in old home week and the festivities of our family reunion. I couldn't wait to tell him the news. I figured it was the perfect way to start things off . . .

"So, Michael, have you heard about the newest addition to Monaco's nobility?" I filled him in on what transpired with Donald.

When I finished, he just stared at me.

Finally, Michael told me, "Gee, Ted, maybe you should be careful in what you say about this; you certainly don't want to offend the *aristocracy* . . ."

It turned out Griffith had brought his own Monegasque connection into our reunion—a local attorney. I had to wonder if this guy had his sights set on becoming a knight, too! But it didn't take long of us talking for me to see that he didn't appear to be bought and paid for by the Monaco establishment. He wasn't dancing on the same smarmy scrimmage line as team Blot-Manasse.

We talked some more.

All three of us knew what the results of the evasion trial would be, but there was still always the underlying chance that at any time a truth mine could be uncovered and I could get the fuck out of there.

Even with a pending evasion trial being a formality, my latest actions demanded re-actions from the Monegasque legal system. The local attorney was obliged to ask me about how I executed the escape.

"I can't answer that," I told him. "And if they or you keep pushing me, I'm back on a hunger strike. I'm not going to play any games this time."

They repeated their new inquisition once every six weeks or so. They *had* to find out about every step in my evasion from their rock-solid maximum-security prison.

Was there a maintenance officer involved?

Was this person involved? That person?

Was my attorney involved?

Was someone from the outside involved?

How did you get the blades in?

"I'm not saying anything," I'd say over and over.

How did the blades come in?!

"I'm not talking about the fucking blades!" I'd repeat. "Sorry . . ."

I probably should have told them that Manasse helped me.

"I'm strip-searched before and after I go to see my attorney, but, oh, yes, by now I know which guards will be on duty when I come back, and which guards do and don't do the most probing searches. I know who is lazy."

Yep, I could have arranged for my attorney visits to be on certain days so I'd be examined by the most deadbeat guards. "Sure, Manasse gave me the blades! Yessir! And I just slid them all up my ass and these lazy-ass fat guards missed 'em. You bet! Give ol' Sir Donald a call!"

The main issue was that my evasion was a huge embarrassment for them. Here was Ted Maher, a nurse, escaping through multi-levels of bars, with cameras everywhere, an official and comprehensive bed check every hour, and their crack penal team didn't do a damn thing about it.

Unfortunately, they did have me back in their greasy grasp and they were going to make the most of it. They were going to hang me out and hang me up again. It was more torture of forcing me to watch the noose sway in the wind.

More waiting.

I had an old sentence to fulfill and some guaranteed new time to be added to my stay in the luxury of Monaco.

They were not going to spend years investigating a simple evasion, but they could spend years dangling me by a hook. What did a numbing limbo and a complete cut-off from life do to the average person?

I think they were hoping I'd kill myself.

The PR didn't matter now. My escape proved my guilt in front of the world, didn't it?

The man is obviously crazy, isn't he? If he offs himself, oh *bien*.

So there I sat, through Christmases, anniversaries, birthdays, sunshine, blue skies, and sacred moment after moment of life—locked down in a lie.

2005

It was during that introspective time that I received a depressing communication from the state of New York. I was being divorced and the names of my children were being changed.

Spectaculaire . . .

It was hard to lose myself in anything; from exercises to optimism, nothing meant much. But I never gave up. I dried the tears and kept pushing.

Nothing will break me.

While I was in the *Aix-en-Provence* prison, I kept up the habit of trying to educate myself. In the French system, I'd initiated a language training program. I figured I'd formalize the rough French I had been learning for so long in the trenches. Every month, I'd get a new cassette tape with further *merveilles français* for me to absorb. And over there, when you took classes, you could actually qualify for a reduction in your sentence.

When I rebounded to Monte Carlo, the service was supposed to be transferred.

Nope.

Not in Monaco.

"We can't allow you to have these tapes," I was told by the prison's new governor, the suddenly elevated Christian Zabaldano. "We don't have the time to examine them; there may be something *mauvais* on them that you shouldn't have."

I looked at him, resorting to a base, yet very direct and readily understood statement: "You're such assholes here . . ."

From that point on, he and his goons would take away anything that would help me to educate myself and keep my mind going. Or to chronicle my story. As before, they wanted to break me.

That would not happen.

There was a CNBC television program with Erin Burnett centered on the stock exchange. I got hooked. I gave myself a quick-pick education in business. I coupled that show with the who's who of the financial crooks and swine drifting in and out of the jail. I tapped into their experience. I learned how to buy euros. "You think that the yen is going to fall? Well, do this . . . do that . . ."

I gave myself a theoretical ten grand to work with and it became my fantasy league. I'd speculate. I'd look at current conditions: *That would make this weaken, this would cause an increase . . . I'm going to buy this much in this currency and so much of that . . . North Korea just sent up a missile, so that's going to affect this or that . . .*

I got adept at studying the tiny fast numbers on the screen and fathoming what they all meant. I started every month with another on-paper ten thousand, building it up to twenty in one month, a hundred big ones the next.

It was mind-exercising games through CNBC and Erin Burnett. And I studied up on everything about Burnett and another CNBC guy, Bob Pisani.

Pisani had actually been the executive director for a law firm where Michael Griffith once worked. Griffith became a superstar lawyer while Pisani crunched high numbers on CNBC. And I'd gotten to know them both in that cell.

Small fucking world . . .

Summer 2006

A German businessman and Monaco resident, Martin Marschner, was booked into the prison. He wasn't happy. He was being accused by his seventeen-year-old step-daughter of molestation. These accusations *coincidentally* came on the soiled heels of Marschner's discovery—and disapproval—of the affair she was having with her forty-year-old school bus driver.

I ran into Marschner in the prison yard.

"You're Ted Maher, aren't you?" he asked. "I'm so sorry for what this country has done to you."

It was an echo of Kate.

"Who are you?" I asked.

I got the story.

Marschner's wife, Jacqueline, worked on-staff in the Prince's palace—ground zero for all of Monaco's financial secrets and stashes.

Martin occasionally helped his wife with some math.

He knew.

He knew a lot.

He knew about things like veiled wire transfers and underground banking in Monaco.

He knew the truth.

As he talked to me, I realized that even more people out there knew that truth.

Later, I would even get a letter from Jacqueline expressing her *support* for my fight. *After* her retirement from service to the Prince, of course . . .

Kate.

Martin Marschner.

Jacqueline Marschner.

They knew.

They *knew*.

Three years later, Martin Marschner would have his name cleared and become the first inmate of Monaco's prison system to be monetarily compensated by the Monegasque courts for "wrongful incarceration."

Late 2006

I'd been in suspended animation. I'd been going through crawling motions of living. It seemed like so long ago—it *was* so long ago—when there'd still been that assumption that this would certainly be worked out and the truth would be known, and I could get on with life.

That hapless hope had been nothing more than the sour punch line to a tasteless joke. I was here again, seeing and living what this gilded palace of sin was about each and every day. This jail was like a microcosm of the Monegasque way.

On my first "tour" of this facility, I wanted to explode, witnessing what the nanny state of Monaco could do to people; not just with Donald Manasse and the judicial authorities, but with the blue-collar worker bees as well. (Of course, there are no real Monegasque blue-collars, they're really more *lapels d'azur*.)

Either way, blue or white, if you were Monegasque, you were on the payroll. If you were the town drunk or you were cleaning up trash, you were on the payroll. If you did twenty years as a janitor, you got your full pay for the rest of your life. That was the drug of being Monegasque. If you had a job doing anything, after twenty years or so you got your full paycheck until you died. Not percentages like pensions and Social Security, but the full Monty of your compensation for the duration.

So at a young age, you can lead the good life on the Côte d'Azur, because you are Monegasque. It's great for them, sure, but it breeds puppets. Nobody goes against that system.

It breeds people who look the other way, allowing those who are taking care of them to do anything they want just as long as that care keeps on a-comin'!

It breeds corruption. Any system that is based on extreme wealth has to at least stay creative and diligent in proliferating ways to keep the gold flowing.

Whenever you decide to inbreed, you risk the possibility—*probability*—of giving birth to a mutant. These little kinks in the process are what elevated Zabaldano into power as the new prison *directeur*.

The old governor, Charlie Marson, had fit the mutant-puppet profile well. So had his son, Renaud, who worked in the facility as a guard, enjoying some good old-fashioned nepotism via his then-well-positioned daddy.

Neither of them, however, was Monegasque.

But Zabaldano was, and he had been floating around the hierarchy of the local *force publique* as part of some special police force. He put his heroic public-service talents to the test on one of the Côte d'Azur's more chilly days, leading twenty young cadets out into the wilderness for intense mountain training. Zabaldano, the Monegasque answer to Buffalo Bill, managed to get the whole party lost and wandering like blind lemmings. It took forever, but Zabaldano's scouts finally charted stars or followed pigeons or something and eventually made it back to the urban sector of paradise.

Most of them had to be immediately hospitalized for hypothermia.

"What the hell do we do with this guy now?" became the big question for Monaco. "Where do we put him?"

Well, sure, make him the security director of the jail system! He will be responsible for any breaches in security or lack thereof.

Oui!

Right after I escaped, whom did they fire? Zabaldano? Nope, they canned Charlie Marson! Then Zabaldano was promoted to governor! Now normally, you'd fire the person responsible, but Zabaldano is Monegasque!

Renaud was soon gone, too. Without his papa to protect him, the non-Monegasque kid was ripe for some perilous picking.

Puppets.

Corruption.

One of the guards who I marginally got along with mentioned that he played football with Renaud and that the poor boy was still very upset about the evasion and what had happened to his and his dad's jobs.

I told the guard that the next time he saw Renaud, to tell him something for me.

"I can do that, Monsieur Maher," he said. "What would you like me to tell him?"

"Tell him," I said with a smile, "that I'm sorry they fired your daddy's ass but, hey, *that's the way we do it in Monaco!*"

Early 2007

My second trial began, preceded by some Patricia Richet–esque interrogation by former courtroom rookie-of-the-year, Jean-Christophe Hullin. It was my first face-to-face meet-'n'-greet with the magistrate; at the "big" trial, we were never formally introduced.

"Nice to meet you," I said to him with a smile. "You were the judge of instruction who closed my original file, right?"

Yes . . .

"Like I said—" My smile waned. "Nice to meet you . . ."

The new proceedings were not Monaco's Trial of the Century II. They weren't much of anything really, except an opportunity to stretch me on their ridiculous golden rack just once more for old times' sake, grinding out a few more screams of pain.

The maximum for simple evasion without guns, without a knife, without a helicopter, without threatening anybody, without hurting anybody, was one year. If I had used a weapon of any kind on anyone, I'd be doing seven or eight more years. But I was a threat to nobody; I just up and left. So, let's get this over with. Slam dunk.

Coupable!

But wait, there was something unexpected to liven up the party: Lily Safra.

The "poor" widow.

She had her head barrister, Marc Bonnant, send one of *his* head assistants to the trial with a large dossier of doom. His delivery was material similar to a victim impact statement in the United States, claiming poor Lily was seriously *injured* by my escape.

Then Bonnant himself showed up with *another* assistant in tow.

Griffith saw Bonnant. "What are you doing here?" he asked.

"Mrs. Safra was injured," he told Michael.

Bonnant then addressed the court with his assertion: "Mrs. Safra was injured because she expected Mr. Maher to serve his full ten-year sentence. When she heard he escaped for over eight hours she was mentally confused and angry; it produced serious psychological problems. For the hours that he was gone, she was psychologically injured!"

"When I heard Bonnant claim Lily was injured," responded Michael openly, "the first thought I had was that it must have happened when Ted escaped from the window and he jumped—did he land on her head? Did he dent her car?!"

Bonnant, with a straight face, finished giving his statement to the court, and the three judges adjourned for ten minutes. They came back, and in a surprise move, they basically threw him out of court.

They seemed tired of me, of my case, and of all the *des conneries* stinking everything up. They just wanted to put me away again, wash their hands in Pilate's bowl, and sweep away the blood curse once and for all.

So that's what they did.

I got nine months tacked on; Luigi got twelve in absentia. If he ever gets out of *il carcere in Italia* and meanders back to Monte Carlo, he'll finish up his seven and a half years there for armed robbery, and then another year for busting out.

In the meantime, *Bang!*

I was back in a cell.

But with some real darkness suddenly around every edge. No doors were going to open anytime soon, and the Monegasque seemed to be blatantly hoping I'd die. And the truth along with me.

It had been seven and a half years since the end of 1999 to where we were now, rolling into summer of 2007. My lawyers had informed me that in Monaco, a prisoner generally must serve seventy-five percent of their sentence before a parole period can come into effect. Tack on nine months for the evasion, and by all accounts I should be out of there early in 2008.

But, of course, another of those delightful surprises I should be used to by now coiled up in the corner and readied to strike.

One quiet afternoon, I was brought to the medical center where my old pal, the nurse, came in with my file and started to do a blood test. And he was talking about getting me ready for a physical and—

I interrupted.

"Just what the fuck are we doing here?" I asked.

"Oh, that's what we do before we transfer a prisoner," he told me. "I've got to give you a physical to make sure everything's fine with you because we can't send a prisoner that's sick to another—"

I interrupted again.

"What are you talking about?!" I got up in his face. "A *transfer*?!"

I found out that Monaco was preparing to ship me to France for the final months of my incarceration! I guess they suddenly realized that I had a fairly short time to go and, damn, it looked like I was probably not going to kill myself. So, hell, they'd just help things along and send me back into the maw of an ugly French general prison population.

Since there was little chance of the hero act I pulled the first time seeing a random repeat, the bastards are right: I wouldn't make it a second time.

I went *off*!

Guards gathered.

"I know you want me and my story to die, but now, here, at the end of my sentence, you fuckers are going to throw me into the fire to be killed in France? Well, I'm not agreeing to go there. I'm *not* going there. I'm not eating, and I'll fucking die right here for everyone to see, so you better make other arrangements. I've spent more time in this jail than anybody else in its history and now, when I'm this close to the end, you're giving me your own little death sentence by shipping my ass off to a French prison? It's *not* going to happen!"

I got a hold of Griffith's local lawyer and he jumped right on this *and* right on the procurer. After relating just how I felt about their *offer* of a trip back to France and that I had already stopped eating again and maybe, just maybe, they really didn't want the world to see me die here—guilty, crazy, or otherwise—they made a "special arrangement" for me to spend the last months of my sentence there.

Right there.

Right where all the shit began, so many years ago.

CHAPTER 45
REDEMPTION

July 31, 2007

I had never given up thinking that "at any time a truth mine could be uncovered, and I could get the fuck out of there." But the long lull in action on that front had admittedly tempered my optimism and energy.

Until one summer morning in the Mediterranean heat.

Opening up a newspaper and seeing your picture is a rush; maybe a reporter snapped you at a grand opening or a sports event or something. But when you open the paper and see your life right there in front of you, synapses and senses start to scream.

What I saw wasn't Ted Maher buying a hot dog at a Yankee game.

This was it. This was the uncovering of the truth mine and I was leaping right on it and shit was going to blow!

On that hot morning the French newspaper *La Figaro* was giving us a few words from Judge Jean-Christophe Hullin. Yes, we were hearing from his *honor,* the magistrate—now exiled—who had presided over my Trial of the Century and the evasion proceedings.

Turns out Hullin had been due for reinstatement for another term as a Monegasque judge of instruction. But even though he had gone along with crucifying me, he apparently wasn't completely toeing the party line and in sync with that *de gauche à droite,* "from the left to the right," business. Monaco didn't reinstate him.

Au revoir! Adieu!

How can you do this to me? I'm sure he was thinking. *Look what I've done for you! The business you have is flowing because of me!*

Sacré bleu!

So he was out of his job and had to leave Monte Carlo and go back to France with his reputation and legacy between his legs.

So I guess he figured he had nothing to lose; it was time to tell the truth.

Nothing hurts liars like the truth.

NEW CLAIM IN SAFRA DEATH

The trial of male nurse Ted Maher—convicted of the 1999 murder of multibillionaire Edmond Safra—was fixed, according to one of Maher's defense lawyers. Michael Griffith tells Page Six that the explosive 2002 trial in Monaco is under investigation by the principality's judiciary after a bombshell revelation by Jean-Christophe Hullin, chief investigative judge on the case. Hullin recently disclosed that a hush-hush, pre-trial meeting was held among himself, Monaco's chief prosecutor and another member of the defense team headed by Griffith. The three allegedly agreed Maher should be convicted and get 10 years in jail. A jury of three judges and three laymen did just that. "It's a terrible situation—just disgusting," said Griffith. "Poor Ted has spent eight years of his life for a trial that was fixed."[148]

—Richard Johnson, Paula Froelich, Bill Hoffmann,
Corynne Steindler, *The New York Post*, July 31, 2007

Hullin's "disclosure" made headlines everywhere. As soon as the prison authorities saw the story—right after the initial "Holy shit!" shock—they tried their damnedest to suppress that steamy "collector's edition" of *La Figaro*. But a copy got to me anyway.

I was elated, but also furious about still being locked up. I yelled at every guard, every official: "Why am I still in here? I'm an innocent man! Why am I still here? Don't try telling me that whole 'This is the way we do it in Monaco' crap! I'm an innocent man!"

Then the media thundered in like wild dogs.

News conferences with my local attorney were set up. Publications like *Libération* told the story along with tons of magazines from all over the world. International television covered it.

The news was simple: Ted Maher was wrongfully charged and condemned for something he didn't do. The whole trial was prearranged, and it was something that Hullin had a hand in.

The media was in shock. After all the far-reaching and not-such-a-stretch conspiracy theories, they realized that at least one thing was solid and true: this whole thing *was* orchestrated. I was right: I was nothing more than a sacrificial lamb for the image of Monte Carlo and whoever was really behind the death of Edmond Safra.

Shortly after Hullin's confession, the chief of police in Monaco was also fired. Then I remember *he* came out with a press release damning Monaco; stating that he was told not to reveal certain facts during the trial.[149] Facts that could have affected the outcome!

The entire exposé was sounding more like a Saturday Night Wrestling Slam Down than a legal system.

I was busting apart. I told the local attorney, "We have to take this to the next level. Now!" But we were being told that they had to continue to hold me pending *another* investigation: an examination of what Hullin was claiming.

No!

What was being said wasn't from some disassociated nut or even me; it was coming from their own judge! Then things got really nasty. *I* got really nasty. The guards would come in and I would accuse them of holding me in a concentration camp—my imprisonment was now internment. I never shut up about telling them they were wantonly punishing an innocent man.

Then I started writing letters: to the minister of justice, the bishop, priests, US Secretary of State Condoleezza Rice, the secretary of state of Monaco. I mailed out registered and notarized letters that cost me every dime of the small amount of money I had left or could scrounge up. I sealed them with tape along all the sides to make sure these letters remained untampered with until they got to where they were going.

And I couldn't say, "Hey, let's go to the copy machine!" There was no copy machine. I had to write every single letter by hand, and if I didn't do it at the right time, the guards would seize it.

They screwed me until the very end.

The State Department was finally starting a hefty push on Monaco, but the righteous-royal principality was stonewalling. They were ignoring our State Department. The United States was demanding a response and you might think this gopher-hole-sized country would answer the most powerful country on Earth.

But nothing.

Zero.

The United States kept at it. The State Department understood what Hullin had said and what it meant. I was innocent. An imprisoned American was innocent. They realized they had to do something, and they had to do it quickly.

And I was pushing even harder: "If you don't let me out after what that judge has said, guess what I'm going to do? I've done it before! I'm going on a hunger strike and this time I'm not coming out of it until I get to America. You can think about that. I already have a track record, and everyone has been notified that the judge has come out and cleared my name and I want my ass out the door tomorrow! And if I don't have an answer immediately, I'm going to be back in the hospital again to not only die on your doorstep, but to die as an innocent man!"

Then Zabaldano came to me.

"Ted, we really are getting things almost ready to find a way so that we can get you a conditional release . . ."

I pounced on him. "A *conditional* release?!"

"Well," he tried to explain, "it's something that would help us both to make this latest awkwardness more palatable."

The translation of that was that they *still* wouldn't have to cop to their corruption. Why, it was just an amazing coincidence that they'd been planning all along to grant me this conditional release. Hullin's revelations had nothing to do with anything.

"This conditional release requires specifics that you have already attained," Zabaldano went on, "having served at least seventy-five percent of your sentence and a few other simple provisions. It also states that if you ever came back to Monaco, we would have to put you back in prison."

Came back?!!

"If I ever came back here," I told him, "I'd come back with an army!"

He stared at me, looking scared to death.

"I'm *never* coming back here, you idiot!"

I had to laugh to myself, though, about the prospect of coming back with an army. I wouldn't need but five trained men to take over that splotch on the map. Close down the three entrances in, nail down their communications with a scrambler, shut down and control the electricity, and you could paralyze the works. They wouldn't be able to do anything. Put a gun to Prince Albert's brain, tell France to stay out of it or we blow Al's head clean off, put a dog leash around his neck and make him a pet.

This is the way we do it in Monaco now . . .

I snapped out of my fantasy and told Zabaldano again that I want out of here, stat!

Again he started to drone, "You know, Ted, you've really caught us at a bad time with all of this. The minister of justice isn't here. It's July and August. I mean, everybody leaves Monte Carlo, there's so many authorities on vacation and—"

"I'm not listening to any bullshit excuses!" I screamed. "You get a hold of whoever you need to get a hold of, and you get this *conditional release* thing or whatever else you've got rolling, because I'm getting out of here one way or another!"

Even with my innocence now broadcast to the universe, it took days and then even weeks of letter-writing and shouting and jumping up and down and threats and just plain anger to finally touch, for real, that sweetest of all gifts: freedom.

I pressured them and I pressured them. Ultimately it wasn't lawyers or politicians or anyone else who got Ted Maher out of Monaco; it was Ted Maher who got himself out of Monaco—not once, but twice.

And it would not turn to ashes this time.

The reasons I spent so much of my life locked away are many, I suppose, and virtually all of them are still kept in truth-check within the minds and ambitions and vengeance needs of those who were really behind the death of Edmond Safra. *And* in the cold conscienceless designs of those who helped to cover it up.

Maybe there was even some cooperation among these rotten rogues as they achieved their individual ends; one filthy hand washing another in a common realization as to just who they could use as the perfect scapegoat.

Lily Safra has clung to my guilt especially tightly.

WIDOW'S PIQUE AT KILLER'S RELEASE
SAFRA'S WIFE LIVID OVER "FIXED TRIAL" CLAIM

The widow of billionaire financier Edmond Safra is fuming over allegations by her husband's newly freed killer that he was wrongfully convicted after a fixed trial.

"She is more than hurt, she feels indignation," Lily Safra's lawyer Marc Bonnant said yesterday . . . "To say the trial of the one who murdered her husband was fixed, it's totally unbearable for her."

An outraged Safra called her lawyer this week to gripe about Ted Maher's statements to *The Post* after he was released from prison after serving nearly eight years—specifically claims that his trial was fixed.

Bonnant called the idea of a fixed trial "totally wrong, absurd and slanderous."

"Monaco is not a barbarian country," he said. "You can't fix trials in Europe."

—Eric Lenkowitz, *The New York Post*, August 18, 2007

Absurd? Maybe. *Wrong?* Absolutely. *Unbearable for Lily?* I bet.

CHAPTER 46
EIGHT AND A HALF HOURS

August 16, 2007

It was the day before my younger son's birthday.

For the final time, Zabaldano came to turn the key that unlocked my cell.

But a day or two before this was when the urgent arrangements and real hustle began: *We just need to get him the fuck out of here!*

I had to give Zabaldano's guards all the material possessions that were going home with me—those two duffel bags full of nothing that represented my life. Then, in one last minor kick to my emotional nuts, they uprooted me and moved me to another cell for my last day. They evidently feared that maybe I'd stashed something in there to bring home with me; something that might cause them some issues.

Still, none of this last-minute crap mattered. Everything that was of any importance I carried right in my mind and memory.

The US State Department sent Ellen Thorburn with a new passport for me, since my original had long since expired. They wouldn't, however, arrange my transport.

So I arranged a flight from Nice to New York via a stopover in London. That was a convoluted mess, though, because they wouldn't just give me a phone to use. I had to go through this bitchy social worker who in turn had to be the one in contact with my sister and mother, who in turn had to wire money for the plane ticket and expenses.

But even that wasn't good enough.

"No, Mr. Maher," the prison authorities told me when they saw the itinerary, "this will not do."

They weren't warm on the plan, because the route had a layover and they were afraid I'd slip out somewhere along the way and come back! So they got the social worker back on the phone to airlines and I wound up with a nonstop. That cost my mother even more money for the "safer" straight-through schedule and penalties for the musical chairs of changing flights around.

Will this really ever be over? I asked myself over and over.

By the time my cage was finally opened, I had served about 93 percent of my sentence, taking into account the potential period for parole. In the added years of physical and mental darkness since I had escaped and been betrayed, I had done more than my share of mathematical calculations.

And those figures were never easy to think about. It was tough trying to look at the actual cost of something so precious as life amid the many prices we all have to pay for the privilege of just living. What is worth it and what is not? I had just done years of hard time for something I was innocent of; was there value there? Was there a learning experience or *something?*

My thoughts and questions were still full of haze, but at least I was going to be free.

———————

I had to depart from Nice because Monaco has no real airport; but they do have their high-class look-who's-coming-and-going-now heliport. I'd first be flying from there to the international airport in Nice.

And *everybody* would know who was leaving on that helicopter.

I was brought to the heliport by a special entourage of police. For the first time in years, I was outside of prison walls without being either handcuffed or chased down as a fugitive.

My God—maybe this was really happening!

The social worker escorted me all the way to the Nice departure point. Then she had to make sure I absolutely got on that plane and watch until I faded out of sight heading west.

They obviously still feared in the back of their minds that I would return to wreak vengeance. But they didn't have to worry about that. Not yet. Because if I'd dropped myself into some sort of crazy violence and gotten killed, my *real* revenge could never have happened.

My revenge is here.

In exposing the truth.

———————

I was on the helicopter, and they started to strap me in.

Hmmm . . .

In my time and experience, I had seen two helicopters crash, killing all onboard. Who knew the extent of just what these people were capable of? And why weren't we driving to Nice instead of taking this chopper?

Collateral damage anyone?

What were the costs of secrets and shame?

I wouldn't allow them to strap me in. I kept one hand on the door release. Once we were flying a hundred feet above the water, the first hiccup I heard or felt from this 'copter and I was out that fucking door.

Alone!

"Ah, Mr. Maher," the social worker shouted above the noise, "you're paranoid, no?"

I ignored her and kept my hand on that release. Then I jumped on her—with my thoughts. She had whined and pushed through the entire end game. But no more. Like those shrinks back in the hospital and like Donald Manasse, I threw the darts at her about *the truth.*

"You've wrongly imprisoned me all these years, and you're a Monegasque citizen. Aren't you so proud of your country? You're here because you don't want to buck the system or you'll lose your pension. You want to talk about what's right and what's wrong? I've lost almost eight years of my life for your wrongs, and you know I'm right about that! You *know* it!"

It was a short hop to Nice, and in spite of the social worker, the sweat, and the other ominous possibilities, we made it. As soon as I stepped out of the helicopter, I was handed my actual plane ticket by French authorities. At that point, the French National Guard began their monitoring of my *dernier adieu*. Along with that bunch, came the eyes of French undercovers from god-only-knows what agencies.

My only link to the authority of Monaco was now the social worker. But when we got to the final security checkpoint before the gates, that was it. She had no golden ticket and no jurisdiction in France; she was going no further. She'd have to watch this final scene from there.

It was a stirring sendoff.

"It's been nice knowing you. Have a nice life!

"And don't worry, *mes amis*, I am indeed leaving. I won't be back. I only want to return to America, land of the free, home of the brave.

"I just want to be happy again."

I didn't board until the last minute. I wasn't going to be trapped *anywhere* again.

I kept seeing the same people walk by me in the waiting area, and I knew there were even more eyes on me as I stood quietly in that French airport feeling every click of every clock in the place in every part of my body. No one said anything until I was finally boarding.

"Have a good flight, Mr. Maher," a stranger in a black suit whispered, turning and then drifting into the crowd.

I stopped and stared at him as he disappeared.

Don't worry, I will . . .

I had just eight and a half hours to freedom.

CHAPTER 47

DETAINED (PART 2)

After the seemingly endless flight, I was more than ready to land. In fact, I had been waiting to touch sweet American soil for years and years.

As we began our descent into New York City, my eyes teared at the sight of the Statue of Liberty. I knew firsthand the price of freedom.

I was also hovering over the place my Special Forces training began years earlier, in Fort Dix, New Jersey. As the plane touched down, I felt like I'd come full circle.

I exited up the gangway and had to pause. Was this whole structure *shaking?* No, *I* was shaking. From excitement. I was seated up front and I found myself following the two pilots and the crew through a veritable wall of security. I was still under the sick spell that this was just that same dream I'd had so many times and that I'd wake up and be in *that cell. God, no!*

I was drifting, and that drift took me right through customs alongside the crew without being checked! I snapped back.

I wasn't dreaming! This was real.

But then I came full circle on something else. And that's my inherent honesty and my desire to be normal and *me* again. I needed to turn back—to do the right thing. Even after all those years—after all I'd suffered doing those *right things*—I could never avoid or deny that *instinct.*

So I went back to clear customs the proper way.

And once again, it cost me. It once again cost me my *freedom.*

Here I was, *detained.* Strip-searched. Harassed. But ultimately—I still hoped—I was actually "free."

———

"You *do* realize I was wrongly convicted, don't you?" I finally asked.

They just kept searching. And then they left me alone, for most of that hour and a half.

Alone.

Again.

I knew that my mother and sister were in the airport somewhere, waiting for me, and that provided some comfort. So did the thought that someday the truth about all of this would be known. Written. Chronicled. Understood. Accepted.

I had other thoughts as well.

But they were interrupted by the door opening. I was about to find out the reason I'd been *detained*—and I discovered that my welcome wagon included one more unhappy surprise.

Another New York City police officer came in—a great big guy.

"Mr. Maher," he said, "do you know why I'm here?"

"Not a clue, officer," I replied. "What's the problem?"

He handed me some papers.

Greetings from the State of New York, I read. *You've been ordered by a judge in Poughkeepsie to stay three thousand feet away from your wife and your children.*

A restraining order.

Heidi evidently pleaded with a judge, telling him she was afraid for *her* children. I'm a murderer, she insisted. I escaped from prison.

In keeping with the karma-bitter bite of these last ten years—the day I arrived home was my son's birthday and I had planned on surprising him. But now, that wasn't going to happen.

Welcome home, Ted . . .

———

Sitting, stripping, standing, and even smiling in that cell-like airport holding room, I was gutted by the thoughts, memories, and ripsaw rewinds of what it's like not to be free.

When the guards finally let me go, I breathed a huge sigh of satisfaction at my final, *final* release from anyone who still had that power to chain me and cage me and *detain* me.

Now I needed to see my family.

During all of this, my mother and sister had been placed in a "secure" section of JFK. I was frantic to find that *secure* spot—which I did.

We were *overwhelmed* with *all of this.*

All of it.

Our emotions showed it. Despite all the shocks and setbacks we'd suffered throughout the so-wrong situation, in that moment we were simply *happy.* Those bastards hadn't broken me, and they hadn't broken my mother or sister. We were still a family, joyful to see each other and joking around.

"You haven't changed at all, have you?" my sister said, smiling. But there was caution. Her husband had expected I'd come out "a bit messed up" after all I'd been through.

But if anything, I *knew*—even now, still just a few hours into freedom—that I would have an appreciation for things in life that many people take for granted.

Some things, however, were still hard to appreciate.

We were finally heading for the exit at JFK but someone, somewhere had done some public relations work and informed the media of my arrival. The *New York Post* was there and who knows who else. Questions were being asked. Microphones shoved into my face. I just needed to leave! I just needed to leave with my mother, my sister, those two bags of pre-prison clothes that for eight years I was never allowed to wear, and my *freedom!*

We broke loose of the media, but we still had to drive from New York to Connecticut, up through the automotive hive that is I-95. I didn't care; I could have sat in traffic for hours. I was free and it was over.

But it wouldn't be long before that little ideal would be crushed. The enemy had allies and they were all reloading fast.

CHAPTER 48
A FETTERED FLIGHT

Now that it was over, I imagined myself a phoenix, rising from the ashes of the entire fiery trauma. But that restraining order at the airport was just the *first* sign that my wings had been clipped. I was still caged in so many ways.

I've certainly been in fights and battles before in my life. But since the night of Edmond's and Vivian's horrible deaths, I haven't *stopped* fighting. First, I fought to save my own life. Then I fought like hell to try to save theirs. I fought to stay out of prison. When that failed, I fought to get free.

Since returning to the United States, what I've been fighting for is to reveal the truth.

But first, I needed to engage in a war to be part of my children's lives.

No time to bask in freedom. Get back in the ring and keep pounding to survive!

To do that, I had to confront Heidi as soon as possible. But there was that legal matter of having to stay three thousand feet away from her! Plus, I had no job and no money, and legal sparring is expensive. My sister and mom could help somewhat, but I had no serious substantive living clout. I was marching into this fight with near zero in the way of ammunition.

At that point, I *still* didn't know what Minnie had done to upset Heidi. I had brought myself to understand and accept that she needed to distance herself from me and what had happened. Fine. But I was still the father of my children and I wasn't a murderer. So what could possibly have pushed her to the extreme level of anger to take the children away from me? (And—I would learn—turn them against me.) I had been wrongfully incarcerated and now that I was free, I had a right to be a part of my kids' lives.

I was in Connecticut with my mother and sister. I had to appear in the Poughkeepsie, New York, court to go over the details of the restraining order. I borrowed my sister's car and headed toward the area that once was my home; where I once lived with my family. I absolutely had to take a tour of the heart—Poughkeepsie via Stormville.

I stopped at the house I built, knowing that Heidi had sold it long ago. I walked over to the nearby stream. Looking at the little bridge I built over it, I began to get something back from all of this; a warm mix of sadness and satisfaction just from seeing the stream again. I also began to wonder . . .

Where were Heidi and the kids living now? I didn't know, but according to my assigned social worker (attached to me because of the restraining order) they definitely didn't live with Heidi's mother.

Snap out of the memories. Get yourself to that court.

The way out of my old neighborhood took me past my former mother-in-law's house, but in the words of the social worker, "No Mahers live there."

Maybe not, but they are *all* there. *My family!*

I saw them and they saw me.

I wanted to jump out and hug my children; children I hadn't seen in *eight* years! But I couldn't. I had to be three thousand feet away! This was torture. *More* torture.

I drove by.

I raced to the court while Heidi raced to the phone . . .

Murderer!

Escaped from prison!

Stalking his ex-wife!

Throw out a dragnet!

The police radios were burning up while I was directly in the middle of the posse at the Poughkeepsie civic center! I finished with the hearing, wrapped up things with my attorney, and then it was back to Connecticut. *Fast.*

Just before the New York/Connecticut state line, they came out of nowhere: cop cars to the front, rear, and side of me.

Guns at my window!

"Keep your hands on the wheel!"

"Freeze!"

"Do you know why we stopped you?"

"Well, I don't think it was for speeding. What's the problem?"

"You were stalking your ex-wife and you violated a restraining order! Get out of the car!"

Cuffs were locked on.

I was transported back to Poughkeepsie where I was now in jail for the first time ever on American soil; just a little over a week after Zabaldano opened what I figured would be my last cell door. I was brought before the judge the following morning for a bail hearing.

"Bail is set at fifty thousand dollars!"

My mom and sister had to come up with ten percent of that to get me a bond to get me out.

And the media wasted no time pulling the pin. *The Poughkeepsie Journal* went so far as to report that according to Heidi's restraining order, I was both bipolar *and* schizophrenic! Admittedly my head *was* spinning, but that was the only issue with my mental health.[150]

What ultimately saved my ass—*this time*—was my attorney contacting the social worker and having her send a formal statement to the court attesting to the fact that she had told me that my family did not live in my former mother-in-law's house, so I could not have expected to see them there as I was merely driving by.

Of course, on school district records, the kids *did* live there so they could keep attending the schools they had been enrolled in before Heidi sold our house. But I guess *that* kind of larceny is okay.

I was out of jail and back at my sister's. I couldn't sleep. Within two weeks, I'd been in jail on two continents, and I couldn't even see my own children. I was breaking out in cold sweats, having flashbacks about being back in Monte Carlo. I'd been free for mere days before being back in jail again. I needed something to occupy my mind. I started playing with my sister's computer; but I was short on cyber-skills—a lot had happened in the world of computers since I'd begun rotting in prison.

I started to fumble and learn—*task-bar trial and end-user error.*

I learned how to "Google" my name.

I was amused by some of the shit I found.

But some of the shit brought me to Heidi.

And to public records.

And to the $365,000 house she bought.

What?!

On my next trip to the Poughkeepsie court, I went into city hall and got the details—in particular, the dates surrounding this real estate transaction.

And the math involved.

I saw the deed from the old house; our home. Heidi's name was on it along with a final price of a cool $300,000. Okay. Good deal. But in New York, I was entitled to fifty percent of the net.

I also seemed to have missed out on my half of the money she received in the sale of my bulldozer. And my half of the $75,000 that was generated when the rest of my construction equipment and pneumatic tools were sold. Oh, and no capital exchanged hands, with me at least, when our two income properties over in Middletown were snapped up. The same financial non-stats were wrapped around the liquidation of both our cars. Everything was adding up to a neat and tidy zero-sum gain for "convict" Ted Maher to return home to.

Heidi, on the other hand, was doing just great for a single mom. She was even able to finish her master's degree. Records showed her working on scholarly treatises and theses while I was starving in a foreign jail. Timelines proved she was in high-level negotiations to get top dollar for our various properties while I was being tossed pittances from priests for an occasional piece of fruit.

But still, even with the sale of everything, a lone mother of three, working as a nurse, and spending the fortune it takes for a master's degree would go through the money she received from all those sales pretty handily as the years went on. There had to be something more involved that allowed her to buy that new house.

The timeline turned its dirtiest when it showed that the new house was acquired just two weeks before Heidi pulled out of her lawsuit against Lily Safra. Could it be that some kind of deal was slid under some table that circumnavigated Griffith and her other lawyer—and their fees—and that prevented certain individuals from exposure to certain kinds of embarrassment and inconveniences?

A few years later, I *finally* got confirmation that the answer was yes.

According to Lily's 2010 biography, Lily and Heidi "agreed to an undisclosed out-of-court settlement . . . With [Heidi's] settlement from the lawsuit, she quietly purchased a new house in Stormville . . ."[151]

That was *one* mystery solved.

———————————

I kept digging.

I was on another mission.

I found out that the restraining order (RO) against me stemmed from Heidi getting a judge to agree with a doctor friend of hers that our children had post-traumatic stress syndrome because of *what their father had done.* I made some legal inquiries and was told that I certainly had the right to get my own doctor, my own counter-witness, and fight the diagnosis and the RO. But, oh, that will cost you about five grand for starters . . .

Money, laws . . . screw all that.

I had to confront her.

It was a strategic part of the mission, but in this mission, there were strict territories and battle zones. The only time that the three-thousand-foot perimeter became a demilitarized zone is when we were in court together, hashing out the restraining order.

That's when I "struck."

I *legally* engaged my ex-wife in conversation in the corridor: "Heidi, I've told you many times before, when you look into my eyes you will know the truth. In those first years, you would tell me on the phone that you believed me and that there was no way I could have been guilty. I thanked you. I loved you. I told you that sometime, some way, someone will step up and clear me.

"That has happened.

"And then, as I felt you withdrawing from me and you threw Minnie and whatever she was doing in my face, I told you that one day you'd find out that her stupid game was all bullshit, too."

That's when Heidi revealed to me the details of what happened with Minnie.

As I'd surmised, Heidi had just needed a reason to disavow me, and Minnie had given her one.

But *what exactly* had she given her?

One of the few things of mine Minnie had kept was a box of notes and letters—love letters, I guess you could call them—that I had given her before and during our marriage.

Those alone could set off a few nerves.

But Minnie was more underhanded than that.

She'd doctored them up a bit—including surgery on the dates and other details—giving Heidi the impression that Minnie and I had stayed in "touch" *after* my marriage to Heidi and that my relationship with the ex was X-rated!

"What?!" I cried. "I spent fifty grand to make you the legal guardian of my son and you think I'm still having an affair with his mother?! Are you for real?! Those cards and shit? Look closer at them, Heidi. I guarantee they're old things I gave her when we were together." I began pleading. "Look in my eyes and you'll know that I'm telling you the truth! Heidi, you've taken my fucking heart out and stabbed it and stabbed it and stabbed it! I spent four extra years in prison because of what you did! Why?!"

No reaction.

None.

I stared at her and I thought, *What if you hadn't betrayed me, Heidi? What if I had escaped cleanly and touched down four fucking years ago at JFK?*

Those bastards in Monaco did this to me!

My escape, with the backing by the State Department would have made a powerful statement that they believed in my innocence. No stain on my character.

I'd be able to get employment easily.

This all would have been so different.

So fucking *different!*

———————

Operation Confrontation and Regeneration continued with Minnie. She—along with the rest of the world—knew I was back in America. She managed to get in touch with me through my family.

She wanted to see Matthew—something even *I* hadn't been able to do.

I spoke with her. I had a suggestion: "Minnie, maybe you should go to some big women's magazine and write an article for them titled something like: 'How to Destroy a Marriage: An Ex-Wife's Revenge!' And after it's published, I'll pick up a copy and make sure that Heidi sees it. It'll clear some air and, possibly, that kind of truth-testimony could lead to your seeing your son again one of these days . . . *Maybe*."

I had faced both of them. I was exhausted, drained, and completely unsure as to where any of it would go. This is the point where I began to sit and think. This is where I felt my face and my head-in-my-hands really take on the look of the "murderer" in the morbid-looking photos that the tabloids loved.

While I was in prison, and especially during my initial arrest and trial phases, the rags were fond of publishing zombie-esque black-and-whites of this monster, Ted Maher. I guess they thought their artistic spins made me look more like a criminal. But if you look closely at those photos, they show a man in that time-panicked human stage of I-just-can't-believe-this-is-happening. Those photos were the unclaimed puppy in a cage waiting for the shelter to put him down, not Cujo with flesh between his teeth.

It was during that head-in-my-hands horror over Heidi and Minnie's mayhem when another phase of that second reality attacked.

Little by little, as I started to reclaim my life, I was hammered and halted by the indelible brand of having once been condemned as a murderer.

I sincerely thought that after Hullin turned both himself and the Monegasque machine inside-out that my name would be cleared. And since I was free, I could join in.

Hullin had told the truth and now *I* would tell the truth. Simple.

After the initial media madness at JFK, I settled in and began granting requests from shows like *48 Hours* and *Dateline NBC* for interviews. Hullin and I were both getting all the media coverage in the world. Truth and publicity: what could be better than that?

The TV shows would challenge me, though: "You signed a confession, didn't you? You said you did this, you said you did that, didn't you . . ."

Well, yes, but . . .

I would explain.

And explain.

But long assertions and studied details evidently don't sell commercials, so most of the cleaning-up of new truth was left out while a lot of the old dirt of murder and melée was rubbed in.

I was even asked if I was living in fear now that I was home and free: "Couldn't that kind of exposure lead to your own murder by those you claim are really responsible for Safra's death—just to keep you quiet?"

My answer was always no.

Because what would that do to this entire mess? If somebody killed me then everyone would know damn good and well that I was *damn good and well* telling the truth! All of the suspicions would turn back to the Russians or the Palestinians or to Lily or to anyone else on the cast's call-back list of showtime hopefuls! All the shit would begin again. More investigations. And maybe the curtain would rise on the truth this time. So no, I wasn't going to lose any sleep worrying about somebody killing me.

But after all the performances and press hoopla quieted down, I realized that while redemption may be a pure, cleansing holy water, the word "murderer" is an even more potent drop of dark ink. With my face and so many different versions of my story told on television and in papers and magazines, and on these new and growing things I wasn't really familiar with called websites, steady jobs nursing children were hard to find.

Impossible was really the word.

Even with continued legal help from Michael Griffith and others, and a government-endorsed name change, I still had to face the truth and ethics of those "full disclosure" sections on résumés. No prospective employer, especially in my sensitive profession, wants to see things written in like "I respectfully must decline to answer the following questions: please call my lawyer," or "By the way, I spent 2814 days of my life in a foreign prison for something I didn't do."

Even on the occasions when I did get a job under my new identity and became established and appreciated for my work, someone would recognize me on one of those shows and gasp.

And run, not walk, to a supervisor in scared shock.

The shows *still* run.

I have been effectively blackballed from the caring work I love so much. In a horribly isolated way, I have discovered that vindication doesn't necessarily mean victory.

The nerve-shredding stress level of this fight has been horrible and high. A decade of living was stolen from me and a brutal brand burned into my reputation and dignity.

I have examined the costs of this "crime" over and over.

This has always felt like—and in the rawest of realities *was*—a reverie of fiction. So it's fitting that a scene from an old movie has worked its way into this haunt.

In Clint Eastwood's *Hang 'Em High,* his character of Jed Cooper is lynched for something he didn't do. Cooper is badly hurt and savagely scarred, but he survives.

He makes it a quest to confront those who tried to kill him and to exact *his* brand of revenge. Finally after search and struggle, Cooper is face-to-face with one of them.

"You don't remember me, do you?" Cooper asks.

The man answers no.

Cooper uncovers the deep scar around his neck from the rope. "When you hang a man," Cooper tells him, "you better look at him."

No one looked at *me.* No one looked at who *I* was when I was "lynched" by Monaco and the cadre of corruption that flowed around Safra and his money. I was just an easy target like Cooper.

And, like Cooper, I was forgotten. *Cinch the rope. Drop the gallows floor. Cure the problem. Get back to the good life.*

But, also like Cooper, I didn't forget.

How could I? How could he? You can't *accept* having the most precious gift of all crushed and spat upon. I understood *what* drove Heidi to do what she did, but I'll never understand the weakness that allowed it. I understood the caustic concepts of jealousy and envy that caused Minnie to do what she did, but I'll never understand the coldness and uncaring that allowed *that*.

I understood the siren-intoxication that can come from insane wealth and absolute power but I will never, ever understand *any* concept that uses a human life as a bait or sacrifice.

"When you hang a man, you better look at him . . ."

And I'd take even *that* to the next level. As the slack in the hangman's rope of Monegasque authority and arrogance and pride stiffened, *I* looked at *them*.

I was taken to the top, allowed to breathe the sweetest air, and then pushed off the edge. My life had been stolen. My family blasted to pieces.

It would be three years before I would talk with Matthew again; and to this day—over two decades since I left for Monaco and a decade since my release—he is the *only* one of my children I've gotten to be in contact with.

My sister showed him articles about what Hullin had admitted. He gave me a big hug and through tears he told me, "Oh, Dad, I'm so sorry! Mom just brainwashed me so much I just didn't know what to believe." He told me Heidi essentially kicked him out of the house and he wound up living in a car for months.

I guess that's because he never really was *hers*.

Maybe, as the others grow into adulthood, I can see them, too. That remains my life's greatest wish.

My sister also arranged for me to see a psychiatrist—echoing her husband's concerns that some *issues* might surface. *I* know I haven't gotten to this stage in my life, enduring what I've endured, just to collapse or kill myself or lose it. I am a *very* strong person.

But I submitted to a complete two-and-half-hour mental probe, and at the end of the evaluation, the doctor told me that she had never met anybody in her professional career who—considering what I'd been through—was saner and more stable.

"So basically," I concluded, "we just flushed three hundred eighty-five bucks down the drain."

"Pretty much," she agreed.

But that's okay. Because although my future continues to be mired in a dark crawl, with obstacles layered in my path like in that cell "window" I cut through piece by piece by piece, I can never—and *will* never—forget staring into the eyes of Zabaldano in the harshest heat of all this. I can never, and will never, forget telling him in a voice that was meant for everyone who had a golden or bloodied hand in what was done to me: "You *won't* break me! No matter what you do, I'll never turn into some feeble little nothing, lying curled up in a ball, filthy and shaking in the corner."

I was right.

THE SEARCH FOR TRUTH

E ven after two decades, this maw of a mystery becomes ever wider and deeper
by the day. The real killer or killers of Edmond Safra have not been brought
to justice, and the person still paying for it is me.

As La Belle Époque burned to gilded cinders, my life also went up in flames.

Despite Judge Jean-Christophe Hullin's conscience-clearing revelation about the
sham nature of my trial that led to my release, I remain cast as a world-recognized
murderer who has spent hard years in prison.

I've changed my name.

I've changed my home.

I've changed my appearance.

I've learned to drive a truck so I can make an honest living while spending vast
amounts of money and time attempting to return to my first love caring for newborns. I've fought legal battle after legal battle with bureaucracies and state officials
and their attorneys, endeavoring over and over and over to clear my name and regain
my nursing credentials.

But in the public's eye and in the mind of legislators, the kind of guy who gets
caught up in the type of wild web that ensnared me is more suited to be separated
from society, not healing children into it—regardless of what the final, *final* verdict
may have been.

In addition to its personal effects on me, the global repercussions of Safra's death
continue to spin as well.

In November 2011, Michael Griffith, in conjunction with the International Bar Association, planned a mock retrial for me at the organization's annual conference in Dubai. Griffith assembled an all-star roster of seventeen distinguished professionals from all over the globe to play the roles of lawyers, judges, and witnesses in order to show what *would* have happened had my original trial been executed fairly—without a collusive judge silencing Griffith and quashing evidence left and right, aided by a member of my own defense team.

But Lily Safra exploded. Although the trial would have no legal bearing, my guess is she didn't relish a revisiting of her controversial actions leading up to her husband's death. However, I should say, a "visiting," given the complete lack of an investigation into her role—another "interesting fact" she wouldn't want scrutinized (especially with her having become one of the world's wealthiest widows from the second *awkward* death of a wealthy husband). Lily threatened to sue the entire event, with her lawyers publicly condemning the proposed proceedings as "grotesque . . . shameless and discreditable."[152] Her media rants and legal action worked: The event was canceled in the eleventh hour, voiding Griffith's highly detailed production and disappointing everyone involved—especially me.

But the ultimate in compelling new clues pointing to a possible answer to this ongoing enigma began in 2013 with a two-fold monster development—a pair of international squabbles that have rocked the politics of two of the planet's most powerful countries: (1) The US government's current "Russia probe" and (2) the controversy-cloaked Magnitsky Act, signed into US law by Barack Obama in 2012.

Every dirty detail intricately woven throughout each has a common element: the dubious banking dealings of Edmond Jacob Safra. And together, these two transcontinental tribulations provide a myriad of reasons why some person or some group would want him killed.

The first part of this "monster development" centers around Republic National's "major client" whose alleged misdeeds hampered Safra's bank sale to HSBC right before his death: economic forecaster Martin Armstrong.

Armstrong posits a complex yet completely canny theory that Vladimir Putin had Edmond Safra killed. This *assassination* was in retaliation for a plot orchestrated by Safra and Russian oligarchs to take control of all of Russia's assets.

One aspect of that complexity—and a more-than-legitimate reason for Armstrong's delay in coming forward—is that in relation to his own entanglement with Safra's bank, he was imprisoned from 2000 until 2011 in the most blatant abuse of judicial power in US history, now being reviewed by the Supreme Court.

The 2014 documentary film *The Forecaster* reveals Armstrong's insider intel on Safra and Putin, outlining a cohesive scenario of international power plays and crime. It's a story that—like mine—takes concentration to follow.

Maybe that's why the truth is so difficult to find.

But it's sure as hell worth the study.

Over the years, Armstrong was invited by Safra and others to join the "Billionaire's Club,"[153] described as "a very powerful community amongst the investment bankers in New York who . . . try to rig the game to create a perfect trade, at the expense of entire economies." [154]

Part of this "rigging" involves colluding with individual politicians and whole governments.

"The only way to succeed is by controlling the political powers," explains Armstrong. "Unfortunately, we do not live in a real democracy; for we do not elect the treasurer, head of the Federal Reserve, SEC [Securities and Exchange Commission], or Attorney General. These are positions that are the spoils of politics that can be bought like a hooker."

Armstrong's analogy is "colorful," and the results of that reality are just as sloppy and rank smelling.

As alluded to during my trial, by the media, et cetera, Safra and the Russians were tightly tangled in many ways.

Back in 1996 is when Safra teamed up with financier and economist William Felix "Bill" Browder to cofound Hermitage Capital Management (HCM) to invest exclusively in Russian companies. The fund was controlled by Safra's Republic National Bank, a.k.a. "Republic."

Probably not coincidentally, '96 is also when Safra and Republic were at the center of that infamous "Money Plane" scandal I mentioned, in which the United States allegedly sent up to a billion dollars *a day* (carted in bags of crisp, clean one-dollar-bills still in Federal Reserve wrappers) to the Russian mob![155]

But anyway . . .

During this period, Armstrong ever declined invites to join the "club," including declining to invest $10 billion of his clients' holdings into HCM, having correctly forecasted an upcoming Russian financial crisis. The country's financial collapse a short time later, in August 1998, decimated the club members' own investments (leading to a US bank bailout), and the club blamed Armstrong because his forecast had appeared publicly—on the front page of the London *Financial Times*—in June 1998.

Thus, a long-term battle was waged between the club and Armstrong, who started outing their plays in his economic reports.

Things came to a head for both Safra and Armstrong *(and me)*, when the group enacted a new plot.

Pay attention, 'cause now we're getting to the really juicy stuff . . .

Armstrong asserts that in August of 1999, Safra and Russian oligarchs conspired to take control of all of Russia's assets by entrapping then–head of state Boris Yeltsin into embezzling $7 billion from Russia's International Monetary Fund (IMF) loans—money specifically lent to Russia to enable Yeltsin to help his people—and then blackmailing him into giving up the presidency and naming one of their cohorts as his successor.

Yeltsin had previously announced his intention to run for reelection in 2000.

The scheme was put into motion when Yeltsin took the bait and the tainted $7 billion—earmarked as a "fee for refurbishing the Kremlin"—was wired through Edmond Safra's hated rival, the Bank of New York. This in itself was fishy, because most large Russian transfers went through Safra's Republic National Bank. According to Safra's assigned role in the conspiracy, he reported the transaction as money-laundering to the US Justice Department, who launched a full-scale investigation, presuming that the Russian mafia was behind any misdeeds. [156]

This is when the conspirators confronted Yeltsin, threatening to spill the borscht about *his* role in the crime—specifically his having stolen from his own people—unless he complied with their demands. If he did, they'd protect him. Their demands were for him to step down and name as acting president their club crony, business tycoon Boris Berezovsky. Wait! Remember him? Safra's buddy, the "godfather of the Kremlin," who fell out of Russian favor before Edmond's death? Yeah, that guy . . .

In response to these threats, Yeltsin turned to then–virtually unknown Vladimir Putin—the director of the KGB's successor agency, the FSB—who promised to "take care of everything" if named Yeltsin's successor.

Yeltsin immediately set the shady stage: On August 9, 1999, he appointed Putin as one of three first deputy prime ministers. Later that same day, Yeltsin appointed Putin as acting prime minister and announced his desire for Putin to be his successor. *Still later* on in that same long day, Putin agreed to run for the presidency.

By December 3, Edmond Safra was dead. A key conspirator and "club" kingpin had been "taken care of."

And on December 31, Yeltsin indeed resigned and named Putin as acting president. Putin was formally elected to the presidency in March of 2000 and his first decree was lifelong immunity for Yeltsin on any and all corruption claims against him while he was president.[157]

Berezovsky fled to London,[158] where he would later be found dead of a "suicide or homicide"[159]—loudly touted as a Russian hit.[160]

London, where in 1606's *Macbeth*, Shakespeare observes that "Confusion now hath made his masterpiece."[161] Maybe, but centuries later, there's so much more to this story that could completely redefine "confusion" and "masterpiece." So let's back up a little bit . . .

While the Belle Époque fire was the end of the line for Safra, a lot more bloodied intrigue ensued in my—and others'—continuing sagas in its aftermath.

Right away, the suspicious death of a lead player in the conniving "club" had many in high financial circles running scared.

"[Everyone was asking, if] Edmond Safra who's worth billions of dollars and has got ex–Israeli defense forces, ex–[Secret Intelligence Service protection], can get himself killed . . . what hope have I got?" attests Neill Macpherson (a member of Armstrong's corporate finance team and stepfather to multimillionaire supermodel Elle Macpherson). "It was absolute chaos and madness."[162]

I have to admit, it's gratifying to find out, even years later, that someone besides me was looking at this entire cluster mess as "suspicious."

And that they *still* are.

Back in May 1999, when Safra started liquidating his assets (per Lily's urging, right before willing her the majority of his estate), he began the process of selling his Republic National Bank to HSBC.

As one of Republic's best and biggest futures clients, Armstrong ended up at the center of a serpentine storm that sent the sale off track.

At the end of September, after the failed Yeltsin/Berezovsky coup, a complex series of international inquiries and clerical errors led to Republic accusing Armstrong of hiding losses (in essence, implementing a Ponzi scheme) in accounts maintained by him and Republic. During the ensuing inquiry into the alleged misconduct, HSBC sent in their own auditors and determined that Republic's claims had been misrepresented; so they withdrew from buying the bank, sending its stock price plummeting. Safra then became determined—desperate—to push the sale through before the truth got exposed that the crimes had actually been committed by Republic's own employees (who'd been forced to throw Armstrong under the banking bus when he'd been the one to report $1 billion missing from his own accounts). So that's why, in the end, Safra agreed to a $450 million reduction in his own personal shares to seal the deal with HSBC.

Two months later, when Safra's mysterious death created a high risk of investigation into all his activities, his "club" partners in crime (who, like Safra, held sway with politicians) rightly worried about all the skeletons in their vaults. Armstrong knew a lot, had evidence, and wasn't on their side. Naturally he needed to be silenced. Quickly. *Lock him up!*

Within days of Safra's demise, Armstrong's office was raided, as the US attorney conspired with the court appointed receiver, Alan Cohen, to imprison Armstrong.

Armstrong was forced to turn over all evidence gathered in his dealings with the "club," including over forty tapes of recorded phone calls (intended for self-protection, not prosecution).[163] Armstrong's personal computer was confiscated for another ulterior motive: the feds (and their club cohorts) wanted access to the source code of Armstrong's eerily effective economic modeling software, which he'd used to accurately predict trends, key economic events *to the date*, and even wars.

When Armstrong refused to hand it over—knowing it would be used for pernicious purposes—he was held in contempt of court . . . for *seven years*. This, despite the statute's stating that imprisonment for contempt can last only up to eighteen months. Armstrong's was the longest federal civil contempt of court imprisonment in American history.

Held without trial—or, in his case, even charges? Boy, do I know that feeling . . .

He was only released when the Supreme Court ordered the government to explain what was going on.

Though Armstrong's continuing ordeal takes a slight tangent from the Safra scandal, it's another eye-opening example of the absolute corruption that absolute power brings to the banks. It's also another example of an innocent man losing a decade of his life due to others' schemes and CYA-actions.

During this time, as HSBC (Republic's new holding company) cooperated in continued investigations into the allegations against Armstrong, it was uncovered that (Surprise! Surprise!) Republic's own staff had been illegally trading in Armstrong's accounts; the bank was also responsible for the missing investor funds. Thus, the club members—and Safra, posthumously—were caught with their hand in a very big cookie jar.

However—per Armstrong's government-bank inter-reliance explanation—the government wouldn't criminally prosecute Republic or HSBC. So instead, Republic was granted a plea deal:[164] admission of guilt and full restitution of the missing funds—to the traumatic tune of $606 million—in return for absolute immunity.[165] No sanctions or punishment whatsoever. To boot, the deal included a lifetime gag order slapped on Armstrong, to prevent him from revealing his version of events or helping his clients sue HSBC. Plus, due to some transaction-trickery, he was cheated out of $400 million dollars of his own legally earned profit.

But even after all *that*—with all client money restored and Republic's admission of guilt—Armstrong continued to be held.[166] So he was finally compelled to plead guilty to conspiracy in Republic's crimes, even though they had taken full responsibility.[167] Armstrong's forced plea was bizarre. He was given a script to read, like a hostage, stating that he had "failed" to tell his clients that Republic—and not Armstrong—took their money for its own benefit.

Again, I know that sinking feeling . . .

Adding injury to insult, his requested credit for time served—which he'd been assured he would get—was denied. He was sentenced to five additional years as a result of his plea.

In full, Armstrong spent eleven wrongful years behind bars. In all that time, no official charges against him were ever filed (except for those generated by the plea deal) nor was any evidence against him ever presented.

Damn! They didn't even go through the charade of a trial like they did for me. But we do have in common that he, too, was caught in a web of wonkiness so complex and nefarious, most mere mortals can't—or don't have the time to—even wrap their heads around it.

But now . . . I hope you're still riding shotgun here, 'cause we're gonna shift a few more gears and drive this truth-truck right into today's Russiagate scandal . . .

The allegations leading to Russiagate state that the infamous Trump Tower meeting was intended to negotiate a quid pro quo: Russia would help Trump get elected in return for Trump's promise to lift sanctions imposed on Russian citizens by the 2012 "Magnitsky Act": a highly publicized and politicized federal measure authorizing the US government to punish those it deems human rights violators—especially officials responsible for the in-prison death of Russian accountant Sergei Magnitsky—by freezing their assets and banning them from entering the country.

Regardless of what did or did not go on in that 2016 meeting between Trump campaign members and Russian representatives, it's undisputed that the Russian president wants the sanctions imposed by the Magnitsky Act lifted. Not only are many of the individuals adversely affected by the Act directly connected to his government, but much of Putin's personal wealth is believed to be tied up in foreign assets and therefore threatened by the sanctions.[168]

So, how the hell did we get here?

Well, we have to go back to Safra's old "partner in crime," Bill Browder.

After Safra's death, Browder embarked on series of deals that gave him complete ownership of the pair's company, Hermitage Capital Management. By 2008, Browder was considered the largest investor in Russia.

Sergei Magnitsky was a tax advisor for HCM.

The accepted saga proliferated by Browder is that the Russian police raided his office to seize the incorporation documents of three of his Russia-invested companies managed by HCM. They then used these docs to transfer corporate ownership to themselves, to profit from a $230 million tax refund owed to the companies by the Russian government. When Magnitsky valiantly stepped up to expose this corruption against Browder, he was arrested.[169]

Eleven months later, Browder alleges, Magnitsky was beaten to death in prison, just eight days before the expiration of the one-year term he could be held without trial.

Browder then lobbied the US government for retaliatory legislation, leading to the passage of the Magnitsky Act.

Since then, Sergei Magnitsky has become a celebrated international martyr, who *did* suspiciously die in prison, after—at the very least—not receiving adequate medical care.

But was Browder's cry-inducing chronicle of Sergei Magnitsky's death and the entire Russian theft of his companies absolutely accurate?

Well, over two hours of investigation into that very question are contained in Andrei Nekrasov's 2016 docudrama *The Magnitsky Act—Behind the Scenes*—a film that's faced bans and protests, especially by Browder. Ultimately, the film is a sort of *mea culpa*: Nekrasov began his work by portraying the story of Sergei Magnitsky in its accepted form, as told to him by Browder; but then he started doing double takes as so-called facts fell apart and even reversed themselves.

In the first portion of the film, Browder appears sympathetic and credible as a victim of Russian persecution and theft. But by the documentary's end, the viewer needs a shower—Browder could not seem slimier.

Could it be he—or one of his "club"—had Magnitsky silenced for knowing too much about their continued attempts to control Russian assets?

It seems more than possible.

And the key point? So much multinational slime and secrecy and greed and corruption orbited around Edmond Safra and the mega-finance, power-driven galaxy of graft and grudges in which he operated, that to believe his death—timed smack dab in the messy middle of shady deals and shadier enemies—was actually caused by *me*, a hired nurse, pulling a stunt to seem like a hero is beyond ludicrous.

Obviously, far higher powers than me were at work.

And there's quite a list of individuals who have crossed the highly-potent Vladimir Putin—directly or indirectly—who have ended up deceased:

- Safra.
- Magnitsky.
- Berezovsky.
- Alexander Perepilichney: A Browder-embroiled businessman whom US intelligence reports indicate with "high confidence" was likely "assassinated on direct orders from Putin or people close to him."

On the stickier side of that stroganoff, Putin blames Browder (dubbing him a "serial killer"!) for the deaths of the *three* key players in Browder's Russia dealings (specifically, his actions running counter to his public narrative of the Magnitsky story!): Octai Gasanov, Valery Kurochkin, and Sergei Korobeinikov.[170] If Browder played a role in Magnitsky's death and others, Putin's accusation may not be too far-fetched.

But what about Lily in all this? Safra's rush to sell off his empire just before willing the bulk of his fortune to her, followed immediately by his mysterious death, has always been a bit of an eyebrow-raiser to say the least. Not to mention her suspicious actions leading up to Safra's death: the last-minute change to my schedule, giving security the night off, leaving open the valance . . . It begs the question: Was she being threatened like I was, or was she in cahoots with Putin or Browder and their criminal contortions?

Martin Armstrong shared his own convictions with the late Dominick Dunne.

"[Dominick Dunne] told me he was in a restaurant in Paris and someone came up to him and said, 'be careful the questions you are asking," Armstrong writes in his blog.[171] "They tried to blame Safra's male nurse . . . After a fake trial, he was sentenced to prison. He was later released by the [Monagasque] high court stating that the prosecutor and judge conspired to deny him a fair trial and he was just . . . sent home to the States. That was the end of the case. Nobody else was ever charged . . . . So do I think that Safra was murdered? Absolutely! He was killed on December 3rd and they began the contempt proceedings on me—to stop any trial [against the "billionaires club"] . . . within three days."

Wow! It's quite a story. And I admit a glimmer of hope in finding out who was behind the ill-fated events of December 3, 1999—and *why*. I am so grateful and respectful of Martin Armstrong's knowledge and research and experience.

And although my release may have represented "the end of the case" for prosecutors, there is no end of the case for me as I continue to try to put my life back together.

There is no end of the case for whoever holds the secrets and answers that keep them basking in power and in whatever riches they've enjoyed thanks to Safra's death and the blame placed on me.

And hopefully, there is no end of the case when it comes to their fear that one day the truth *will* be uncovered.

NOTES

INTRODUCTION
1. Greenfeld, Karl Taro. "Murder by Fire." *TIME*, December 5, 1999.
2. Vincent, Isabel. *Gilded Lily: Lily Safra: The Making of One of the World's Wealthiest Widows*. New York: Harper, 2010.
3. Dunne, Dominick. "Death in Monaco." *Vanity Fair*, December 1, 2000.
4. Carrie Coolidge, "Book Review: The Making of One of the World's Wealthiest Widows," review of *Gilded Lily: Lily Safra: The Making of One of the World's Wealthiest Widows*, by Isabel Vincent, *Daily Finance* (June 29, 2010), accessed April 22, 2015, http://www.dailyfinance.com/2010/06/29/book-review-the-making-of-one-of-the-worlds-wealthiest-widows/.
5. Vincent, *Gilded Lily*.
6. "World's costliest flat sold for 200 mn pounds." NDTV, September 14, 2010, accessed April 22, 2015, http://www.ndtv.com/world-news/worlds-costliest-flat-sold-for-200-mn-pounds-431347.
7. Cowell, Alan. "HSBC to bay $10.3 Billion for Republic." *The New York Times*, May 11, 1999.
8. Watson, Russell. "Death in Monaco." *Newsweek*, December 12, 1999.

CHAPTER 2
9. "On This Date: November 21, 1989 The MGM Grand's Fire Disaster." *Las Vegas 360*, November 21, 2014, accessed May 13, 2015, http://www.lasvegas360.com/2956/on-this-date-november-21-1980-the-mgm-grands-fire-disaster/.

CHAPTER 7
10. Brennan, Morgan. "The Most Expensive Billionaire Homes In The World." *Forbes*, March 29, 2013.
11. "Villa Leopolda." *Wikipedia*, last modified March 29, 2015, http://en.wikipedia.org/wiki/Villa_Leopolda.
12. "Lily Safra's House (Villa La Leopolda)." *Virtual Globetrotting*, accessed May 12, 2015, http://virtualglobetrotting.com/map/lily-safras-house-villa-la-leopolda/.

CHAPTER 10

13. World Bank Group, "Monaco." The World Bank Data, accessed August 12, 2019. https://data.worldbank.org/country/monaco?view=chart.
14. "Life Expectancy for Countries, 2014," Pearson Education, publishing as Infoplease, accessed April 23, 2015, https://www.cia.gov/library/publications/the-world-factbook/rankorder/2102rank.html.
15. Monaco, Unemployment Rate." Ereport.ru, accessed August 12, 2019, http://www.ereport.ru/en/stat.php?razdel=country&count=monaco&table=ueecia.
16. "Law Enforcement in Monaco." *Wikipedia*, last modified November 17, 2013, http://en.wikipedia.org/wiki/Law_enforcement_in_Monaco.
17. "Monaco penthouse flat sells for £199 million." *The Telegraph*, September 11, 2010.

CHAPTER 11

18. Vincent, *Gilded Lily*.
19. Vincent, *Gilded Lily*.
20. Vincent, *Gilded Lily*.
21. Vincent, *Gilded Lily*.
22. Vincent, *Gilded Lily*.
23. Vincent, *Gilded Lily*.

CHAPTER 12

24. Maugham, W. Somerset. *Strictly Personal*. New York: Doubleday, Doran & Company, 1941.
25. "Monaco." Encyclopedia of the Nations, accessed April 23, 2015, http://www.nationsencyclopedia.com/economies/Europe/Monaco.html.
26. Warren, Katie. "15 astounding facts about Monaco, the tiny French Riviera city-state where 32% of the population is made up of millionaires." *Business Insider*, May 22, 2019, accessed September 8, 2019, https://www.businessinsider.com/mind-blowing-facts-about-monaco-wealth-2019-5#1-with-an-area-of-just-078-square-miles-and-a-population-of-38300-monaco-is-one-of-the-densest-countries-in-the-world-1.

CHAPTER 15

27. Vincent, *Gilded Lily*.
28. Vincent, *Gilded Lily*.

CHAPTER 19

29. "Kidnappers Free Banker." *Sun Sentinel*, July 13, 1994.
30. Charap, Sam. "Safra Widow Restores Synagogue." *The Moscow Times*, July 3, 2001.
31. Dunne, Dominick. *Justice: Crimes, Trials, and Punishments*. New York: Broadway Books, 2002.
32. Klebnikov, Paul. "The day they raided Aeroflot." *Forbes*, March 22, 1999.
33. Greenberg, Eric J. "We Have Lost Our Crown." The New York Jewish Week, December 10, 1999, accessed September 7, 2019, https://jewishweek.timesofisrael.com/we-have-lost-our-crown/.

CHAPTER 20

34. Investigative Report on the deaths of Edmond Safra and Vivian Torrente, compiled at the request of Monaco's Chief Examining Magistrate Patricia Richet, 2.
35. Vincent, *Gilded Lily*.
36. Investigative Report, 3.
37. Investigative Report, 3.
38. Investigative Report, 5.
39. Vincent, *Gilded Lily*.
40. "Ted Maher." Academic, accessed May 7, 2015, https://enacademic.com/dic.nsf/enwiki/8587607/Ted_Maher.

CHAPTER 21

41. Investigative Report, 3.
42. Investigative Report, 4.
43. Investigative Report, 22, 25.
44. Vincent, *Gilded Lily*.
45. Vincent, *Gilded Lily*.
46. Vincent, *Gilded Lily*.
47. "Decision for an Indictment Delivered by the Court Chambers on 18 June 2002," *Public Prosecutor v. Theodore Maher*, trans. Micheline Campos, 9.
48. "Decision for an Indictment Delivered by the Court Chambers on 18 June 2002," *Public Prosecutor v. Theodore Maher*, trans. Micheline Campos, 9; Vincent, *Gilded Lily*.
49. Investigative Report, 10.
50. Investigative Report, 11.
51. Investigative Report, 2.
52. Investigative Report, 31.
53. Indictment, 9.
54. Investigative Report, 2–3.
55. Dickey, Christopher. "A Bad Bet in Monte Carlo." *Newsweek*, August 5, 2001.
56. Indictment, 8.
57. Anthony, Andrew. "The Strange Case of Edmond Safra." *The Observer*, October 29, 2000.

CHAPTER 23

58. Dan, Uri. "Slain Financier Made a Fatal Error Mistook Rescuers for the Attackers" *New York Post*, December 5, 1999.
59. "Nurse admits setting fire that killed Monaco banker." *Deseret News*, December 6, 1999.
60. Kennedy, Helen and Tracey Tully. "Safra aide confesses Nurse from N.Y. sez he started fatal fire," *New York Daily News*, December 7, 1999.
61. Dickey, Christopher. "A Bad Bet in Monte Carlo." *Newsweek*, August 5, 2001.
62. "Nurse's 'black thoughts' bring rich banker's death." *Lubbock Avalanche-Journal*, December 12, 1999.
63. "Nurse's 'black thoughts' bring rich banker's death." *Lubbock Avalanche-Journal*, December 12, 1999.

64. Anthony, Andrew. "The Strange Case of Edmond Safra." *The Observer*, October 29, 2000.

65. Sancton, Thomas. "The Charade of Death," *TIME*, December 12, 1999.

66. "Nurse's 'black thoughts' bring rich banker's death." *Lubbock Avalanche-Journal*, December 12, 1999.

CHAPTER 24

67. "Maison d'arrêt." Wikipedia, last modified February 24, 2014, http://en.wikipedia.org /wiki/Maison_d%27arr%C3%AAt.

68. "Committee against Torture hears response of Monaco," The Office of the United Nations High Commissioner for Human Rights, May 23, 2011, accessed May 13, 2015, http://www.ohchr.org/EN/NewsEvents/Pages/DisplayNews.aspx?NewsID =11050&LangID=E.

CHAPTER 25

69. "Monte-Carlo SBM." Good & Co, accessed April 23, 2019, https://good.co/company /monte-carlo-sbm-societe-des-bains-de-mer.

70. "Monte Carlo Société des Bains de Mer, accessed April 23, 2015, http://www.montecar losbm.com/resort-en-2/.

71. "Politics of Monaco." Wikipedia, last modified March 24, 2015, http://en.wikipedia.org /wiki/Politics_of_Monaco#Judicial_branch.

72. Winslow, Robert. "Monaco." Crime and Society: A Comparative Criminology Tour of the World, accessed May 12, 2015, http://www-rohan.sdsu.edu/faculty/rwinslow/europe /monaco.html.

73. Springer, John. "American nurse faces charges in the death of billionaire Edmond Safra." Murderpedia, June 21, 2001, accessed April 23, 2015, http://murderpedia.org/male.M/m /maher-theodore.htm.

74. Nupress, Nita and Phil Dragoo. "American Green Beret Vet TED MAHER Held HOSTAGE by Monaco for 629 Days." Free Republic, August 24, 2001, accessed May 12, 2019, http://www.freerepublic.com/focus/news/517660/posts?page=214.

CHAPTER 26

75. Autopsy Report of Vivian Torrente, conducted by Dr. Woltiewiev and Dr. Ohayon. Translation by Alessia Vittone.

76. Prosecutor's Report, 3.

77. "Ted Maher, 5th discussion," *Public Safety Administration and the Principality of Monaco* (December 6, 1999), trans. Alessia Vittone, 1.

78. "Ted Maher, 5th discussion," *Public Safety Administration and the Principality of Monaco* (December 6, 1999), trans. Alessia Vittone, 1.

79. "Ted Maher, 5th discussion," *Public Safety Administration and the Principality of Monaco* (December 6, 1999), trans. Alessia Vittone, 1.

80. "Ted Maher, 5th discussion," *Public Safety Administration and the Principality of Monaco* (December 6, 1999), trans. Alessia Vittone, 1.

81. Investigative Report, 34.

82. "The Money Plane." BernLeaks, accessed August 25, 2019, http://www.worldcorruption .info/eng/moneyplane.htm.

83. Gentleman, Amelia. "The fixer: how Berezovsky pulls the strings in Russia." *The Guardian*, April 17, 2000.

84. Daniels, Vic. "Edmond Safra Blamed for Nurse's Death." HITC, accessed August 26, 2019, https://amp.hitc.com/en-gb/2002/12/07/edmond_safra_blamed_/.

85. Vincent, *Gilded Lily*.

86. Dominick. "Death in Monaco." *Vanity Fair*, December 1, 2000.

87. "5 Little-known Interesting Facts about Monaco." Hotels.com, accessed September 4, 2019, https://www.hotels.com/articles/ar015445/fun-facts-about-monaco/.

88. "Why Is Monaco Considered a Tax Haven." Investorpedia, accessed December 17, 2019, https://www.investopedia.com/ask/answers/060316/why-monaco-considered-tax -haven.asp.

89. "Monaco: Personal Taxation." Lowtax, Global Tax and Business Portal, accessed December 17, 2019, https://www.lowtax.net/information/monaco/monaco-inheritance -and-gift-taxes.html

90. *Dateline*. "Billionaire's mysterious death in Monte Carlo." NBC, March 23, 2008.

91. Sancton, Thomas. "A Deadly Cry for Attention." *TIME*, December 20, 1999.

92. Dunne, *Justice*.

93. Michael Griffith, in discussion with coauthor, Jennifer Thomas, Dubai, November 2, 2011.

94. "Our Work," *Amnesty International,* accessed June 9, 2015, http://www.amnestyusa.org /our-work.

95. "Our Work," *Amnesty International,* accessed June 9, 2015, http://www.amnestyusa.org /our-work.

96. "Our Work," *Amnesty International,* accessed June 9, 2015, http://www.amnestyusa.org /our-work.

97. "Notable Cases," *Michael Griffith Lawyer,* accessed April 23, 2015, http://www.michael griffithlawyer.com/notablecases.html.

CHAPTER 29

98. Shakespeare, William. *The Tragedy of Hamlet, Prince of Denmark*. New York: Simon & Schuster, 2012.

99. Affidavit submitted to the United States of America Department of State by Heidi Maher (May 8, 2001), notarized by Gelsomina Bentivegna, New York, 6–11.

100. Order to Show Cause submitted to the Supreme Court of the State of New York by Heidi Maher (April 13, 2001), notarized by Kerry P. Straley, New York, 10.

CHAPTER 30

101. "Hydroxylidocaine." U.S. National Library of Medicine, accessed on September 9, 2019, https://pubchem.ncbi.nlm.nih.gov/compound/3-Hydroxylidocaine.

102. *High Noon*. Directed by Fred Zinneman. New York: United Artists, 1952.

103. Springer, John. "American nurse faces charges in the death of billionaire Edmond Safra." Murderpedia, June 21, 2001, accessed September 8, 2019, http://murderpedia .org/male.M/m/maher-theodore.htm.

CHAPTER 33
104. Paul, Jenny. "Maher Trial Starts Today." The Riviera Gazette, November 21, 2002.
105. "Monaco's 'trial of the century' ends with 10-year sentence." Associated Press, December 3, 2002, accessed May 4, 2015, http://www.smh.com.au/articles/2002/12/03/1038712929683 .html.
106. Indictment, 17.
107. Indictment, 21.
108. *Dateline.* "Billionaire's mysterious death in Monte Carlo." NBC, March 23, 2008.
109. Dickey, Christopher. "A Bad Bet in Monte Carlo." *Newsweek*, August 5, 2001.
110. Michael Griffith Interview.
111. Michael Griffith Interview.

CHAPTER 34
112. Michael Griffith Interview.
113. Indictment, 13.
114. Michael Griffith Interview.
115. "Prosecutor's Report," *Public Prosecutor vs. Theodore Maher*, trans. Elle Phillipe, 5.
116. "World's costliest flat sold for 200 mn pounds." NDTV, September 14, 2010, accessed September 19, 2019, http://www.ndtv.com/world-news/worlds-costliest-flat-sold-for-200 -mn-pounds-431347.

CHAPTER 35
117. Prosecutor's Report, 9–10.
118. Prosecutor's Report, 15–16.
119. Prosecutor's Report, 17.
120. Indictment, 21.
121. Prosecutor's Report, 13–14.
122. Prosecutor's Report, 19.
123. Dupuy, Philippe and Brad Hunter. "Safra Guard Claims Cop Bungle Led to Fire Death." Free Republic, November 26, 2002, accessed April 23, 2019, http://www.freerepublic .com/focus/news/796306/posts?page=3.

CHAPTER 36
124. Prosecutor's Report, 8.
125. Vincent, *Gilded Lily*.
126. "The Safra Mystery." *Law & Ordnance*, August 1, 2009, accessed April 23, 2015, http: //lawandordnance.com/The-Safra-Mystery.html.
127. "The Safra Mystery." *Law & Ordnance*, August 1, 2009, accessed April 23, 2015, http: //lawandordnance.com/The-Safra-Mystery.html.
128. "The Safra Mystery." *Law & Ordnance*, August 1, 2009, accessed April 23, 2015, http: //lawandordnance.com/The-Safra-Mystery.html.
129. Vincent, *Gilded Lily*.
130. Dupuy, Philippe. "Prayer Halts Safra Trial." *New York Post*, November 28, 2002.
131. Dupuy, Philippe and Brad Hunter. "Brother Bares Anguish Over Lost 'Father' Safra." Free Republic, November 29, 2002, accessed September 4, 2019, http://www.freerepub lic.com/focus/news/798300/posts.

132. Dupuy, Philippe and Rita Delfiner. "Firebug's 'Ominous' Remark." *Free Republic*, November 30, 2002, accessed September 4, 2019, http://www.freerepublic.com/focus/news/798300/posts.
133. Dupuy, Philippe and Rita Delfiner. "Firebug's 'Ominous' Remark." *Free Republic*, November 30, 2002, accessed September 4, 2019, http://www.freerepublic.com/focus/news/798300/posts.
134. Lynn, Christina. "Widow's horror tale of fatal fire." *New York Daily News*, November 30, 2002.
135. Autopsy Report of Vivian Torrente. Conducted by Dr. Woltiewiev and Dr. Ohayon.
136. Investigative Report, 18.
137. Investigative Report, 2.
138. Autopsy Report of Vivian Torrente. Conducted by Dr. Woltiewiev and Dr. Ohayon.
139. Donald Manasse to Michael Griffith, November 29, 2002.

CHAPTER 37
140. Indictment, 17.
141. "Daniel Webster Quotes." Brainy Quotes, accessed May 10, 2019, https://www.brainyquote.com/authors/daniel-webster-quotes.

CHAPTER 39
142. Duthé, Géraldine, Angélique Hazard, Annie Kensey, and Jean-Louis Pan Ké Shon. *Suicide in French prisons: trend, level and risk factors.* Princeton: Princeton University, 2010. Accessed December 17, 2019. https://epc2010.princeton.edu/papers/100309.

CHAPTER 40
143. Dunne, *Justice.*
144. Dunne, *Justice.*

CHAPTER 42
145. Paul, Jenny. "The Not So Great Escape." *The Riviera Gazette*, January 30, 2003.

CHAPTER 44
146. "The Foundation Council," Stelios Philanthropic Foundation, accessed May 11, 2015, http://www.stelios.com/foundation-council/blog.html.
147. "Royal Orders and Decorations," Prince's Palace of Monaco, accessed May 11, 2015, http://web.archive.org/web/20071003011135/http://www.palais.mc/wwwpal.nsf/0/dabb699db0a67de1c1256ba7002eb448?OpenDocument.

CHAPTER 45
148. Johnson, Richard, Paula Froelich, Bill Hoffman and Corynne Steindler. "New Claim in Safra Death." *New York Post*, July 31, 2007.
149. Michael Griffith Interview.

CHAPTER 45

150. Christine Pizzuti, *The Poughkeepsie Journal*, Aug 24, 2007.
151. Vincent, *Gilded Lily*.

EPILOGUE

152. Gatecrasher. "Lily Safra's lawyers say mock trial of late billionaire husband's murder would be 'grotesque.'" *New York Daily News*, October 29, 2011.
153. Armstrong, Martin. "Looking Behind The Curtain: The 'Real' Conspiracy" FOAFOA. April 9, 2009. Foafoa.blogspot.com. http://fofoa.blogspot.com/2009/04/martin-armstrong-on-goldman-sachs.html.
154. By Armstrong's former client Larry Edelson.
155. "The Money Plane." BernLeaks, accessed August 25, 2019, http://www.worldcorruption.info/eng/moneyplane.htm; Friedman, Robert. *Red Mafiya: How the Russian Mob Has Invaded America*. New York: Little, Brown and Company, 2000.
156. Dejevsky, Mary. "Russian mafia 'laundered $10bn at Bank of New York.'" *Independent*, August 20, 1999.
157. Traynor, Ian. "Vote gives Putin chance of life-long criminal immunity." *The Guardian*. November 29, 2000.
158. Harding, Luke. "Boris Berezovsky: a tale of revenge, betrayal and feuds with Putin." *The Observer*, March 23, 2013.
159. Cowell, Alan. "Russian Businessman's Death Remains Mystery, Coroner Says." *The New York Times*, March 27, 2014.
160. Parfitt, Tom. "Boris Berezovsky death: friend suggests he may have been victim of Russian hit." The Telegraph, March 24, 2013.
161. Shakespeare, William. *The Tragedy of Hamlet, Prince of Denmark*. New York: Simon & Schuster, 2012.
162. *The Forecaster*. Directed by Marcus Vetter. Germany & Switzerland: FILMPERSPEKTIVE, GmbH, 2014.
163. Armstrong, Martin. "Four Banks Plead Criminally Guilty to Currency Manipulation." Armstrong Economics, May 21, 2015, accessed September 6, 2019, https://www.armstrongeconomics.com/international-news/north_america/americas-current-economy/4-banks-plead-criminally-guilty-to-currency-manipulation/.
164. Barrett, Devlin. "Bank to Pay $606m for Swindle." *New York Post*, December 18, 2001.
165. Barrett, Devlin. "Bank to Pay $606m for Swindle." *New York Post*, December 18, 2001.
166. *The Forecaster*.
167. De La Merced, Michael. "Jailed 7 Years for Contempt, Adviser Is Headed for Prison." *The New York Times*, April 28, 2007.
168. Ma, Alexandra. "Putin hinted he wanted Trump to give him access to one man — and it reveals his greatest weakness." Business Insider, July 17, 2018, accessed September 8, 2019, https://www.businessinsider.com/trump-putin-bill-browder-magnitsky-act-press-conference-2018-7.
169. "Attack On Hermitage, $230 Million Tax Theft." Stop the Untouchables. Justice for Sergei Magnitsky, June 23, 2012, accessed September 8, 2019, www.russian-untouchables.com/eng/group-crimes-p6/.

170. Townsend, Mark. "Putin accuses British anti-corruption campaigner Browder of three murders." *The Guardian*, November 18, 2017.
171. Armstrong, Martin. "Dominick Dunne – Death in Monaco." Armstrong Economics, November 21, 2018, accessed September 8, 2019, www.armstrongeconomics .com/?s=Dominick+Dunne.